D0534682

PRAISE FOR *Living With Bears*

"As someone who lives, hikes and fishes in bear country, I highly recommend this book. Following the helpful tips and guidelines will help make both bears and people safer. *Living with Bears* is also an invaluable guide for city governments, schools, and wildlife professionals and management agencies."

> – *General H. Norman Schwarzkopf, Spokesman for the National Be Bear Aware and Wildlife Stewardship Campaign*

"*Living with Bears* is urgently recommended by the thousands of 'problem' (victimized) bears that needlessly die each year in North America. This insightful, well researched and witty book will guide and inspire humans to live in greater harmony with bears."

> – *Steve Herrero, author of* Bear Attacks: Their Causes and Avoidance, *and Past President of the International Association for Bear Research and Management (IBA)*

"If you live in bear country (and, unless you're an inner-city resident, you probably do), you owe it to bears to read this smart, useful and long-overdue book. Don't let them die because of your or your neighbors' mistakes."

> – *Ted Williams, Editor-at-Large,* Audubon, *and Conservation Editor,* Fly Rod & Reel

"For bears and humans to coexist successfully, we must ensure the bear's natural integrity and wildness. Education is a key element in accomplishing this task. *Living with Bears* gives a clear understanding on bear behavior and provides essential information for humans to protect themselves and their property, while giving bears the opportunity to live the long, natural, healthy lives they deserve."

> – *Tori Seher, Wildlife Biologist, Yosemite National Park*

"To enter bear territory without understanding bears should be illegal. This book is a must-read if we want to coexist with bears."

> – *Ann Bryant, Executive Director – BEAR League, Lake Tahoe*

CALGARY PUBLIC LIBRARY

OCT == 2006

"... a spirited encyclopedia of skills and attitudes for living and traveling safely and considerately in bear country. Its voice is straightforward, accessible, and appealing to young readers and veteran naturalists alike. And best of all, with internationally recognized black bear expert Tom Beck as advisor and contributor, *Living with Bears'* biological credibility is unimpeachable."

    – David Petersen, author of Ghost Grizzlies: Does the Great Bear Still Haunt Colorado?

"Anyone living in bear habitat should have at least two copies—one for handy reference and one to loan to the neighbors. This book will save me dozens of phone calls a year—now I will just tell folks to get THE BOOK, and read it."

    – Tom Beck, bear biologist

"At The Center for Wildlife Information, our mission is to help people learn to live responsibly and safely with wildlife, especially bears. *Living with Bears* is filled with practical information that does just that. It's a great handbook for anyone spending time in bear country."

    – Chuck Bartlebaugh, Director – Center for Wildlife Information

"I believe that anyone who picks up *Living with Bears* will be motivated to work toward preventing conflicts with black bears. And just as importantly, they will have the information they need to do it."

    – Patti Sowka, Director – Living with Wildlife Foundation

"Linda Masterson has put together a book that is concise, knowledgeable and easy-to-read. And her timing is perfect. This book is a godsend to those attempting to demonstrate to the 'smarter of the two species' the need and ability to live with bears."

    – Bryan Peterson, Executive Director – Bear Smart Durango, Colorado

Living With Bears

A Practical Guide to Bear Country

LINDA MASTERSON

PIXYJACK PRESS LLC

Living With Bears: A Practical Guide to Bear Country

Copyright © 2006 by Linda Masterson

No part of this book may be reproduced, stored in a retrieval system or transmitted in any form, or by any means, electronic, mechanical, photocopying, recording or otherwise, without prior written permission of the publisher, except by a reviewer, who may quote brief passages in review.

Published by PixyJack Press, LLC   PO Box 149, Masonville, CO 80541 USA

FIRST EDITION 2006

ISBN 0-9773724-0-5 (ISBN 13-digit: 978-0-9773724-0-9)

9 8 7 6 5 4 3 2 1

Library of Congress Cataloging-in-Publication Data
    Masterson, Linda.
      Living with bears : a practical guide to bear country / Linda Masterson.
        p. cm.
      Includes bibliographical references (p.   ) and index.
      ISBN 0-9773724-0-5
      1. Black bear--Behavior. 2. Bear attacks--North America--Prevention.
      3. Human-animal relationships--North America. I. Title.
      QL737.C27M3522 2006
      599.78'5--dc22
                    2006003608

Printed in the U.S.A. on ECF (Elemental Chlorine Free) paper with soy ink.

Distributed to the trade by Johnson Books (division of Big Earth Publishing), Boulder, Colorado. 1-800-258-5830   www.johnsonbooks.com

Cover bear photos by Bill Lea. Bear crossing sign from Lake Tahoe, photo by Ann Bryant. Back cover photo by Paul Conrad, The Aspen Times. Book design by LaVonne Ewing. Beartoon illustrations by Sara Tuttle.

CAUTION TO READERS: PixyJack Press, Linda Masterson, Tom Beck and the dozens of bear experts and organizations from the U.S. and Canada who consulted on or provided information for this book assume no liability for accidents, injuries, or property damage caused by bears. Understanding and following the recommendations provided in this book will lessen the likelihood of a bear encounter that results in injury, death or property damage, but bears are individuals, and much like people, there is no way to predict or insure the specific behavior of an individual bear under all circumstances. Every effort has been made to assure the accuracy of the information in this book. The publisher and author cannot be held responsible for any errors.

For black bears everywhere,
and all those who make it easier for bears and people to peacefully coexist.

And for my husband Cory,
my partner in all things great and small.

TABLE OF CONTENTS

continued

Beary Smart Solutions CASE STUDIES FROM NORTH AMERICA

continued

FOREWORD

The American landscape has changed markedly in the last three decades, both physically and socially. Overall these changes benefited black bears and resulted in major shifts in emphasis for wildlife biologists. Few of us who were working with black bears thirty years ago could imagine the scope and nature of these changes. We were primarily concerned with conservation of bear populations, preventing over-hunting, and learning as much as possible about the secret lives of this amazing creature with the advent of a new technology—radio telemetry. While I suspect our well-intentioned endeavors may have helped a few black bear populations, in the whole the species benefited most from other forces in American society.

The great emigration of Americans from rural lands to urban/suburban centers during 1930–1970 was a boon to bears, especially in the East. This allowed many thousands of acres of hard-scrabble farmland and cutover forest to revert to forest lands. Since farmers had long used both gun and trap liberally to reduce wildlife depredations, these land tenure changes removed a major source of bear mortality. Black bears have relatively low reproductive rates and young females seldom travel far from birth areas, so the initial spread of black bear populations was slow. However, a critical mass seemed to be achieved in the 1980s and since then the recovery of black bears along the entire Atlantic seaboard region has been impressive.

Concurrently, agricultural changes throughout the central and southern Rocky Mountain region certainly improved things for black bears. The range sheep industry declined precipitously in this region during the 1970s. As the sheep industry waned, the level of predator control directed towards black bears declined significantly. Social acceptance of widespread predator control also declined, as evidenced by the commission of several scientific advisory panels and eventually the restriction of most poisons on public land. Black bear populations rebounded.

Just as things were looking good for black bears, a portion of urban/suburban Americans decided to "move back to the country." But the new country dwellers were different. Whereas earlier generations had been living off the land, the new generation only wanted to live on the land. They did not need to produce a livelihood from the land; thus their presence did not necessarily reduce the habitat for many species of wildlife. In fact, the presence of wildlife was most often seen as a valuable feature of the land. The wildlife species we refer to as habitat generalists responded positively to these cumulative changes; among them white-tailed deer, raccoons, red foxes, Canada geese, and black bears. But even in Eden there is a dark side.

Over half a century ago the principal philosopher of wildlife management, Aldo Leopold, urged the American public to enthusiastically adopt a land ethic. He believed such an ethic was critical for the preservation of both wildlife and our relationship to the natural forces of life. I fear we have made little, if any, progress toward that end. We still don't live in harmony with most wildlife. We want our wildlife to be close and visible, but we don't want them to cause us extra work. It only takes one chewed up flower bed for the "beautiful doe" to become the "damn deer." Or one broken down fruit tree, or one dumped trash can for the awesome black bear to decline to the status of "nuisance bear."

I have long believed in the power of words. Is there any doubt as to the guilty party when agencies refer to "nuisance bear" problems? Initial attempts to resolve the "bear problem" nearly always started with increased hunting, primarily because of the subculture bias of wildlife managers and hunters. It is truly unfortunate that increased hunting doesn't solve the problem. Early in my career, I proposed my agency refer to these conflicts as "nuisance human" events. I soon grew accustomed to the look of disbelief and consternation among my fellow wildlifers. But with time and patience (which I admit I am a bit short of) the problem soon became identified as human-bear conflicts. More accurately describing the problem opens up new alternatives, including altering human behavior.

For many years now some bear biologists have stood up at bear workshops and loudly proclaimed that teaching people how to live with bears should be the number one bear management research objective. For a variety of reasons, agencies generally ignored such calls. Wildlife management agencies tend to be both conservative and reactive. Thus, until lots of bears were figuratively biting them in the butt, they were reluctant to act. But now the large numbers of bears and people have led to perpetual problems of major proportions. We presently find ourselves limited to the few research projects addressing this subject plus the collective anecdotal wisdom gained through experience.

Collectively, over two decades, we have learned a lot about living in harmony with bears. Forced to deal with lots of human-bear conflicts, park service employees and various committed citizen activists have been the source of creative approaches. Thus, most of our knowledge has come from trial-and-error rather than formal scientific experiments. Such modest roots in no way diminish the applicability of these techniques. The limitation of such practical knowledge is that it is difficult to synthesize and report.

Fortunately for all of us living in bear habitat, Linda Masterson abandoned her urban/suburban life and moved to the mountains of Colorado's northern Front Range. She quickly volunteered for a new Colorado Division of Wildlife volunteer group called Bear Aware. The area she lives in is basically poor bear habitat. However, the recent influx of homes has served to improve the bear habitat, as the homes are a source of ample quantities of high-quality food. Add to that a major drought, and the volunteers got lots of experience in helping neighbors deal with persistent black bears. Linda saw a dual need that could be remedied. Citizens needed a source for information on how to live safely with

black bears across a range of activities. The black bears needed a more responsible human reaction to their behavior; after all, they were just being driven by their bellies. Ideally, both large-brained, simple-stomached, omnivorous species would benefit.

The information was available, but not readily so. Much of the knowledge is in informal reports, anecdotes, or the memories of participants. Good stuff; but very time consuming to collect, edit and critically examine. Not surprisingly, Linda discovered that the experts don't always agree. Disagreement among scientists is quite common, even when dealing with experimental data. When dealing with mostly anecdotal information, disagreement often becomes the norm. But she was a persistent researcher, kept asking questions, and finally distilled the best information into this book. Along the way, she fell victim to the same pitfall as nearly every bear biologist— she became addicted to bears. These awesome creatures dominate our lives.

Fortunately she avoided the boring writing style common to most biologists! Written text must be readable; a characteristic rather obvious to all but the editors of professional journals. After all, we have the most engaging subject matter I know of. Good medicine doesn't have to taste bad; and good information doesn't have to put you to sleep. Linda has done an exceptional job of researching the nature of the problem and solutions that actually work. To top it off, it is fun to read. Even the most jaded of you will smile, or maybe even chuckle occasionally.

I suggest you buy two copies. One to keep and mark up, dog-ear the pages, use it. The other to loan to your neighbors; for you will quickly learn that to resolve human-bear conflicts you need the collective power of a large neighborhood. As an added benefit, you'll get to meet your neighbors. You might even find one you like.

You and the bears both stand to benefit.

— *Tom Beck*
Dolores, Colorado

© *Tom Beck*

PROLOGUE

I grew up on the shores of Lake Erie, well before black bears began wandering back into the Buckeye State. I spent a couple of decades of my adult working life in Chicago, where the only bears were Walter Payton, Gary Fencik and their colorful coach, Iron Mike Ditka.

Professionally, Chicago was very, very good to me. I paid her back by escaping at every opportunity. I spent countless long weekends and longer vacations hiking everywhere from Great Smoky Mountains National Park to the Rockies. If I so much as glimpsed a black bear, it went into my hiking log, and I considered myself very lucky.

My husband Cory Phillips and I used our mid-life crises as a springboard, and traded our corporate jobs and hundred and ten year old townhome in Evanston for a log home on a ridge top in Colorado, and the freedoms and uncertainties of self-employment.

One of the first things we did in our new home was sign up for the Colorado Division of Wildlife's Volunteer Program. That first year we counted big horn sheep and winter waterfowl and made blue bird nesting boxes. Colorado and much of the West was in the grip of a devastating drought. That summer the papers were filled with stories of bears wandering into towns and invading homes, looking for food wherever they could find it. People were losing their patience. Bears were losing their lives. That was the summer weary wildlife officers and an innovative education coordinator brainstormed better ways to help people learn to live with bears, and Colorado's Bear Aware Program was born.

We missed that first year, but the following spring we joined the fledgling group, attended an all-day training class, and enthusiastically threw ourselves into our new job of helping human and ursine neighbors get along.

It didn't seem right that bears had to die because people wouldn't lock up their trash or take down their birdfeeders. The more people we talked to, the more apparent it became that neither newcomers nor natives really knew much about the do's and don'ts of living with black bears.

Being both an optimist and a writer, I convinced myself that education was the answer. If I could give people the information they needed, along with a good dose of inspiration and motivation, most people would see the light. The information came from thousands of references, research studies, personal interviews, Web sites, biologists, wildlife managers, and agencies and organizations. The inspiration and motivation came from learning how parks, communities and others developed smart, workable solutions to their bear "problems" that made the world a safer place for both bears and people.

Although at the time I had no idea just how well-known and well-respected he was in the world of bear professionals, I talked at length with Colorado's bear biologist, the legendary Tom Beck, who urged me to pursue the project, telling me that at the last Western Bear Biologists conference he'd attended, the biologists and other bear experts there from the western states had all agreed on one thing: teaching people to get along with bears was the single most important thing that could be done to insure black bears would continue to have a place in our ever more crowded world.

The idea of writing a practical guide to living with bears simmered in the back of my mind while my life filled up with new clients, new projects and new responsibilities. While I was thinking it over and wondering how I'd find the time to tackle such an ambitious project, Beck took an early retirement, and retreated to his organic farm and orchard in the Four Corners region.

But as Beck says, bears get under your skin; the more you know about them, the more you respect, admire and appreciate them. And the less patient you become with people who don't understand that it's we humans who hold the keys to both the long-term survival of black bears as a species, and the welfare of every individual bear that's trying to make a living in people country.

Beck still cared deeply about the bears he'd spent twenty-five years studying. And even though he was no longer on the state payroll, he was more than willing to put in what would turn out to be hundreds of hours helping me separate bear myths and misconceptions from reality. His name opened doors, and black bear professionals across the continent made time to talk with me about bear "problems"—and solutions.

One of the myths that pervaded most strongly, even among some professionals, was the "all bears are created equal" theory—the tendency to lump black bears and their bigger and decidedly different cousins, grizzly bears, into a species described generically as "bears."

While the two do have some things in common, black bears and grizzlies respond very differently when surprised or pressured, and the rules of close encounters are different as well.

Early settlers soon decided that the larger and more aggressive grizzly bear was a threat to be eliminated, whereas black bears were merely a nuisance. Grizzlies were mercilessly hunted and pushed out of most of their historic range. Their low reproductive rates and need for vast tracts of wilderness eventually doomed them to a life confined to a few areas in the lower 48, where they remain on the Endangered Species List, and Canada and Alaska, where there's still more room to roam.

Today there are perhaps 50,000 to 55,000 grizzly bears remaining in just a handful of areas in North America—and upwards of 900,000 black bears found in over 80 percent of the U.S. and virtually all of Canada. Unless you spend a lot of time in what little remains of grizzly country, your chances of encountering a grizz are pretty slim.

Black bears are much more adaptable, and willing and able to live in much closer proximity to people. With black bear populations healthy or growing across much of the continent, and people populations on the increase as well, people and black bears are encountering each other more often. And like the early pioneers, we have a choice to make.

Black bears can survive—and even thrive—on the fringes of civilization, or sometimes right in the midst of it. The real question is whether people are willing to learn to live with them, or whether as a species they'll once again go from wildlife to be treasured to nuisance to be eliminated.

I don't want to contemplate a world where the amazing black bear survives only in parks and zoos. So this book is dedicated to giving people the information they need to learn how to peacefully coexist with black bears, and the inspiration and motivation to want to.

— *Linda Masterson*
February 2006

© *Paul Conrad* / The Aspen Times

chapter 1

Welcome to Black Bear Country

Where the Bears Are

In New Jersey a suburban mom comes home and discovers a black bear rummaging through her refrigerator. In Lake Tahoe a bear slips into a summer cabin through an unlocked cellar door and turns the basement into its winter den. In New Mexico a bear wanders into the lobby of a motel and heads toward the pool, where startled guests chase him up a giant rubber tree plant. In Colorado a bear browses through the freezer in the garage and makes off with all the Haagen Daaz, leaving the store brand ice cream untouched. In Arizona a young camper is rudely awakened by a bear licking the remnants of a chocolate bar off her face. In Pennsylvania a bear emerges from its winter den and discovers a housing development has taken root in what a few months ago was the forest. In British Columbia five "nuisance" bears get a one-way ticket to the great garbage dump in the sky.

It's just another day in black bear country.

From the suburbs of Orlando to the forests of British Columbia, there's little doubt people are encountering black bears more often these days, often with consequences that are unnerving for humans and deadly for bears. Why are human-black bear encounters on the rise? And what can you do to prevent encounters from turning into conflicts?

The first question could be the subject of an entire book all by itself. The short answer is that the sheer number

© Tim Halvorson

of people living, working and playing in places bears call home has gone up dramatically over the past decade or so, and in many areas the bear population has gone up as well.

In much of the U.S. and parts of Canada, a new generation of pioneers is hitching up their 4x4's and migrating to the edges of cities, and beyond. Sparsely populated places that used to be "the country," "the woods" and "the mountains" are sprouting clusters of housing developments and sprawling suburbs that put people in much closer proximity to bears.

A wireless world has created an opportunity for people to live and work anywhere. Rapidly climbing housing prices have pushed people out to the fringes of the suburbs and beyond in search of an affordable roof over their head, and a better quality of life. The trend to second and even third homes has spawned a housing boom in ski and resort communities and around just about every gateway city nestling up against a national or provincial park.

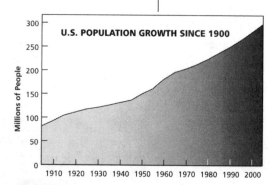

The human population boom is one reason more people are encountering bears these days.

Oftentimes people from cities and suburbs who move out into bear country are astonished to find they're now sharing space with a variety of four-footed neighbors, and some of them are just as challenging to get along with as the two-footed ones they left behind.

Even old timers and locals who've lived in bear country for years often remark that the peaceful coexistence with the local wildlife they enjoyed a decade or two ago isn't so peaceful anymore.

"We've lived here thirty years, and this is the first time we've ever had bear problems," one of my Colorado neighbors lamented. "We're not doing anything any different. What's going on?"

A quick look at the county records revealed the human population of the canyon they live in had grown from a few hundred people to several thousand over that same time frame. A stream running through the canyon provides a steady source of water. Chokecherries, serviceberries and wild raspberries crowd the banks.

It's a good place to be a bear. So the ursine residents did their best to adapt to the rising tide of people who built homes and planted gardens and fenced in meadows in the midst of their habitat. But the chances of bears meeting people as they run the human obstacle course in what used to be the bears' back yard have increased a thousand fold.

In some parts of North America, not only are there more people living or playing in bear country, there are also more bears. When Europeans first arrived, black bears could be found wherever there were forests—most of the continent except for the Great Plains and the frozen tundra.

In America, the early pioneers were intent on farming; black bears were just another varmint standing in the way of progress. There were no hunting seasons or rules and regulations; bears were plentiful and bounties so common some hunters made a good living turning in bear pelts. Toward the end of the 19th century black bear hides fetched $8 a piece, and meat went for eight cents a pound. Wildlife was a commodity to be used, or a problem to be exterminated. The concept of wildlife conservation was decades away.

By the late 1800s black bear populations had been decimated in much of the eastern U.S. Eventually managing wildlife as a renewable resource replaced exploitation and extermination, and state and federal management agencies were born. Then along came the Industrial Revolution; millions of acres of marginal farmland were abandoned and eventually reclaimed by second-growth forests. These new forests matured over the next century, and bears once again had a place to live.

National and provincial parks were set aside to preserve and protect our natural resources. They offered people unspoiled places to come and experience nature, and provided a safe haven for wildlife. Parks are

President "Silent Cal" Coolidge with Yellowstone National Park Superintendent Horace Albright getting way too close to black bears near Roosevelt Lodge in the 1920s. Imagine the Secret Service putting up with this today.
National Park Service

often surrounded by forests; many of those forests quickly became home to communities that sprang up to serve the needs of the tourists. Today towns like Estes Park, Colorado, the gateway to Rocky Mountain National Park, that were once tiny hamlets people passed through on their way to enjoy the scenic wonders have grown into sprawling mini-cities with thousands of full-time residents, tens of thousands of part-timers, and literally millions of visitors.

People have been training bears to peer into cars in search of a handout since the automobile replaced the horse and buggy.
National Park Service, 1962

Green belts and open spaces have become common—often mandated—amenities in new developments. These natural areas make excellent travel corridors for wildlife as well as people. With open land harder and more expensive to come by, in many places green-belts aren't really big enough to provide a safe harbor for wildlife; they can actually increase the odds of people and bears encountering each other, as both species try to make use of the remaining precious natural space.

Black bears are highly intelligent, adaptable and resourceful. Nature has equipped them with a nose that can detect a food source literally miles away, and the size, strength and endurance to regularly roam over many miles searching for meals. Bears spend most of their lives looking for the calories they need to survive, with a few time outs now and then to mate or find a cozy place to sleep the winter away.

Bears are naturally wary of people, and other unfamiliar things. But they're also naturally curious, a trait that makes them willing to constantly explore their environment in the hopes of finding something new to eat.

When a bear follows its super-sensitive nose to an overflowing garbage can, a bird feeder filled with sunflower seeds, a pack stuffed with peanut butter sandwiches and granola bars, or an apple pie cooling on a windowsill, it learns that overcoming its natural wariness of people pays off. The bear spends a few minutes someplace it doesn't really want to be, and leaves with a quick and easy meal. Bears are fast learners; when they find food in a backyard or campground, they usually come back for more. And because they're smart enough to go through a sort of bear deductive "reasoning" process, they'll check out all the other backyards or campgrounds they come across.

Once bears learn to include people-places in their mental checklist of food sources, problems for people and bears inevitably follow. Bears determined to get their paws on human food do hundreds of thousands of dollars worth of property damage each year; occasionally people are injured in the process.

Bears that lose their wariness of people often wind up losing their lives as well. Every year in North America thousands of healthy black bears are destroyed for becoming "problems" and "nuisances."

It doesn't have to be that way. Most human-bear conflicts can be prevented, if people are willing to be half as adaptable and resourceful as the furry natives.

Bears are flexible thinkers. Once they learn the rules, as long as natural food sources and denning spaces are available, most bears can be taught it's in their best interests to avoid people. People often seem both less adaptable and less willing to change their lifestyles and habits to make room for bears, and to help keep bears wild.

WHERE THE BEARS ARE

Where do black bears live? As one bear researcher succinctly put it, "Anywhere they can."

According to noted bear expert Steve Herrero's latest calculations, there are about as many black bears in North America as

Learning more about what causes human-black bear conflicts and what you can do to prevent them is what this book is all about.

Michael Seraphin; courtesy of the Colorado Division of Wildlife

there are people in the state of Montana; around 900,000. Some experts believe the population is evenly split between the U.S. and Canada; others think about 60 percent of black bears live north of the U.S. border.

Since bears don't travel in herds that can be counted from the air, or dutifully turn in census forms every decade, even bear researchers who spend their entire lives studying *Ursus americanus* don't know exactly how many black bears there are in any particular state or province or forest.

"Population estimates for animals that are fairly easy to monitor, like deer and elk herds, routinely run plus or minus 20 percent. Bears don't run out of the forest in herds when we fly over them—calculating the number of bears in any one area is challenging. While some methods of estimating bear populations may be more reliable than others, they are all simply educated guesses," says highly respected bear biologist Tom Beck, who served as the scientific and technical reviewer for this book.

We do know that today black bears are found in every province in Canada except for Prince Edward Isle, and in at least 41 of 50 states in the U.S., including places like Kentucky and Ohio, where bears haven't been seen since Daniel Boone's days. ❖

ADAPTABLE

"One word describes the black bear—adaptable. The American Black Bear occupies a greater range of habitats than any bear in the world. It occurs on tundra and ice pack in Northern Labrador, in temperate rain forest in coastal British Columbia and Washington, in the oak forests on the edge of the Sonoran Dessert in northern Mexico and Arizona, in the cypress swamps and Everglades of Florida, throughout the northern hardwood forests of eastern North America and all across the breadth and width of the immense boreal forest of Canada that stretches from Newfoundland to Alaska."

WAYNE LYNCH, AUTHOR OF
BEARS: MONARCHS OF THE NORTHERN WILDERNESS

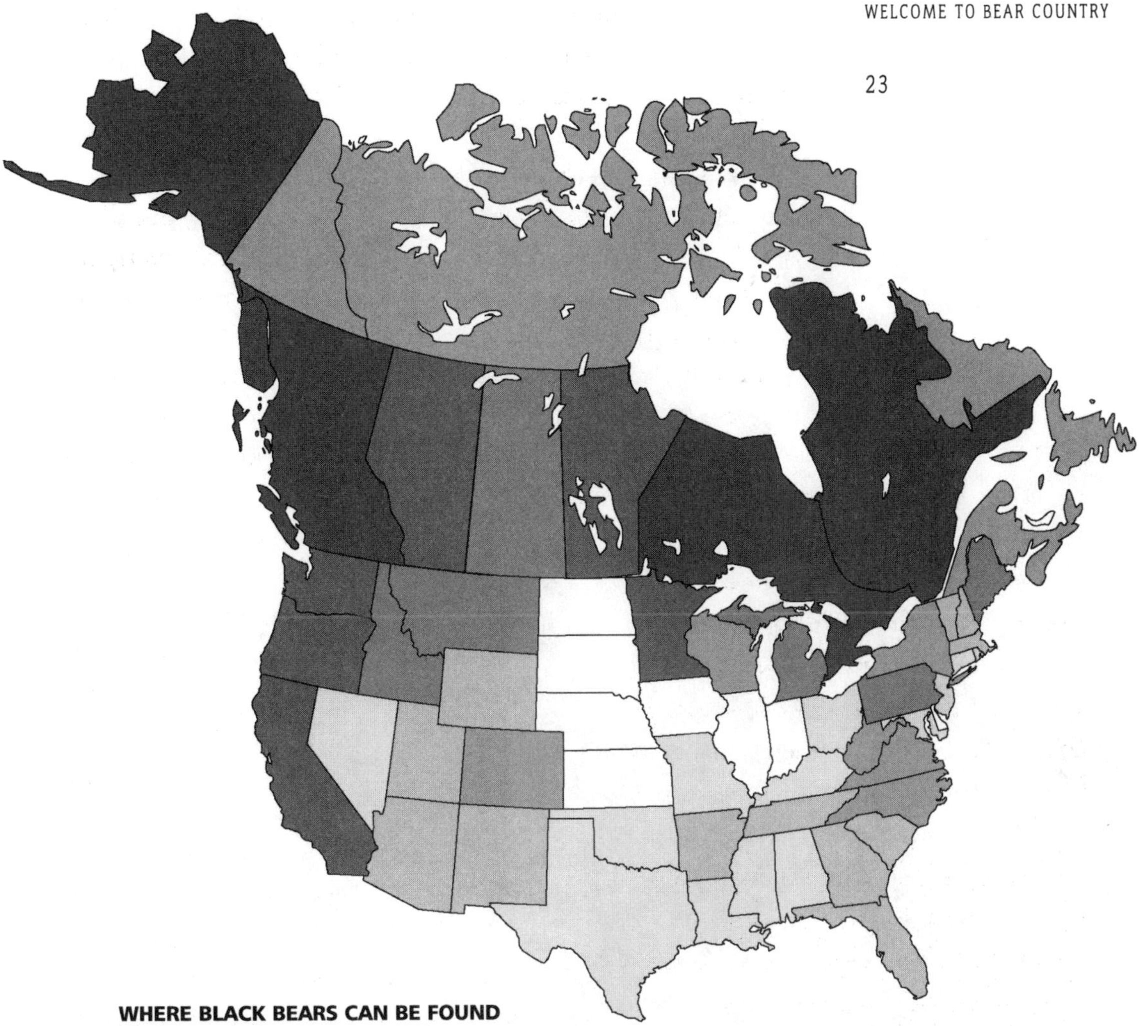

WHERE BLACK BEARS CAN BE FOUND IN THE UNITED STATES & CANADA

There are approximately 900,000 black bears in North America today, according to the latest population estimates. Even states without resident bear populations often have bears passing through. Bear in mind that counting the number of bears in a state or province is not like counting the number of jelly beans in a fishbowl. Bears travel long distances, either alone or in a small family group, and generally remain within the cover of the forest, so they are hard to spot from the air.

- No resident bears
- Under 1,000
- 1,000 – 5,000
- 5,000 – 15,000
- 15,000 – 25,000
- 25,000 – 50,000
- more than 50,000

For a look at estimated bear populations by state and province, see pages 236-237.

© *Paul Conrad* / The Aspen Times

chapter 2

The Bear Essentials

Bear Biology Lesson

Bears are a marvel of natural engineering; uniquely equipped to thrive and prosper in a world of extremes. My husband and Bear Aware partner Cory Phillips is from Minnesota, where the natives say there are just two seasons: "Winter's Coming" and "Winter's Here." For bears, the two seasons are "Hibernation's Coming," and "Hibernation's Here." Bears spend "Hibernation's Coming" trying to put on enough weight to survive up to six months of "Hibernation's Here."

A BEAR'S LIFE

Bears can live twenty-five years or more in the wild; their life span varies from region to region, but averages about eighteen years. Bears also grow, mature and mate at different ages in different areas; in food-rich habitats like the acorn forests of Pennsylvania bears grow more quickly and mate earlier than bears that live in places where food is harder to come by.

National Park Service

Compared to many mammals, black bears are slow reproducers; once a female reaches maturity sometime between age three and five, she'll give birth to an average of two to three cubs every other year.

As it is for most young animals, the world is a dangerous place for little bears, and even with plenty of available food, on average

25

about one in three cubs dies before its first birthday. In bad food years, survival rates are even lower. Cubs fall out of trees, drown, are hit by cars, starve to death if something happens to their mother, and fall victim to a number of predators, including coyotes, mountain lions, wolves, grizzly bears and other black bears.

Adult bears do occasionally die of old age, or more rarely of disease, but hunting, poaching, the destruction of "problem" bears, and vehicular bearicide account for most adult bear deaths.

© Derek Reich

HOME ON THE RANGE

Bears have loosely defined home ranges—the territory where they forage for food, mate and raise their young. The size of a bear's home range can vary from a mere square mile to over 100 square miles (260 sq km) or more. Ranges in western North America are generally bigger, although no one is sure why. It's not uncommon for adult male bears in Colorado to roam over 250 square miles (650 sq km).

Females have smaller ranges than males, from one to 80 square miles (207 sq km). When juvenile females are ready to leave home they'll often be allowed to "move in next door," or occupy part of their mom's home range; adolescent males are booted out, and may have to travel a hundred miles or more to find a place of their own.

Mature males mate with as many females as possible, so their home range is usually much larger, from 8 to 250 square miles (20 to 650 sq km). Because bear ranges overlap, bears rely on a social hierarchy based on dominance to keep order—with smaller, more submissive bears going out of their way to avoid rubbing the top bears the wrong way.

WHY DO BEARS ROAM?

Bears are slaves to Mother Nature's cupboard, and quickly learn which parts of their range have good food at which time of year. But how far bears wander doesn't always have much to do with how much food is available, or how good it is. Noted bear biologist Tom Beck reports a control study that's typical—he monitored two female cubs born the same year to different mothers with overlapping home ranges, so for the cubs, food availability and weather were pretty much the same. By the time the cubs were four years old, one had a range of 4 square miles (10 sq km); the other had a range of 15 square miles (39 sq km). Beck says there was no apparent biological or environmental reason for one bear to have a territory nearly four times as big as her neighbor.

"A bear a long distance from a scale always weighs more."
NATURALIST ADOLPH MURIE

SIZING UP BEARS

People often swear the bear involved in an unexpected encounter weighed a thousand pounds and stood eight feet tall, which is a good indication of how well things grow in our imaginations. Their bulky builds and heavy fur coats make bears look bigger than they are; in one study seasoned bear biologists overestimated the size of their subjects by as much as 25 percent. Little wonder wide-eyed homeowners usually miss the mark.

In reality, a healthy adult black bear can weigh from under 100 pounds (over 45 kg) to over 600 (272 kg) or more. Bears, like humans, are sexually dimorphic; males in an area typically weigh about a third more than females. Depending on habitat and time of year, females weigh in between 120 and 250 pounds (55 and 114 kg), and pack on most of their bulk during their first three

© Tim Halvorson

years of life. Males generally weigh between 180 and 300 pounds (82 and 136 kg), and if enough food is available, they gain weight up until their tenth birthday, or even beyond.

The biggest wild black bear on record is a ten-year-old male that weighed 880 pounds (400 kg) when it was shot by a hunter in North Carolina in 1998. A black bear hit and killed by a car near Winnipeg, Canada in 2001 weighed just over 856 pounds (388 kg), but officials estimated his live weight would've been over 886 pounds.

How big a bear grows depends on the quantity and quality of food that's available. In Colorado, Beck discovered that bears living in the lodgepole pine and spruce/fir forests of Middle Park where the pickins' are slim are about 20 percent smaller than bears browsing the lush green understory of the aspen and scrub oak forests on the Uncompahgre Plateau.

Bears are almost always at their thinnest and scruffiest in late spring, when they're still living off their winter fat reserves, and hit their high weights for the year just before denning in late fall.

From the tip of its highly sensitive nose to the end of its short stubby tail, an adult male can measure 6 feet (182 cm) or more and stand 3½ feet (107 cm) high at the shoulder—about the height of your average four-year-old. A female is usually 4½ to 5 feet (137 to 152 cm) in length, and stands about 3 feet (91 cm) high at the shoulder.

WHAT COLOR IS A BLACK BEAR?

The black bear is a species, *Ursus americanus*, not a color. Black bears come in every color from snowy white and

In Alaska and British Columbia, black bears are occasionally a frosted glacier blue, a color phase that probably dates back to the last ice age, when their blue-gray coats would have provided great camouflage against the frozen landscape. British Columbia is also home to the rare white Kermode or Spirit bear. The Spirit bear isn't an albino or a separate species—just a mutation in the chromosome responsible for coat color that's only found in bears living in a few islands off the coast of British Columbia.

© Tim Halvorson

glacier blue to black as a moonless night sky, and just about every shade of brown. In the eastern third of North America, black bears are usually black, with brown muzzles; about one in four sport a jaunty white chest blaze. Head west, and black bears are more likely to be brown. In sun-drenched Arizona, 95 percent of black bears are some shade of brown. Researchers tracking individual black bears have even documented cases of bears changing colors through the year, or from season to season. Cubs of all different colors can be born in a single litter. No matter what color coat they're wearing, they're still black bears.

CARNIVORE OR OMNIVORE?

Scientifically, black bears are classified as carnivores, in the same category as dogs, cats, weasels and raccoons. But unlike other carnivores, the diet of the average black bear is less than 10 percent meat. And much of that comes from winter-killed deer, scavenged carcasses, and that high protein treat the hit TV reality show, *Fear Factor*, has made famous: bugs.

Bears have big skulls—the longest and most massive of all the carnivores—but have neither the flesh-cutting cheek teeth of other predators nor the grinding molars and efficient stomachs of herbivores like elk and deer. That's why bears have to eat so much to get the nutrition they need, and why they eat the most tender, newly developing and most digestible parts of green plants.

A black bear may have the digestive system of a meat-eater, but even though bears can run at speeds of up to 35 mph (56 kph) over short distances, they just don't have the feet for efficiently hunting and chasing down a meal.

Bears have five toes on each foot, with non-retractable claws. Take a good look at a black bear track, and you can see a bear's hind foot is eerily similar to a human footprint. That's because bears walk

Tracks left by bear feet and bare feet can look remarkably similar.
© Tom Beck

in plantigrade fashion, using their whole foot, heel to toe, much like we do, except normally bears walk on four feet instead of two.

Other predators like mountain lions and lynx walk on their toes; that's one reason they're much better at bringing down speedy prey. Black bears are at a disadvantage chasing down dinner because they run like people, instead of your average predator.

Bears are built for strength, not speed. They have thick limbs, huge shoulders and short backs and feet. Rather than tapering from hip to foot like a cat's, a bear's thick muscles stretch the entire length of the leg, making sprinting for any distance a challenge.

Black bears have short claws made for climbing trees, digging and ripping.
U.S. Forest Service

THE POWER OF BEARS

Bears are incredibly strong, with jaws that can crunch through the bones of an adult deer, and powerful limbs that can rip a 10-inch (25-cm) log to shreds, dig out a winter den or flip over 100-pound (45-kg) boulder searching for grubs. Even young bears are surprisingly strong; a six-month-old cub is a good match for most humans.

WHAT'S FOR DINNER?

Bears are often described as opportunistic feeders. That means that much like your average two-year-old child, a hungry black bear will eat or drink just about anything with calories. Bears are hard-wired to spend the summer and fall gaining weight, and they adapt as best they can to whatever natural— and unnatural—foods are available.

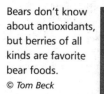

Bears don't know about antioxidants, but berries of all kinds are favorite bear foods.
© *Tom Beck*

The bulk of a bear's diet consists of nuts, berries, tender young grasses, and plants called leafy forbs, which translates to "anything green that isn't a grass or a tree." Bears also scavenge carcasses when they can find them. In some areas bears emerging from their dens depend on winter-killed elk and deer while they're waiting for green-up; after a mild winter bears often have a tough time finding enough early spring food.

Bears love protein-rich grubs, insects, and nice fatty larvae. If you see rocks that have been turned over, that's a pretty good indicator a hungry black bear has been by.

THE ANNUAL FEEDING FRENZY

During the spring and summer, an average-sized black bear will get by on about as many calories each day as a human of the same size—perhaps 2,500 or so. But in late summer and early fall when berries and acorns begin to ripen, black bears become eating machines. Bears need to gain as much fat as possible before they turn in for the winter, and they're biologically programmed to "eat while the eating's good." During this time called hyperphagia, bears will forage up to twenty hours a day, trying to get the 20,000 or more calories they need to gain 3 to 5 pounds (1.4 to 2.3 kg) a day. That's a lot of berries—up to 30,000 a day. During the fall bears often travel outside their spring and summer ranges to seasonal feeding grounds where berries, acorns or other natural foods like spawning salmon are abundant. In years when natural foods are in short supply, some bears may be more likely to investigate human food sources.

BEARS IN LOVE

Bears typically mate in June or early July, when dominant males roam through their expansive territories seeking out females in heat. I once watched a love-struck male lumbering along at the heels of the object of his affection. Every once in a while she stopped and looked

A REGULAR BEAR

In California's Happy Valley east of Redding, one bear made a daily trek to a woman's front porch, leaving a nice big pile of bear scat near the front door before heading back to the woods.
SAN FRANCISCO CHRONICLE JUNE 10, 2001

© Tim Halvorson

Cubs learn
everything they
need to know to
survive from their
mothers, and don't
normally leave home
until after their
second winter.

back over her shoulder; when he caught up, off she'd go again. I watched them disappear into the ponderosa pines, and can only assume he eventually had his way with her.

It's not uncommon to see bears traveling in pairs this time of year; the female won't mate until the timing is perfect. Once she finally says yes, the pair may stay together for a couple of days, and mate several times. Females will also mate with more than one male; in fact cubs from the same litter can have different fathers—a great way to keep the gene pool going.

One of Tom Beck's employees once watched a female bear they were radio-tracking mate with a small and very happy suitor. Afterwards the pair hung out together for about twenty minutes—until a very large male came along. The smaller bear sized up the competition and beat a hasty retreat. The big guy swaggered in and mated with the female, and eventually they disappeared over a ridge.

A LITTLE BIT PREGNANT

Unlike people, bears really can be "a little bit pregnant." Because when it comes to having babies, Mother Nature has worked out a plan that works perfectly for bears.

The physical demands of a summer pregnancy would be a real handicap to a bear that by fall must spend up to twenty hours a day searching for food. So even though her eggs are fertilized in June, they don't implant into her womb until she's safely in her den, and has put on enough weight to see herself and her cubs through as much as six months without food. If it's been a lean year, or the bear is sick or injured, the embryos are reabsorbed so the mother bear has a better chance of surviving to breed again.

If the bear is in good shape, the embryos implant and begin to grow, and after one of the shortest pregnancies on record for a mammal the size of a bear, sometime in late January or early February one to six cubs—most commonly two to three—are born, each about the size of a chipmunk. Older, more experienced bears tend to have larger litters than first time moms; it's tough enough for an inexperienced mother to keep an eye on one rambunctious bundle of energy, never mind three or four.

The female rouses long enough to lick the cubs clean and consume the afterbirth, and then slips back into hibernation. There's no rest for the cubs; they must nurse and grow bigger and stronger before they'll be able to venture out into the world in the spring.

A newborn bear looks like a pink, hairless rodent. It weighs between 8 and 12 ounces (249 to 373 grams), and is a mere 1/300th to 1/500th the size of its mother. Compare that to the average human baby weighing in at 6½ to 7 pounds (2.95 to 3.17 kg)—already nearly 6 percent of the weight of a 120-pound (54.4 kg) adult.

Nourished by rich mother's milk that's 33 percent fat, the cubs grow quickly. By the time they poke their curious noses into the world for the first time, they're three to four months old, and about the size and shape of big, fluffy puppies, with bright blue eyes that gradually change to brown as they grow older.

Male black bears have nothing to do with rearing their offspring, and sometimes kill cubs. The ever-vigilant female and her youngsters form a tight family bond and will be inseparable until the cubs are ready to strike out on their own, usually after their second winter.

DO BEARS REALLY HIBERNATE?

Human mothers will recognize the look of long-suffering patience on this bear's face, and can surely sympathize with having so many hungry mouths to feed. *© Jenny Ross*

That question has been debated for years by bear biologists. Hibernating mammals like bats, marmots, squirrels and rodents almost go into a state of suspended animation; their body temperature drops drastically and metabolic processes slow nearly to a halt. They wake up every week or two, drink some water, go to the bathroom, nibble some stored food and go back to sleep.

But a bear's body temperature drops only a few degrees, and they don't eat, urinate or defecate. Bears often change position in the den, and some even wander out into the world for brief periods, then go back to sleep. Hibernating mother bears routinely nurse and even clean up after their cubs while they're "asleep," something any new human mother can easily relate to.

If a denning bear is startled, it can be awake and running in minutes, so don't ever crawl into a bear den.

A LONG WINTER'S NAP

Bears don't den because it's cold; they put themselves to sleep for the winter because of dwindling food supplies. In far Northern Minnesota or Canada, bears can be in their dens for up to six months out of every year. In milder climates like the Sierras, they might den from mid-December until March or early April. In places where it's warm all year and there's plenty to eat like Florida's Ocala National Forest, with the exception of pregnant females, most bears don't den at all, although they spend a lot of time lounging in day beds and taking it easy.

A denning bear is a marvelous example of recycling at its best. It can go as many as two hundred days without eating, drinking, or visiting the outhouse. Bears have a unique ability to reuse protein byproducts, so they truly live off the fat reserves they worked so hard to acquire, and lose fat, not muscle, while they sleep. They also recycle calcium back into their bones, avoiding the bone loss that's typically a byproduct of long periods of inactivity. If humans had the same ability, no one would

WHAT DOCTORS HOPE TO LEARN FROM BEARS

In 1998 Tom Lohuis and Hank Harlow of the University of Wyoming and Colorado bear biologist Tom Beck did a study that helped prove that while a bear loses an average of 25 percent of its weight over the winter, a bear's muscles only atrophy slightly. A human being on six month's of bed rest loses a lot of muscle. Scientists hope that by studying the bears' unique physiological ability to hibernate without losing muscle or bone mass they may be able to improve astronauts' life in the weightless world of space, and even find ways to help the human body better adjust to organ transplants and heal from major wounds.

have to worry about holiday weight gain. You'd just go to sleep in January fat, and wake up fit and trim in June.

Bears make their dens in natural caves, snow caves, hollow trees and logs, or shallow caves they've dug out beneath tree roots. In some areas bears "nest" in a tree-hollow far above the ground. Bears have even been known to gather a bed of twigs and vegetation on the ground and patiently wait for old man winter to cover them up with an insulating blanket of snow. And most bear biologists have a story or two about a bear that settled in for its long winter's nap beneath some unsuspecting homeowner's deck or porch.

When it's time to leave the den, adult males are generally the first bears out and prowling around; females with cubs are normally the last to emerge.

SMARTER THAN YOUR AVERAGE DOG

Yogi Bear had a famous line: "Hey, Boo Boo, I'm smarter than your average bear." That would make Yogi an ursine genius, because your average bear is pretty darn smart.

Bear biologists who've measured bears' IQs say that the average black bear is significantly smarter than a German Shepherd, widely regarded as the smartest dog. Bears have the heaviest brains, relative to body length, of any carnivore.

Bears are also naturally very curious, and will explore just about anything new they come across in the hopes it might be edible. Scientists believe a bear's curiosity and intelligence are important tools that help bears squeeze the most possible calories out of their environment, identify and

"The intelligence of this animal never fails to amaze me. I observed and photographed this bear moving a log into place so she could walk across it and get to the other side of a creek without swimming. This was an animal using a tool to accomplish a task— an ability normally accredited to only humans and chimpanzees. Bears are truly amazing."
BILL LEA, WILDLIFE PHOTOGRAPHER

avoid danger, and find mates. But if you've ever watched a bear playing "slide down the snow bank," or "tree teeter-totter," it's hard not to believe that sometimes bears just wanna have fun.

Bears also have excellent memories, and will return unerringly year after year to a place that has provided food, whether it's a berry patch or a garbage dump. Mother bears patiently teach their cubs where to find the calories they need, and what times of year to visit each source. We live in an area where chokecherries and service-berries ripen in August, and each August, just like clockwork, bears appear to feast on the ripening fruit. For three or four weeks, copious piles of seed-laden bear scat festoon our road. By September the bears have moved on.

CAN BEARS REASON?

There's plenty of evidence that bears can recognize a wide variety of objects, from beehives and berry bushes to coolers and campers, and learn and generalize to a simple concept level.

So if a bear discovers a bird feeder in one backyard and nothing bad happens when it bats it down and gobbles up the seed, it will check out other yards hoping to find more bounty. If it does, the bear "reasons" that this must be a place with a good crop of "bear-feeders," and keeps looking. And since it found a good meal once, it's likely to come back for more.

Bears have an acute sense of smell, and can scent a person as much as a mile away.

A NOSE FOR FOOD

"A cookie crumb fell in the woods. The eagle saw it. The deer heard it. The bear smelled it, and went looking for the rest of the box." That's not exactly how the old American Indian proverb goes, but it does highlight a bear's single most powerful sense: its nose.

Think you have a pretty good sense of smell? Imagine being able to stand on your back porch and smell the scent of

© Tom Beck

chicken grilling on your neighbor's barbeque 5 miles (8 km) away. A bear's nose has 100 times more nasal mucosa area than yours, and is seven times more sensitive than a bloodhound's famed sniffer. According to Gary Brown's *Great Bear Almanac*, a black bear in California was once seen traveling upwind 3 miles (4.8 km) in a straight line to reach the carcass of a dead deer.

Bears can detect molecules of food so small they're invisible to the naked eye. Sniff out a candy bar stuffed under a car seat—from outside the car. And tell the difference between people and animals by trace scents left in footprints.

So is it any wonder that the leftovers from yesterday's dinner decomposing in your garbage send out tempting smell signals a hungry bear finds easy to follow…and hard to resist?

Even adult black bears climb trees with ease.
© Tim Halvorson

ALL EARS

It's pretty hard to administer a hearing test to a conscious black bear, but scientists believe that bears hear in the ultrasonic range of 16 – 20 kilohertz or higher—much better than we do.

DO BEARS NEED GLASSES?

Bears can see about as well as we do, although there is some speculation they might be a bit nearsighted, and that's why they often stand up and sniff the air when they're trying to identify something. Being nearsighted might actually help bears locate berries, grubs and other small delicacies. Bears also see in color. Watch a bear delicately stripping berries from a branch or licking up ants scurrying out of an anthill, and you'll have no doubt a bear can see what it's doing.

ALL-AROUND ANIMAL ATHLETES

Bears can run up to 35 mph (56 kph) for short distances, and despite what many people seem to believe, have no trouble running downhill. Or uphill. Or across the hill. World class Olympic athlete Mo Green can hit about 23 mph (37 kph), but the average human is lucky to manage half that. Bears are also good swimmers. And unlike grizzly bears, even adult black bears are great tree climbers. You can't outrun, outswim or outclimb a bear. ❖

Bears don't sweat, so they love to cool off in a stream, lake or the occasional backyard pool. They're also good swimmers.
© Cory Phillips

JUST HOW SMART ARE BEARS?

I had one very large female that regularly visited leg-hold snares. She'd pick up rocks and drop them on the trigger, firing the snare. Then she'd  go in and eat the bait. All this after only one prior capture. Quite often she would also leave a bucket-load of scat before leaving. I interpreted her parting gesture to be her opinion of leg-hold snares in general, an attitude I soon came to share with her. *Note: leg-hold snares are no longer in use in Colorado. In fact, Beck helped design a better, more efficient and less dangerous (to the bear) cage trap.*

chapter 3

The Nature of Bears

Understanding Bear Behavior

B lack bears can easily attack and kill people, but very seldom do. They can defend their territory and their young, but are more likely to flee. Bears are neither the growling, slobbering man-eating beasts of movies, nightmares and sensational news stories, nor the cute, cuddly, friendly teddy bears of cartoons and story books. Bears, just like people, have both general characteristics and individual temperaments and personalities. It's ironic that a species whose members range from Jeffrey Dahmer, the cannibal killer, to Mother Theresa thinks bears are unpredictable.

"If you've studied an individual bear, its behavior is almost 100 percent predictable. The bear has developed certain set ways to respond to danger, challenge, opportunity, obstacles," noted bear authority Steve Herrero explains.

A bear's life is dedicated to doing whatever it takes to find food and avoid trouble. So in addition to being naturally shy and wary of humans and other things they're not familiar with, bears are also highly adaptable, insatiably curious, and very intelligent, flexible and resourceful.

© Bill Lea

BEARS ARE SHY

Centuries ago when the grizzly bear roamed over much of the continent, black bears learned to share space by avoiding confrontations at all costs. They took to the forest, where there was plenty of

39

cover and places to hide, and avoided the open plains where they'd have to stand and defend themselves against far bigger and more aggressive predators.

A wild black bear detecting a human nearby will normally turn tail and flee. But bears are also nervous and easily frightened; surprising, cornering or approaching a bear can force it into a position where it thinks it has no choice except to fight back.

REMARKABLY TOLERANT

Even under the most trying of circumstances, black bears are remarkably tolerant of people. Steve Herrero tells a tale that demonstrates both the tolerance of bears and the cruelty of some humans. In 1968 he watched three teenagers chase two cubs up a tree, pelting them with rocks while the mother bear watched. The boys continued shelling the young bears, and eventually the sow climbed up and tried to shield her cubs with her body. At that point Steve the dispassionate scientist gave way to Steve the protector of nature; the boys threatened him with a tire iron, but he stood his ground. Apparently they were willing to take on a bear, but not a hopping mad bear scientist, and eventually they left. He notes if they'd harassed grizzly bear cubs, they would almost certainly have been injured, or worse.

CURIOUS AND RESOURCEFUL

Black bears have to take in a lot of calories just to survive, so naturally bears are always looking for food. Most bears live in places where different foods are available at different times of the year. They're genetically programmed to investigate everything and anything that might possibly be edible, and use their sensitive noses to lead them to the source of any interesting smells. For a bear, a spirit of culinary adventure and endless curiosity are necessary survival traits.

One summer day in Minnesota's northwestern woods a great blue heron strode with wings outstretched through the Vince Shute Wildlife Sanctuary. All the bears in the area immediately climbed trees to escape this "threat."

GOOD MEMORIES

A bear's ability to quickly learn and retain information helps it keep a mental catalogue of all the various food sources in its territory, and when they're usually available. Mother bears patiently teach their cubs where to find food from the earliest spring buds and grasses to the acorns and berries that ripen in the fall. An animal that can remember that buffalo berries ripen the second week in August on the south slope and the third week on the north slope has no trouble remembering that by Thursday night the community dumpster is full of tasty trash.

THE LANGUAGE OF BEARS

Bears may not be able to talk, but they use a wide variety of sounds and body postures to get their point across. Despite what you see in the movies, black bears don't snarl or roar, but they do occasionally use a wide range of vocalizations that all have a specific meaning—to the bear.

Grunting "Clungk, clungk" is the most common bear sound. Bears grunt in amicable situations with mates, cubs, other bears, and occasionally with humans.

Huffing A loud, single exhalation of air through the lips sometimes heard by people who encounter a bear; it means the bear is nervous or afraid. Even cubs huff.

Huff-Huff-Huff See above, and repeat.

Jaw Popping Snapping the jaws and popping the lips. Huffing and jaw-popping often precede or follow bluff charges; rather than being aggressive, it's usually a defensive sound that's an alternative to getting physical, kind of like people yelling.

NICE TRY

In the Smokies bears learned to distinguish between tourists and uniformed park rangers, and promptly ran away when rangers appeared, even when they drove unmarked cars.

BEARS SNORE

No word on whether
Breathe-Right strips are
effective, since, except
for mothers with cubs,
bears sleep alone, and
no one elbows them in
the side and tells them
to roll over.

© Bill Lea

Tooth-clicking A softer version of jaw-popping that people some-times hear when a bear retreats or is bluffing. When used by mothers with cubs it means "Something's wrong, get up a tree."

Bawling Long, loud, hoarse wailing produced by cubs frightened or separated from their mothers. Cubs also scream in distress, whine much like human offspring, and make a deep humming sound when nursing or comfy and warm.

Moaning Sounds like a human moan. Bears trapped in trees for long periods of time often moan in fear.

Moaning and Throat Pulsing If a black bear you've encountered is facing you with its ears back moaning and making a deep-throated, pulsing sound, it's time to be very alert and cautious; the bear is very distressed and could charge.

BEAR BODY LANGUAGE

Bears use their bodies to communicate everything from "Hey, I wonder if that's something good to eat?" to "Back off and get out of my space." Because most people don't speak bear language, it's easy to misinterpret what a bear is trying to say.

Bear standing on hind legs "*Gotta get a better smell of whatever that is.*" Bears stand on their hind legs to get a better look and smell of something unusual they've detected—from a passing hiker to a decomposing carcass. Despite what you see in movies, this is not an aggressive posture. The bear is just using its super-sensitive nose to figure out what's going on.

Bear standing on hind legs, moving head from side to side "*Hang on, it's a really faint scent, I need a better whiff.*

Rotting deer? No, ripe garbage!" The bear's trying to pick up more scent particles in the air; kind of making its own breeze.

Nose up, ears forward, standing on all four paws or standing up on hind legs *"I gotta figure out what that is. It might be good to eat. Or it could be dangerous."* The bear is once again "nosing around" trying to get a better smell of something it doesn't recognize.

Head down, ears laid back, body low to the ground or rearing up on hind legs *"Don't make me do something we'll both regret."* Ears laid back—just as with horses and dogs—mean the bear is nervous, afraid or feels threatened, and might feel like it has to fight back.

Rearing up on hind legs with ears laid back, jaw and mouth wide open to display teeth, moaning, woofing or clacking *"How many times do I have to tell you to get lost?"*

Ears lowered, but not back all the way, no eye contact, cowering with head lowered, trying to look smaller. *"Hey, sorry, I didn't mean to butt in. How about we just go our separate ways?"*

Ears forward, openly approaching, silent and confident Whether directed at prey or people, these are signs of a bear on a mission, and indicate aggressive, predatory behavior. See Chapter 17 for how to recognize and respond to an aggressive bear.

Ears laid back is a sign that a bear is nervous or feels threatened. It means "back off and go away."
© Cory Phillips

BEAR VS. BEAR

While bears have been observed having "boxing matches" during mating season, or tangling over turf or food, black bears seldom fight to the death. Usually the smaller or younger bear shows proper deference to its elders by cowering and backing off.

BEAR UP A TREE

Bears climb trees to munch acorns and take naps; they also take to the treetops to escape from something they perceive as dangerous—like the television crew and mob of neighbors that turn a bear wandering out of the foothills into somebody's apple orchard into "news."

Mother bears routinely send their cubs up trees to avoid everything from potential predators to overly-curious humans. Usually if you see cubs in a tree, their anxious mother is nearby. If you persist in hanging around, or looking for her, you might drive her farther away, or cause a startled cub to take a fatal tumble. Or it's always possible you'll actually find momma bear, and succeed in frightening and aggravating her so much she gives you a swat.

My favorite observation on what to do if you see a bear in a tree comes from the no-nonsense Web site of Minnesota's Department of Natural Resources: "Leave the bear alone. It will come down and go away when it feels safe."

BEAR SIGNS

Bears are big animals, and usually leave signs of their presence. You can learn a lot about bears if you know how to read them. How you react to signs of bear activity depends on where you are, what time of year it is, and what you and the bear are doing. A steaming fresh pile of bear scat on a trail leading through a dense stand of oak brush in the fall means bears may be in the area right now, and you should either turn around, or proceed with extreme caution. Bear tracks on the trail tell you a bear has passed by, but not usually when. Long claw marks on trees are a sign you've found a marking tree, but not necessarily that a bear is close by. A smashed,

A black bear can scoot up a hundred foot tree in under a minute. These bears in British Columbia are getting a bears' eye view of the countryside. *Courtesy of Ken Flett and Larry Pollman*

empty bird feeder lying on the ground is a sure sign a bear has paid you a visit—and you can expect it to return.

Bear Tracks

Black bear tracks are very distinctive; it's hard to mistake them for anything else, except maybe a barefoot human foot print. All bears have five toes. The front foot is short and 4 to 5 inches (10 to 12.7 cm) wide. The hind foot is long and narrow, measuring around 7 inches (17.8 cm), with a rounded heel and a wedge in the instep. Bears can't retract their claws, but sometimes claw marks aren't visible. Bears are normally solitary; if you find more than one set of prints, it could be a mother with cubs or yearlings, or if it's mating season, it might be a male and female traveling together. Or you could simply be on a trail that bears travel frequently. Bear tracks are common in areas with enough rainfall to keep the ground soft; uncommon in much of the drier western part of the continent except during the rainy or snowy season. In any case an absence of tracks doesn't mean there's an absence of bears.

Bear tracks in the mud.
© *Bryan Peterson*

Bear Scat

It's easy to recognize a bear's very sizable droppings. Bears have digestive systems that aren't very efficient; instead of leaving tidy piles of tight little pellets like deer and elk, bears leave big piles that leave no doubt what's been by. Bear scat will usually tell you exactly what the bear's been eating—from berries to bird seed, it all comes out in the end.

    If you want to know how fresh the scat is, turn it over with a stick. If the grass underneath is still green, it's fresh enough that the bear might be nearby.

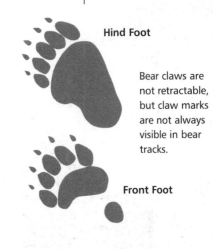

Hind Foot

Bear claws are not retractable, but claw marks are not always visible in bear tracks.

Front Foot

If the underside is dry and the grass is yellow or brown, it's been a while since the bear passed through.

Bears are a lot like people—the more they eat, the more they scat. During summer bears deposit scat piles a couple of times a day. During berry season, the same bear might scat fifteen times a day. So lots of big piles of berry-filled scat don't mean there's a herd of bears in the area.

A bear's sizable dropping are very distinctive. A good look will usually tell you what the bear's been dining on. The cell phone gives you an idea of volume. The tidy droppings are from the spring; the big "cow pie" is from the fall. Bear scat usually doesn't smell bad, so if you're the curious sort, use a stick to break apart droppings, and look for berries, bits of fur and hair, and other evidence of the bear's diet.
© Bryan Peterson

Overturned Rocks and Logs

Bears flip over rocks looking for ants, beetles, grubs and plant roots. If the underside of the rock is still damp, you just missed the bear. Bears also rip into fallen trees and logs looking for insects, and will dig into ant hills and bee hives in search of a fat- and protein-packed meal. In cattle country, bears turn over cow pies in search of bugs.

Marks on Trees

Bears often climb trees for safety, and leave distinctive claw marks going up and sliding down. Sometimes they use trees as scratching posts, leaving claw and tooth marks in soft bark. Bears also "mark" trees in their home range by rubbing, leaving strands of hair, or clawing the tree—all thought to be signals to other bears.

Fish Heads and Entrails

If you find fish heads and entrails along a stream or lake shore, it could be a sloppy fisherman, but it's probably a sign of bears feeding on fish in the area. See Chapter 16 for details on what to do next.

Brush-Covered Carcass

If you find a carcass hidden under a pile of debris, it probably belongs to a mountain lion or a bear. In either case, the advice is the same. Take a good look around, back off until you're out of sight, and then turn around or make a wide detour. Animals work hard for their dinner, and whatever buried the carcass is probably close by. Even a mild-manned black bear might turn defensive to protect its food. If you're in grizzly country, this is a potentially serious situation; vamoose immediately, keeping your eyes peeled for a climbable tree and your ears open. Mountain lions cache carcasses more often than bears do, and are very defensive about protecting them.

WOOFING, MOANING & GRUNTING

If you hear a lot of woofing, moaning or grunting sounds, there's probably a bear close by who's trying to let you know you've gotten too close, and it's not comfortable.

Many years ago, when I only came out West on vacation and knew nothing about bears, I got lost in the forest near sundown. While I was wandering around trying to find my way out, I heard persistent woofing; luckily for me, I never found the "dog" that was "barking" at me. Blind luck must have sent me out of the bear's way, and eventually I stumbled within earshot of a family that had just arrived for the weekend. I've learned a lot about both bears and hiking since then. ❖

Black bears use their short, curved claws to rip into fallen trees and dig out tasty insects and grubs.
© Tom Beck

Whistler, British Columbia, Canada

Getting Smart About Bears

Just about everyone in the breathtakingly beautiful Canadian province of British Columbia lives in bear country. Between 1992 and 1996, British Columbia received reports of over 41,000 human-black bear conflicts; 4,246 bears were destroyed, and another 1,418 were relocated.

The four-season resort town of Whistler, British Columbia, is nestled in a valley bottom in the Coastal Mountain Ranges, right next to Garibaldi Provincial Park. Whistler is in the midst of the kind of habitat black bears love to call home.

"Over twenty bears a year were dying in the community of Whistler because of people's carelessness and negligence; the policy was to destroy bears that came in contact with people. We thought the bears deserved better," says Sylvia Dolson, executive director of the Get Bear Smart Society.

Thanks to Dolson, and a coalition of representatives from government, industry and

> *"There is no need to unjustly fear bears. When we can replace fear and ignorance with respect, then people will become more tolerant, and will be more likely to take the appropriate steps toward human-bear coexistence."*
>
> WHISTLER BLACK BEAR MANAGEMENT PLAN

the private sector, people in Whistler and many other Canadian communities are learning how to peacefully coexist with bears.

By the time you read this, Whistler will probably be Canada's first official Bear Smart Community, which seems only fitting, since the Bear Smart Community Certification Program had its roots in programs developed and pioneered in Whistler.

"The more people learn about bears, the more they respect them, and the less they fear them. You can change people's attitudes and behavior one person at a time. Every individual can make a difference. You can choose to be part of the problem—or part of the solution," says Dolson.

Between April and November—which is also bear season—the tiny town hosts nearly a million visitors who come to hike, bike, golf and windsurf. Tourists and temporary workers are tough to educate and motivate. Predictably, the town had ongoing problems with bears.

In 1997 Sylvia Dolson became a director and co-chair of Whistler's newly organized Black Bear Task Team, charged with developing and implementing a bear management plan. The team also included the Resort Municipality of Whistler staff, the local waste management company, the Conservation Officer Service, Whistler-Blackcomb Mountain staff, and the Association of Whistler Area Residents for the Environment.

With that many people and government entities on one committee, it's amazing they got anything done at all, much less implemented a bear management program that's the envy of much of North America.

Today Whistler has the most extensive black bear management plan of any community in British Columbia. The program includes education for all, mandated bear-proof waste management programs, tough local regulations that are strictly enforced and an aversive conditioning program—a non-lethal way to teach bears that people equal trouble, not food.

There are Neighborhood Bear Watch groups, Bear Smart business and residential certification programs, community workshops and programs, and plenty of bear signage, something Whistler, as a resort community, was at first a bit leery about. What would the tourists who fueled the town's economy think about

signs that reminded them they were playing in bear country?

Educating tourists is an uphill battle, but forewarned is forearmed, and today Whistler-Blackcomb resort, owned by Intrawest, has a comprehensive bear ecology and bear-awareness program as well, with interpretive displays, educational signs and an inviting wildlife center for children. The resort has even attempted to improve natural foraging opportunities for bears by planting fruit-bearing trees and undertaking a program of thinning forests by helicopter logging rather than traditional logging; when trees are thinned out, more light penetrates into the undisturbed understory of the forest, and berry production goes up.

SARA TUTLE

It took several years to get the town's daunting garbage problems, typical of tourist towns everywhere, under control, but by 2000 all waste containers were bear resistant. Whistler doesn't have a household garbage collection system—instead they have two bear-proofed compactor sites, one at each end of town. They're cleaned out daily, out of regard for both bears and people.

Whistler's local waste hauler is Carney's Waste System. Owner Owen Carney has been a big supporter of bear-proofing Whistler, and even designed a brand new commercial bear-resistant bin.

Thanks to a combined effort by The Get Bear Smart Society, the Resort Municipality of Whistler, private businesses and public donations, all the waste containers along Whistler's pedestrian walkways are now bear-resistant as well.

Whistler's municipal landfill has now been completely fortified with an electric fence.

When the fence was installed, the bears showed just how smart they really are. They dove into the landfill from nearby trees and rock piles. They climbed wooden fence posts. They dug under the fence. They scooted through the gate when it was left open.

Determined to outsmart the bears, the town installed concrete barriers to keep them from digging under the fence, nailed spikes into the wooden posts, and installed a cleverly designed gate with plastic handles, so the power is always on. All the trees inside the landfill were removed, so if bears managed to get in, they had nowhere to hide.

The final touch was an electrified cattle grate which trucks can drive over, and people wearing shoes can safely walk over, but gives bear feet a big shock. Now and then a bear overcomes all the obstacles and gets in, but most have finally given up and gone back to foraging on all the natural foods available.

An aversive or negative conditioning program to teach bears to avoid people places got underway in 1999, along with a positive conditioning program directed at Whistler's human inhabitants.

Is it working? The number of bears destroyed in the Whistler area has dropped by 75 percent.

Team Members: back row–Dan LeGrandeur, Eivind Tornes, Wayne McCrory, Ray Longmuir, Ainslie Willock, Catherine Sherlock; front row–Sylvia Dolson, Evelyn Kirkaldy, Lucy the Bear Dog, Loran Visser, Kristi Broadbent.

LAYING DOWN THE LAW

Whistler's Garbage Disposal Bylaws contain some of the toughest provisions in British Columbia, and much tougher provisions than most municipalities in the U.S.

BYLAW NO. 1445

◆ No garbage, food waste or other waste can be stored outdoors, including on the patio, deck or balcony.

◆ All outdoor trash containers have to be wildlife resistant.

◆ All businesses, hotels, apartment buildings and industrial complexes have to store garbage inside a building or wildlife-resistant enclosure.

◆ Feeding "dangerous wildlife" and depositing or storing any "garbage, food waste or other edible waste" is illegal.

◆ Bird feeders must be inaccessible.

◆ Garbage containers for special events have to be picked up and emptied by 10 p.m.

Whistler residents and businesses that don't comply get more than a slap on the wrist; municipal bylaws impose fines of up to $2,000. In serious cases, failure to comply with a written order can earn the offender a trip to court, a $50,000 fine and six months in jail. The Whistler newspaper regularly publishes articles and lists areas that have been issued orders.

Whistler now has its first bear-response officer, and the B.C. Conservation Corps Program is funding three grad students to study black bear aversive conditioning in the hopes of discovering what techniques are most effective, and establishing guidelines for the province and North America. Part of the study will involve radio-collaring and monitoring Whistler's bears, so they'll know what's really happening.

The Bear Smart program focuses on addressing the root causes of human-bear conflicts, reducing the number of conflicts, and ultimately reducing the number of bears that are destroyed due to conflicts.

Canada's Bear Smart Certification program involves a complex six-step process that includes a bear hazard assessment of the community and surrounding area by a bear biologist, a human/bear conflict management plan, a continuing education program directed at all sectors of the community, developing and maintaining a bear-proof municipal solid waste management system, and implementing "Bear Smart" laws prohibiting people from intentionally or unintentionally providing food for, or attracting, bears.

In order to assist communities with pursuing "Bear Smart" status, the Ministry of the Environment offers some funding to local governments and local community conservation organizations, in cooperation with the Habitat Conservation Trust Fund. The Vancouver Foundation, the Animal Welfare

Foundation of Canada, and Community Foundations of Canada all make grants to support local initiatives. Communities provide an office with a phone and Internet hook up, as well as some matching funding, and hopefully a team of Bear Smart volunteers.

Dolson envisions a network of Bear Smart Communities stretching across North America from border to border. They've just begun working with other governments across Canada that want to proactively address their own bear issues. They're also working with Canada's federal police force, the Royal Canadian Mounted Police, in British Columbia and Western Alberta to provide training to all the police officers who work in bear country, with the RCMP providing funding, and the Get Bear Smart Society providing the bear know-how. Canada's federal government is now talking about implementing a national program.

"Governments are just now realizing that it's within our power to prevent these problems," says Dolson. ❖

ABOUT THE GET BEAR SMART SOCIETY

The Get Bear Smart Society—formerly the Jennifer Jones Whistler Bear Society—is a registered Canadian charity, with a large number of supporters. They fund their wide-ranging bear education and problem prevention activities through donations, a municipal grant from Whistler, and whatever foundation grants are available. They also have donation boxes in retail outlets, and produce educational merchandise like Bear Smart playing cards, stickers and magnets retailers can sell for a profit, so they make money, Get Bear Smart makes money, and people have fun learning about bears.

Get Bear Smart has an extensive and enlightening Web site that's a must-visit for anyone who wants to know more about getting along with bears. There's a wealth of information, plus many free materials available for downloading, including resident and visitor guides, and copies of brochures, flyers, booklets and pamphlets that can be adapted to other communities.

www.bearsmart.com   ◆   Donate through *www.CanadaHelp.org*

chapter 4

Cleaning Up Your Act
Stash That Trash and Save A Bear

Ask almost any bear behavior expert what's the biggest cause of human-bear conflicts and the answer is always the same: garbage, one way or another, kills bears.

WHY BEARS LOVE GARBAGE

© Michael Burhart; courtesy of
Bear Smart Durango.

Many people have a hard time understanding why bears are attracted to their icky, stinky trash. It's because just one typical 35-gallon (132-liter) garbage container filled with leftovers and scraps can provide enough calories to feed a bear for a day.

Bears are just like people. It's calories eaten (food) minus calories expended (exercise and basic metabolism) that determines how much a bear weighs. Most people want to be thin. All bears want to be fat. Bears need to gain 30 to 40 percent of their springtime body weight by fall if they're going to survive their winter hibernation.

Imagine the bear bounty offered by a trip down just one alley filled with garbage waiting to be picked up. Or the incredible allure of an open dumpster stuffed to overflowing with a week's worth of bear food. Imagine being a mother bear trying to feed a couple of rambunctious cubs that are growing like weeds. Imagine being a

53

young bear trying to survive on your own. Imagine being truly as hungry as a bear.

If we make it easy for bears to fatten up on the leftovers of the human good life, how can we blame them for taking advantage of an easy meal?

WHY GARBAGE KILLS BEARS

Getting rewarded for getting into the garbage is often a pivotal event in a bear's life. Lured in by the smell of food, the bear overcame its natural wariness of humans. If the bear gets the reward it came looking for and goes away none the worse for the experience, it will be back to the all-you-can-paw-through buffet.

Being an opportunistic feeder, an enterprising bear will also case the joint to see what else smells or looks good. If it discovers more easy-to-get-at goodies—bird feeders, pet food, even things that smell interesting but really aren't, like a greasy barbeque grill—they're added to the menu.

Pretty soon the bear is causing a lot of "problems." It's becoming a "nuisance." As it gets more comfortable around people, it grows bolder. It might start strolling through back yards in the middle of the day, pushing open screen doors, or popping out open or unlocked windows searching for more

Bumper sticker from the Colorado Division of Wildlife.

DEADLY TRASH

Bears everywhere die horrible and needless deaths each year from eating plastic and other packaging materials not meant to be digested by human or bruin. Trash can block, twist or rupture the intestines, resulting in a slow and painful death for the bear. Bears have also died after eating toxic substances people throw out, like antifreeze.

food. In some places bears have learned to open car doors to look for treats; apparently bears realize humans go nowhere without provisions.

Eventually the bear may cause so much damage, or become so aggressive, it will be killed. All because someone who lives in bear country wouldn't lock up their trash.

BEAR PROOFING YOUR GARBAGE

Bryan Peterson, the president of Bear Smart Durango, says studies show that three simple steps can eliminate up to 90 percent of all bear conflicts:

◆ Put your trash out in the morning, never the night before
◆ Store trash in a secure location or bear-resistant container
◆ Clean your trash container regularly

"We lure bears in with an easy meal and punish them with death for accepting our invitation."

SYLVIA DOLSON
GET BEAR SMART SOCIETY

Put Your Trash Out in the Morning

Sure, it's easier to take your trash out to the curb the night before. But having garbage sit out overnight issues an almost irresistible invitation to come and get it to any bears within five or ten miles.

A study done by the town of Payson, Arizona showed that residents who left their garbage out overnight had a 70 percent chance of a bear dropping by. That chance dropped to just two percent for people who stored their trash securely until the morning of pick up.

Do yourself and the bears a big favor. Put your trash out in the morning, as close to pick up time as possible.

A bear can crumple a flimsy, unlocked shed as easily as you can crush a modern day soda can.
© Bryan Peterson

Bear Safe Trash Stashing

It won't do you any good to take your trash out in the morning if it's sitting in an old garbage can next to your garage the rest of the week. Inside a screened-in porch, on or under your deck, in a flimsy shed or garage, or the back of your pickup truck are all bad places to store garbage.

In between collection days or trips to the dump, store your trash inside a garage, basement, or sturdy shed or barn with solid doors that close and lock. If the building has lever-style door handles, be sure to lock it up each night, or replace the handles with old-fashioned round knobs that bears can't open.

Freeze It

If you don't have a really secure location to store garbage, start a trash sack in the freezer for extra smelly items like fish, meat, chicken, bones and fruit. Add it to the trash the morning of pick up, or when you're taking trash to the dump.

The Bear-Resistant Solution

Like mother, like son...or daughter. You're never too young to learn that a pick-up truck full of trash is a great place to pick up a quick meal. © *Mike Fox*

Bear-resistant containers are one of the best ways to defeat bears. They come in a wide range of sizes, from 64 gallons (242 liters) to dumpster size, and range in price from around a $100 to $500 USD or more. It may seem like a lot of money for a garbage can, but it's a small investment compared to the price of cleaning up after a bear. Ordinary metal and rubber trash containers, even ones with locking lids, are no match for a bear.

The Grizzly and Wolf Discovery Center in West Yellowstone, Montana is home to a number of grizzly bears that put bear-resistant products to the ultimate test. Grizzly bears are incredibly strong, as well as curious and patient. A grizzly can punch a hole in the roof of a cabin, rip the door off a car or pry open just about anything it can get its claws under.

Some of the Center's bears were orphaned as cubs, and wouldn't have survived on their own in the wild. Others were "nuisance" bears who had learned that people equal food and were paroled to the Center instead of destroyed. They have individual dens, and roam around a two-acre outdoor habitat where visitors can watch them. Their keepers hide food under rocks and in log piles to encourage them to use their natural foraging skills.

The bears that were once "nuisances" now work for a living by trying their best to get at the food treats hidden inside a variety of trash containers and dumpsters sent to the Center for testing.

The grizzlies take their job seriously, and are happy to whack, bash, poke, prod, stand on, jump on and toss around the containers. If a container can stand up to the determined assault of a grown grizzly bear, it's a safe bet it will be able to take anything a black bear can dish out.

The testing protocol and standards were developed by the Living With Wildlife Foundation; Montana Fish, Wildlife & Parks; U.S. Forest Service; and the Interagency Grizzly Bear Committee. A CD of resources is available from the Living with Wildlife Foundation. See the Appendix for more information.

Determined grizzlies work for their keep putting trash containers to the ultimate test. © *Derek Reich*

Make a Trash Corral

One alternative to bear-resistant containers is a bear-resistant enclosure. A simple chain link enclosure with a lid, metal flanges and hinges, and a sturdy lock—not a simple latch—can defeat the most determined bear. Bears are great diggers, so build your corral on a concrete pad. Go for materials a bear can't claw or bite through—chicken wire or flimsy fencing won't work.

Sturdy, curbside bear-
resistant containers have
locking lids.
© Bryan Peterson

Creative Trash Control

No time to build an enclosure, no money to buy bear-resistant containers? Bears are smart, but most people are smarter. Just about any sturdy, durable, closed and locked metal or heavy duty plastic container can be turned into effective temporary trash storage, including steel storage drums with modified locking lids, tool, truck and storage boxes and cargo trailers. One enterprising man solved the problem by suspending his trash from two trees, campground style, in between pick ups. No word on what the neighbors thought of this particular solution, but it kept the bears at bay.

Give Your Trash Can a Bath

A good spray-down with bleach or ammonia and hot water will go a long way towards eliminating lingering odors that can attract bears. Keep a spray bottle filled with ammonia handy and spray your cans inside and out after every pick up during bear season. Some people attach those handy stick-up air fresheners to the insides of the lids— if you try this, use industrial strength unscented fresheners. Making your garbage can smell like lemons will attract bears, not deter them.

YOU'RE NOT ALONE. UNFORTUNATELY.

If you clean up your act, and your neighbors don't, you may not have any problems, but the bears most certainly will.

Peer pressure is a wondrous thing. Once people know their neighbors frown on them creating a situation that could be expensive, unsanitary, unsightly and potentially dangerous to both bears and people, most folks think twice before they haul 70 gallons of leftovers out to the curb the night before.

If your neighborhood becomes a place where it's not cool to

cause bear problems, you could save the community a lot of aggravation and expense, and maybe save a bear's life.

Many forward-thinking towns, cities and municipalities across North America have taken the decision of whether or not to do the right thing out of the individual's hands by enacting ordinances that make it illegal to allow bears or other specified wildlife access to human food, garbage, pet food, bird seed and other attractants.

For some examples, see the Beary Smart Solutions profiles of the Town of Snowmass Village, Colorado (page 72), Canmore and Whistler, Canada (pages 83 and 48), and Lake Tahoe, California/Nevada (page 171). ❖

Bear-resistant dumpsters at the Falls Creek subdivision, north of Durango.
© *Bryan Peterson*

Unlocked dumpsters are open invitations to bears.
Courtesy of the Humane Society of the United States.

Hemlock Farms, Pennsylvania

Making Room for Bears

Pennsylvania's bear story is typical of many states in the eastern U.S. Twenty-five years ago Pennsylvania had an estimated 4,500 black bears. Over the past several decades marginal farm lands have reverted to forest, creating more spaces and places for bears. Today over 75 percent of the state is covered in second growth forests—ideal habitat for a bear population that's grown to 15,000.

Pennsylvania's human population has

> *"Bears are often needlessly killed, not for what they have done, but for what people think they might do. Many people unjustifiably fear bears, and still believe they cannot survive where humans exist. That is a fallacy."*
>
> BEAR BIOLOGIST GARY ALT

been increasing as well. And like so many other places in North America, as people push out into areas bears call home, more people come into contact with bears.

The story of the community of Hemlock Farms was first told by Wayne Lynch in his beautifully written book, *Bears: Monarchs of the Northern Wilderness.* When the book was published in 1993, the full and part-time residents of about 2,000 homes shared less then eight square miles with twenty resident bears.

Today over 3,000 homes nestle on half-acre lots carved out of prime bear habitat between Albany, New York and Harrisburg, Pennsylvania. In the summer the number of residents swells from 3,000 to 10,000. In order to preserve the natural environment people move to Hemlock Farms to enjoy, homes are surrounded by lots of community green space.

Noted bear biologist and researcher Dr. Gary Alt worked closely with the community for many years, studying both the bears and the

Bears cooling off in a backyard pond. © *Mickey McManus*

people. He often surprised residents by showing them a picture of a bear he and his team had just research tagged that had spent the winter denned up under the family's deck.

Hemlock Farms is a great place to get away from it all without traveling far off the beaten path. The community in the woods is close to a lot of things, including the state of New Jersey and major highways. After September 11 Hemlock Farms experienced a real influx of people who were nervous about city living, and fed up with city taxes.

Mike Sibio, who's worked for the Hemlock Farms community for over twenty years and been the resident manager for the last eight, says that today their biggest challenge is keeping a steady influx of new members informed about potential problems, and helping them understand that feeding animals leads to acclimating them to humans, bear break-ins and conflicts.

"Most of them come from the city; they've never even seen a bear. At first we get bear jams when a bear is sighted, especially in the spring when we have mothers and cubs. But for most people the novelty wears off over time. They hear enough about bears and cubs to give them plenty of space and respect them," Mike said.

The Association makes sure all new residents get a welcome package with all the bear facts. And residents go out of their way to let newcomers know they're serious about keeping their bears out of trouble.

"We try to assist with the education process through programs and handing out literature from the Pennsylvania Game Commission. Working together we are able to avoid the common problems associated with living with bears," Mike explained.

SARA TUTTLE

> One mom in Hemlock Farms successfully raised 29 cubs over ten years, a world's record.

The Association has regulations prohibiting the feeding of bears, requiring residents to put their trash in secure bear-resistant containers, and to use ammonia in their cans to prevent the bears from visiting and spreading the trash around on collection days when the cans are put out.

"Not getting along with the bears is not an option. They are so well adapted, that the placement of a community in their home range doesn't faze them. It's up to people to accept the fact that bears live in close proximity and they need to educate themselves on the do's and don'ts of living with them," Mike explained.

Nobody's perfect, and in the past several years the PGC has had to destroy two different sows that were breaking into houses, lured there by people who broke the rules and fed the bears. Once attracted, the bears quickly made themselves at home, and soon were loitering on porches and breaking in while people were home.

In 2003 the state of Pennsylvania followed the example set by Hemlock Farms, and passed a new ordinance making it illegal to put out food for bears, and illegal to put out any type of wildlife food, including bird seed, that causes bears to congregate in or become habituated to an area. ❖

Note: See the Appendix for a copy of the Hemlock Farm Ordinance.

A nervous mamma bear sends her cubs up out of "danger" near Elm Lake in Hemlock Farms.
© *Dennis Fleming*

chapter 5

Home, Bear-Proof Home

Outsmarting Bears on Your Home Turf

People who live in big cities often install burglar bars on windows, motion detector lights in their yards and high-tech security systems. They wouldn't dream of going to sleep with windows or doors unlocked because they know crime is often a matter of opportunity and convenience, and are willing to do what it takes to outsmart potential intruders.

Most folks don't give much thought to what it takes to live smart in bear country, but every year bear break-ins cost homeowners many thousands of dollars in damage, and often cost bears their lives. With a little preventative care and maintenance, you can protect your home, your property and the bears.

TIPS FOR HOMEOWNERS

The precautions you put into practice will depend in part on the level of bear activity in your area. Someone who lives in one of the woodsy communities surrounding Lake Tahoe or a ski community in Canada has a different level of interaction and exposure to bears than someone living in an area where bears are only occasional visitors.

Checkin' out what's for dinner. © *Bill Lea*

Talk to your neighbors and your local wildlife agency. If bears come through your neighborhood a few weeks a year on their way to the berry patch, you may not need to be on full bear alert except

63

for that particular time period. If bears are around from den-out to den-up, then faithfully taking every possible precaution makes *beary* good sense.

In my neighborhood, bears visit in the spring when young males are out looking for a quick meal and a new home, and in late summer when chokecherries and serviceberries ripen. Most of the rest of bear season we have only an occasional visitor. But we bring our bird feeders in, lock our trash in the garage and shut and lock our first floor windows and doors every night anyway. Less than 5 miles (8 km) away there are homes close to a creek; bears are active in that area all summer long.

This screen would be demolished if the bear that left these claw marks had really wanted in.
© Derek Reich

Close and Lock Those Windows

Close and lock all accessible windows whenever you leave the house, and every night before you go to bed. If you leave a window open even a crack, it's child's play for a bear to slip a paw underneath and push it open. Even if the window is closed but not locked, a bear can easily get a claw between the edge of the frame and the windowsill. Screens are for keeping out bugs, not bears. If you can afford it, replace any single pane windows with double pane glass; you'll save on your energy bills too.

You can leave upstairs windows open unless there's easy bear access—like a stairway leading to a second floor porch or deck. Heat rises, so the heat from downstairs will flow up and out, and cool evening air will eventually flow in.

If you must keep your downstairs windows open at night, or have a cabin or home that's only occupied intermittently, you can install sturdy grates or bars on the outside of any accessible windows. There are lots of decorative choices; as an added bonus, they help keep out human intruders as well.

In a pinch, you can put a heavy wooden dowel in the window track so the window only opens an inch or two. The downside: if a bear wants to rip out your window, it now has the leverage to do so.

If your ground floor windows offer a view into the kitchen or pantry, consider using shutters, shades or curtains during bear season. In Lake Tahoe bears peer into kitchen windows in hopes of spotting the big white box full of food. If they see a refrigerator, they try to get inside. Living without the view from your kitchen window is better than living without your kitchen. Bears are very curious; at the very least cover windows that provide a bear's eye view when you're not at home. Windows at garden level should be secured; sturdy grates are your best protection.

Bears Love French Doors and Screen Doors

French doors are a big hit with bears; in many areas they've learned to push down on the handle and quietly let themselves into the house. If you live in one of those places, replace your lever-style door handles with sturdy round knobs bears can't get a grip on.

It also helps to have doors that open out, rather than in; that way if a bear does manage to open the door it still has to pull it open rather than just lean into it.

Locking a screen door does nothing to keep out a bear. Close and lock all your exterior doors whenever you leave the house, and at night before you go to bed.

Pet Doors Are Used By More Than Dogs and Cats

Mama bears sometimes send their cubs into a home through a handy pet door. Once inside the youngsters scurry about gathering up provisions, and bring them back outside for a family picnic.

Many adult bears can also easily fit through a dog door. Beck reports that the standard winter den entrance in Colorado ranged between nine and fourteen inches high. Your dog door is also plenty

BEAR BELLS

If you live in an area with frequent bear activity and want to leave windows and doors open when you're home, hang a bell on the screen, so you'll be alerted if a bear (or anything or anyone else) is trying to get in. There are also motion-activated bear alarm systems. Bells and alarms won't deter a determined bear, but at least you'll hear it coming.

big enough to admit raccoons, skunks and even some people.

So lock your pet door at night, or install a one way door, where your pet can get out, but can't get back in. Yes, I know that's inconvenient. It's not as inconvenient as cleaning up the mess a bear can make of your kitchen. There are also doggy doors that are activated by a special electronic dog collar.

Cellar and Trap Doors Are An Open Invitation

Crawl spaces make excellent dens. © Bill Lea

In some parts of North America, homes still have root cellars or storage areas with simple, outside trap doors. These doors are equally simple for bears to open, and what better place to den up for the winter than in a nice, snug, weather-tight cellar? If the owners are away, the bear has plenty of time to make itself at home. One bear in Lake Tahoe dragged pillows and comforters from the master bedroom down to the cellar to make a nice little nest. The bear also emptied the cupboards, pantry and freezer, and turned the rugs and floors into a litter box. So lock and secure your cellar door.

FAST FOOD WINDOW

A nervous homeowner discovered a bear trying to raise a kitchen window that was cracked open a few inches, and threw some bread out of another window to divert its attention. The bear stopped and ate the bread, then started pushing on the window from where it had come. If the woman could have delivered a good shot of bear spray, the bear might have left for good. Now the bear knows her house as the "push on the window, get instant bread" house.

JOHN KOEHLER, DISTRICT WILDLIFE MANAGER – BOULDER, COLORADO, 2003

Porches Can Be Dangerous

A screened-in porch, sun room or three-season room might seem like a convenient place to store trash, pet food, birdseed, canned goods, beer and wine or any number of other things. Screens won't keep out bears. If you don't want to clean up a big mess, keep anything that could be an attractant inside, or in a secure building.

Trees Make Great Ladders

Trim back all tree limbs within 10 feet of upper story decks and windows. This helps protect against wildfires, too. In one community bears have learned to climb trees that overhang roofs, jump onto the roof and dangle over the edge trying to open a window—all to avoid bear unwelcome mats (see Chapter 12) on the ground level.

Bears Love To Stair-Step

Bears scamper up staircases with ease. One homeowner in the Crystal Lakes subdivision north of Fort Collins, Colorado built an ingenious "drawbridge" staircase for his weekend home. (He was highly motivated, since they'd had a messy and expensive bear break-in the previous year.) Now when they head back to the city after a weekend in the mountains, they raise the drawbridge.

Is Your Garage An Easy Target?

Garage doors made from lightweight panels are very vulnerable to bears. We have a neighbor who returned from a successful hunting and fishing trip with elk meat and trout that went into the freezer in the garage. One night a bear pushed in one of the panels on the garage door, raided the freezer and had quite a feast.

Black bears go stair-steppin' with ease.
© *Tim Halvorson*

All the guidelines about windows and doors apply equally to garages. Keep your garage door closed at all times—resist the temptation to leave it open because you'll just be gone for a few minutes.

Beck says if you live in an area with chronic bear break-ins, invest in a wooden, shuttered door that closes over your automatic sliding door that you can close at night or when you'll be away for a while. Replacing your garage door might be less expensive than replacing a couple of freezers full of food—and the freezers.

Another alternative is to move your extra freezer and frig inside. Refrigerators and freezers have vents that carry odors to the outside, and there's also ample evidence that many bears have learned that the big white boxes are almost always stuffed full of goodies.

Securing Storage Sheds, Outbuildings and Barns

Security is the key with all structures in bear country. Flimsy doors and windows, poor construction or leaving doors and windows open or unlocked is an invitation to a bear to come on in. Especially if you're storing horse grain or treats, livestock feed, pet food, birdseed, trash or recyclables (yes, empty cans smell good—even if they've been rinsed out) or anything else that smells inside.

Don't store things with odors inside a building that's hard to secure or poorly constructed. That includes things people don't eat, like anti-freeze, paint and petroleum products. You can also install electric fencing around the building.

I know a couple who stashed their horse cookies in plastic Rubbermaid containers near their round pen for years without incident—until the night the new bear in the neighborhood discovered them, and made off with 50 pounds of expensive, high calorie treats.

A little bear-proofing can prevent a lot of damage.
© *Bryan Peterson (top)*
© *Derek Reich (bottom)*

NEW CONSTRUCTION TIPS

If you're building a home in bear country, you can work with your builder or architect to build in a lot of bear-proofing features, which will improve both your life and the lives of the bears in the neighborhood.

To find out about bear activity, talk to the neighbors, your local bear group or your state or provincial wildlife agency. Don't rely on your builder or real estate agent; they're not too keen on telling customers about things like bears, wildfires, water shortages or other facts of life that might seem like warts on the perfect face of Paradise.

Location, Location, Location

If you have a choice, situate your home well away from brush, vegetation, streams, berry patches or fruit or nut bearing trees. Make sure there are no climbable tree limbs within 15 feet (4.5 meters) of your house that might provide access to upper story windows or decks. The less natural cover that's close by, the less likely it is a bear will come close enough to investigate.

© Paul Conrad / The Aspen Times

In the western U.S. many people live in areas with limited shade, lots of meadows and shrublands at lower elevations, and small pockets of conifers on north-facing slopes. Rest assured that every bear in the area will visit these cool, shady slopes on hot days. Positioning your house well away from any conifer stands will help prevent daytime bear visits.

Bear-Smart Landscaping

Don't put in, or allow your builder to plant, fruit-bearing trees or bushes if there are bears in the neighborhood. Don't plant shrubs

that produce berries of any kind close to your house. You can't blame bears for thinking they've discovered a dandy new food source. Once you attract bears to your property, they'll explore to see what else is around. If you absolutely must have fruit trees, consider installing an electric fence to protect them. Don't plant new lawns in clover. Bears just love clover, and you could soon have a bear convention in your front yard.

Choosing the Right Windows and Doors

Some recommend installing all windows at a height of at least ten feet (3 meters) off the ground. Sometimes with walk-outs and wrap-around decks that's not practical, so choose high quality, double or triple pane windows. Avoid casement windows; if you forget to lock them, they're very easy for a bear to open.

Avoid lever-style handles and French doors. Go for old-fashioned, high-quality round door knobs to thwart bears. Install doors that open out instead of in, so the bear has to pull the door open instead of just push it in.

Building In Bear-Resistant Storage

Think through how you're going to handle trash, where you're going to store pet food, bird seed and the like before you build. Don't plan on storing attractants outside or in a breezeway or screened-in porch, unless you're willing to invest in high quality bear-resistant enclosures or containers, and always use them.

Once you've locked your trash cans inside here, no bear can get at 'em.
NoBearCan, courtesy of Living With Wildlife Foundation

HELP! THERE'S A BEAR IN MY HOUSE

What should you do if you come home and discover there's a bear in your kitchen munching its way through your cupboards?

Open all your doors and get out of the bear's way before you start encouraging it to leave. Keep something handy inside and outside each entrance so you can quickly prop open doors; you don't want to be hunting for doorstops while trying to keep one eye on a bear.

Make sure you're not in the bear's escape route, and start yelling and throwing things in the bear's direction—you want the bear to know your home is not its home.

If you're inside the house and a bear comes in, try not to panic. Bears startle easily, and can wreak havoc careening around trying to escape. Don't get between the bear and an obvious escape route. In their mad dash to escape bears have injured people who've gotten in their way. If possible, prop open all exits, send your kids to their rooms or another safe place so they're out of the way, and then defend your space. Do your best to let the bear know it's not welcome. Yell, throw things, make lots of noise, and don't back down. You want to send a message to the bear that this is your den, and it's not welcome.

The Lake Tahoe BEAR League tells people to pretend they're a big grizzly bear that knows a black bear is no match for them, and they won't let it sneak in and raid the food cache. "We get calls all the time from people telling us how tough and powerful they felt watching a bear high-tail it out of their space after they yelled at it," says director Ann Bryant.

If you're going to yell and go on the offensive, remember—don't approach the bear, yell from wherever you are. And conjure up whatever mental image it takes for you to yell convincingly—don't leave any doubt in the bear's mind that you mean business. No screaming, shrieking, crying or sounding like wounded prey, please.

Try to note the bear's size, color, and any characteristics that stand out, like a color blaze. If the bear broke into your home—not just walked in through a door or window you left unlocked—authorities will probably want to try and locate it. ❖

Beck's Bits

I recommend keeping several baskets full of baseballs in strategic locations; they're a lot easier to throw than rocks; not many people have rocks inside their house. Baseballs sting, but unless you've got a killer fast ball, you won't do permanent damage to the bear. Hit up the local Little League for end-of-the-season deals on used baseballs.

The Town of Snowmass Village, Colorado

It Takes a Village to Save a Bear

It's 10:00 a.m. on a warm Saturday morning in July 2005, and Snowmass Village Animal Officer Laurie Smith has already taken four bear calls.

"That was a man who left his pickup truck unlocked in his driveway last night. He was at a neighborhood party and heard somebody honking his horn. He didn't check on it because he was sure it was just a prankster," she tells me.

It turns out the prankster was a black bear who'd gotten into the truck by opening an unlocked door. The pickup was parked on an incline, and the door had slammed shut, trapping the frantic bear inside. In its efforts to escape it ripped out the dash, stripped the inside plastic and paneling off the doors, shredded the seats and finally popped out the rear window, doing a reported $20,000 worth of damage to the truck.

"This is the first year bears have learned to open unlocked car doors," Smith explained. "Bears are so smart; no matter how many ways we try to outsmart them, they're always finding new loopholes."

The man's response to his bear incident is a good indication of how well Snowmass's decade-long bear education and awareness campaign is working.

"He apologized. He said he knew he should have locked his doors, and he just forgot. In the old days we would respond to

> *"The biggest challenge is dealing with the swinging door of people new to Snowmass—and often new to living in an area where bears are a very real part of the local wildlife."*
>
> TINA WHITE, SNOWMASS VILLAGE ANIMAL OFFICER

a bear incident and the attitude would be 'What are you going to do about this bear?'"

"All the callers so far this year, even second-home owners with their kitchen torn apart, tell me they know it's their fault, they forgot to lock a window or a door—they take responsibility," she continued.

About 1,500 people live in scenic Snowmass Village, surrounded by the picture-postcard splendors of the Roaring Fork Valley, in the heart of Colorado ski country. Countless thousands more stream in during all four seasons to ski, snow shoe, hike, mountain bike and otherwise enjoy themselves.

"The high elevation backcountry surrounds us. We hear foxes barking, elk bugling, coyotes howling, marmots chirping. We are blessed with an endless array of wildlife if we protect their habitat. If we remove a bear, there will be another bear: we live in prime bear habitat. People and bears have no choice but to learn to coexist," Smith explained.

Laurie Smith, who's been with Animal Services for over a decade, and fellow officer Tina White, who joined the team in 1997, share a phone, an office and a passion: arming people with the information and motivation they need to share space with the bears who lived there first. With the support of Snowmass' eight police officers and District Wildlife Manager Kevin Wright, a trained professional is on call to deal with human bear conflicts twenty-four hours a day, seven days a week.

But it hasn't always been that way.

Back in the 1970s the number of sheep ranches in the valley dwindled, and the small bear population suddenly had room to grow. By 1990 the human population in the Valley was growing as well, as ranches became housing developments and ski complexes. After years of fairly benign coexistence the bears of Snowmass began dropping into restaurant dumpsters and wandering through the village in search of an easy meal.

In the beary busy summer of 1993, a sow and two cubs were tranquilized so they could

SARA TUTTLE

be moved to another area. But something went wrong, and one of the cubs died. The community was upset; then as now, the locals loved their wildlife, and hated it when something bad happened to one of "their" bears. The Division of Wildlife officer at the time, Randy Cote, urged the Town of Snowmass Village to enact an ordinance requiring bear-resistant containers, and help prevent bear problems.

Animal Services officer Kelly Wood, a former ranger in Yellowstone National Park, got her hands on a copy of West Yellowstone, Montana's ordinance. The town council, the police department and the Division of Wildlife worked all through the rest of '93, and by New Year's Snowmass Village had passed the first bear ordinance in Colorado.

The regulations required bear-resistant dumpsters, or dumpsters in a fully enclosed, bear-resistant shed; curbside containers had to be stored in a house or garage. For the next four years, officers educated, explained, cajoled, begged, pleaded and threatened, but it was tough to crack down on chronic offenders, because they couldn't write tickets. That all changed after the summer of 1998.

"1998 was a very bad year for bears. There was an acute shortage of natural foods, and bears were feasting in open containers all over the county and village. A mom with three cubs was breaking into homes and creating havoc; the cubs never learned natural ways to forage. Early one morning the Division received a call that the bears were ransacking an open dumpster at a construction site. When the bears were euthanized, residents were enraged. But ultimately they took responsibility for the tragic consequences of their actions. That gave us the leverage to push through the tougher ordinance that's in place now," explained Tina White.

PLEASE LATCH

A BEAR'S LIFE DEPENDS ON IT

Above: A bear visit gives a whole new meaning to "the kitchen's a mess."

Left: Refuse Can Sticker

"The best part of my job is seeing the look on someone's face when they see a bear in a natural setting, and can finally understand bears aren't vicious killing machines lurking behind every bush, waiting to pounce on people and drag them off to the wilderness." – LAURIE SMITH, SNOWMASS VILLAGE ANIMAL OFFICER

The new and improved ordinance gave the wildlife officers the ability to hit people in the wallet when nothing else worked; fines start at $50 and escalate to a summons to court. It also makes it illegal to intentionally or unintentionally feed or attract wildlife, clearly defines what a wildlife-resistant dumpster, enclosure, or refuse container is, and mandates that residents with curbside pick up wait until morning to put out their trash, and have empty containers back inside by 6:00 p.m. Refuse must be secured inside a home or garage, or inside a wildlife-resistant container or enclosure approved by the police department. There are also provisions for special events, construction sites, and just about anywhere that generates trash.

The ordinance even tackles the touchy subject of bird feeders in bear country. Between April 15 and November 15 all bird feeders have to be suspended on a cable or other device so a bear can't get at them, and the area underneath has to be kept clean and free of hulls and other debris.

Both officers say that while the heart of the program centers on awareness, education and prevention, their ability to fine chronic offenders gives it necessary muscle. "We let people know we can write a ticket," says Laurie, "but we'd much rather work with them to solve the problem. We'd rather have the person invest in a bear-resistant container than pay a fine."

"Everyone seems to pattern their ordi-

© Paul Conrad / The Aspen Times

nance after Snowmass and adjusts it to their own needs. They were very proactive and sought a solution. They decided they did not want to have any more bears put down due to human error. They took responsibility for where they chose to live and build their town. They got council and citizen support. It works," says CDOW officer Kevin Wright.

IT TAKES A VILLAGE TO RAISE A BEAR

From mid-April to mid-November, Smith and White spend a lot of time dealing with human-bear conflicts—and even more trying to prevent conflicts from developing in the first place. When they see a problem—an incorrectly hung bird feeder, overflowing trash, windows and doors left open—they educate the homeowners on housekeeping in bear country.

The officers in the Snowmass police

department have all been trained in what causes problems, how to prevent them, and how to respond. They regularly go out on bear calls, and are tireless practitioners of aversive conditioning—cheerfully using their marksmanship skills to safely blast bears with painful but harmless rubber buckshot and beanbags.

The town's trash hauler is deeply committed to helping solve the problem of bears getting garbage, and he and his crew have put in countless hours testing designs, retrofitting lids, welding latches and researching solutions.

If the police or maintenance crew see a situation they suspect is

Left: Kevin Wright with a radio-collared bear.

Below: Laurie Smith, Top Hat the horse, Tina White, and Dude the Cahoula bear dog.

going to be bear trouble, they alert Smith and White, who make frequent house and business calls to try to keep potential problems from turning into real ones.

LET'S TALK BEARS

An important part of their job is making sure everyone has a chance to learn about how to enjoy bears—and how to prevent problems.

They do presentations for organizations that range from preschool classes to Rotary club. They have fliers, sandwich boards, newspaper ads, key chains, water bottles and door hangers. They bring in public speakers and host booths at Snowmass' frequent events and festivals. They put up signs in areas that bears are frequenting, and take them down when they've moved on, so people pay attention when they see a posting. They even send out an e-mail alert to area property managers to tell them about bear goings-on.

More than anything else, after a combined twenty years on the job, the pair still has a seemingly endless supply of patience, perseverance, passion and hope. "It's taken a while, but people really have learned to coexist with bears instead of living in fear, or demanding we come and solve their problems. People are accepting the responsibilities of living in bear country," Smith concluded. ❖

Note: See the Appendix for a copy of the Snowmass Ordinance.

chapter 6

The Birds and The Bears

Feeding Birds in Bear Country

Feeding birds is one of the most popular hobbies in North America. Bird feeders provide much needed winter forage for birds, and countless hours of enjoyment for the people who watch them. **But every year, bird feeders kill bears,** because bird feeders attract bears to places they shouldn't be. Bears that find bird feeders learn that people's yards are an easy source of food. Bears are smart, so they'll go from house to house looking for more goodies. Sooner or later they're bound to find a house where the garbage isn't stored properly, or food or other attractants are easy to get at.

Then it's often just a matter of time before the bear gets so comfortable around people it becomes first a nuisance, and then a potential danger. And when agencies have to choose between the safety of people and the safety of bears, bears always lose, even though it's usually people who are to blame.

WHY BEARS LOVE BIRD FEEDERS

Bird feeders are fast-food for bears. They provide an easy, concentrated source of highly nutritious, calorie-packed food. A pound of black-oil sunflower seeds in the shell has 1,740 calories. That means a bird feeder that holds 7 pounds (3.2 kg) of seeds offers a hungry bear over 12,000 calories.

The seeds in a 7-pound bird feeder have over 12,000 calories. No wonder bird feeders are irresistible to bears. © *Nancyjane Bailey*

77

A study in New York State cited bird feeders as the initial lure for bears in 80% of incidents.

Imagine how hard a bear would have to work to get that many pounds of seeds in the wild. Hummingbird feeders are just hanging pop-cans. A 32-ounce feeder (one liter) offers up to 774 energy-packed calories that satisfy a bear's sweet tooth.

Is it any wonder bears are attracted to all the handy "bear feeders" scattered conveniently through our yards?

The best way to keep bears out of your bird feeders is to take them down from March though November, or whenever bears are normally up and about in your area. But for many bird lovers, that advice is hard to take. I know, because I love to watch birds, and unfortunately summer in the mountains is when the widest variety of birds is around for the watching. So what's a bear-loving bird-lover to do?

ATTRACTING BIRDS NOT BEARS

© Alan Olander

There are many things other than food that will attract birds to your yard. Birds enjoy everything from a bird bath to a pond; if you can create the sound of splashing water, even better. It doesn't have to be elaborate; something as simple as a galvanized wash tub with a rock popping out of the water will attract a wide variety of birds. Check out your local home improvement store for a selection of self-contained and solar-powered water features and water gardens, or visit *www.gardeners.com*.

Planting for Birds

There are dozens of annuals, perennials, ground covers, vines and even trees that attract hummingbirds, butterflies and beneficial bees. Check a local nursery to find out which ones will grow best in your area. Or just buy a couple of hanging baskets at the beginning of the season, and enjoy.

Put Up Bird Nesting Boxes

Nesting boxes will guarantee you'll have birds to watch most of the summer. Add to their appeal by landscaping and offering some sort of water feature, and you'll have a three-season bird garden. Put your feeders back outside when the bears turn in for the winter, and you can enjoy watching the birds all year long.

IF YOU MUST FEED THE BIRDS IN BEAR SEASON

Bring Your Feeders in at Night   This isn't as good a solution as taking your feeders down for the season, but it's better than leaving them out at night, when bears are more likely to be about. Buy feeders with seed pans to keep seed and hulls from collecting on the ground, where bears can find them. Store bird feeders inside a secure building from sundown to sunup during bear season.

Hang Feeders Out of Reach   Out of reach means at least 10 feet (3 meters) off the ground, and 10 feet (3 meters) from any climbable tree. You'll still need to use feeders with seed pans, and clean up seed that falls on the ground. And if you rig up some clever pulley mechanism to bring the feeder up and down for filling, make sure a bear can't reach it, or ideally even see it. Brainy bears study people filling their feeders, and duplicate their actions later. If you hang bird feeders on your deck, make sure you bring them in at night and keep the deck clean; it's a cinch for a determined bear to climb your posts—or walk up the stairs.

Hanging things out of reach of a bear is like dangling a particularly tantalizing problem in front of a mathematician. The bear is very likely to hang around, and come back often, to see if it can crack the code and figure out how to get to the prize. So if you try this approach, it's doubly important to make

Proper hanging keeps hummingbird feeders from becoming hummingbear feeders.

sure that while the bear is lounging around your yard trying to figure out how to snag your bird feeder it doesn't find anything else to munch on.

And remember: your bird feeder might be out of reach, but what about your neighbor's? If you can get everyone in the neighborhood to take precautions, bears will move on.

Bearproof Bird Feeding The Vince Shute Wildlife Sanctuary in northern Minnesota is a summer and fall feeding ground for as many as sixty wild black bears. They built a bird feeder demonstration area to show people how to feed birds without endangering bears (see illustration below).

Switch Your Birdseed If you're going to feed birds in bear season, consider switching your bird seed to a premium, millet-free mix. Many birds don't really like millet seed; that's why it often ends up on the ground. Bears aren't as fussy, and millet is very hard to clean up.

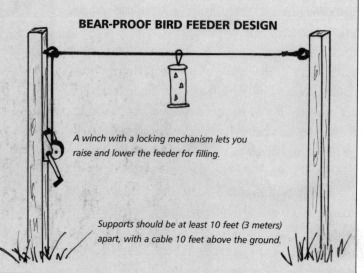

You'll need two sturdy fixed supports, such as 4x4 posts firmly planted in the ground, mature trees or the sides of two building. The two supports need to be a minimum of 10 feet (3 meters) apart. Install a cable a minimum of 10 feet (3 meters) above the ground; make sure the feeder itself can be at least 5 feet (1.5 meters) from either post or support.

BEAR-PROOF BIRD FEEDER DESIGN

A winch with a locking mechanism lets you raise and lower the feeder for filling.

Supports should be at least 10 feet (3 meters) apart, with a cable 10 feet above the ground.

The Living with Wildlife Foundation recommends offering sunflower kernels—shelled sunflowers—which cost more per pound, but last a lot longer. And there are no hulls to clean up—or attract the attention of a foraging bear.

Suet, Peanut Butter and Grease Leave these tasty, calorie packed bird treats for the winter, when birds really need them. Summer sun makes them even more aromatic than usual. And by now you know what that means.

KNOW YOUR LOCAL AND STATE LAWS

When gentler regulations have failed to inspire people to get rid of their bear attractants some areas have passed laws regulating or prohibiting putting out any food that attracts wildlife. In some places you can be ticketed and fined for having a bird feeder out during bear season. ❖

Give the bears a break. Practice bear-safe bird feeding.

WILDLIFE CAN'T READ

When you put out cracked corn for the deer and rabbits, peanut butter and suet for the birds, treats for the squirrels, or fruit for the warblers you've got a good chance of attracting a whole different crowd. In addition to bears, all of the above attracts raccoons, coyotes, foxes, skunks and rodents. Deer, rabbits and rodents attract things that eat them—like bobcats, coyotes, mountain lions and snakes.

Cracked corn left out for the bunnies attracted a much bigger critter. When bears get comfortable in backyards, the results are often deadly—for the bear. If you really love wildlife, please don't feed 'em.
© Linda Masterson

TO DO LIST

Monday
garbage day!
raid trash cans

Tuesday
check security system
at new neighbors

Wednesday
berry foraging

Thursday
dumpster diving

Friday
TGIF party leftovers

The Weekend
campground
crawl

Bear Calorie Counter

	Menu Item	Serving Size	Calories
	Black oil sunflower seeds	1 pound	1,740
✳	Birdseed	7 pounds	12,180
	Hummingbird nectar	16 ounces	385
✳	Purina Dog Chow	25-pound bag	42,425
✳	Shortening	3-pound can	12,430
	Potato Chips	1 pound	2,560
	Jelly Donuts	12	2,640
	Honey	1 cup	1,031
✳	Ice Cream	1 gallon	4,960
✳	Peanut Butter	28 oz jar	4,750
	Bacon	1 pound	2,532
	Chocolate Chip Cookies	1-pound bag	3,200
	Sweet Corn	12 ears	1,080
	Hot Dogs	1 pound	1,456
	Watermelon	10" Whole	2,464
	Huckleberries	1 pound	2,105
	Acorns	1 pound	2,082
	Cranberries	1 pound	1,892
	Hickory Nuts	1 pound	2,051

✳ FOOD FOR THOUGHT

A quick glance is all it takes to understand why people food can be so appealing to a hungry bear biologically programmed to pack in as many calories as possible before winter sets in. It takes a bear many hours of foraging on natural foods to get the 12,000-plus calories it can down in five minutes at a bird feeder.

Canmore, Alberta, Canada

Kicking The Curbside Habit

Set in the Bow Valley between Banff National Park and Kananaskis Country, the historic mining town of Canmore is one of the gateways to the scenic splendors of the Canadian Rockies, and some of the largest protected natural areas in the world. The town has become a center for outdoor recreation and adventures, offering world-class golf, fly-fishing, mountain biking, climbing, hiking and skiing.

Canmore's 11,000 full-time residents and millions of visitors are attracted by fresh air,

SARA TUTTLE

clean water and scenery straight out of a travel guide. Black bears are naturally attracted by some of the best bear habitat around, with plenty of berries for the picking.

Black bears were also attracted by the unnatural food supplies the town offered up: an unbeatable year-round supply of high-quality garbage. Why forage all day in the berry bushes when you can satisfy your calorie needs with a quick trip to the landfill, or a midnight raid on the garbage cans?

By the early 1990s, Canmore was experiencing growing pains, and growing bear problems. Environmental groups and concerned citizens pressured the Town Council to do something about all the bears coming into town. The Waste Management Committee looked into options, and in 1997 recommended that the town discontinue its traditional curbside trash collection and go to a communal "bear bin" collection system.

Nervous that voters wouldn't be willing to sacrifice the convenience of having their trash picked up at their doorstep to prevent conflicts with bears, the Council instead implemented a dual system that gave residents the option of taking their trash out to the curb on collection day, or using the bear resistant containers any time.

The first hurdle was getting residents to agree on where to put sixty big, bear-resistant dumpsters. People worried about noise. They worried about smells. They worried about property values. They thought the dumpsters would be an eyesore. They were afraid they'd be hard to use. Nobody likes change.

But the Council went ahead anyway. They surveyed residents, and provided maps of all the proposed locations. They were surprised to find that most folks were okay with the idea, because they thought the community had an obligation to do a better job of getting along with the bears. The few complaints came from residents who wanted the containers closer to their homes.

The good news: people adjusted nicely, and by summer of 1997, an average of 55 percent of households—up to 77 percent in some neighborhoods—were using the new bear-resistant containers.

The bad news: the dual program was very expensive, because the town had to pay for a complete curb-side program for all residents whether they used it or not, and also had to pay to have the bear-resistant containers picked up and emptied regularly.

The bears didn't respond to change quite as well as the people. In the summer of 1998,

a poor berry crop added to the pressure, and the number of bear sightings and incidents in town multiplied. Fish and Wildlife officials begged the town to completely discontinue curbside pick-up. Citizens wrote letters to the newspaper. Things got so bad the Mayor sent out a letter urging people to use only the bear-resistant containers until the bears turned in for the winter.

Apparently not everyone complied, because by the end of the summer they'd had over 300 bear sightings in town. Nine bears were relocated, and four bears were killed.

The number of residents using curbside service continued to drop, and by September of 1998, another audit showed that only 23 percent of households were now using curbside, despite the fact that the town was paying for 100 percent pickup. When Canmore officials finally decided to go cold turkey they discovered they'd have to double the number of containers they put out if they were going to keep up with the tons of trash generated during the height of tourist season. They bought sixty more containers, and gave existing businesses a year to replace their old dumpsters with bear-resistant ones. New businesses had to get with the program from the get-go in order to get licensed. In May 1999, they stopped curbside pick up.

The number of incidents and problems involving bears and trash dropped from 300 to zero. As an added bonus, the move cut the

**OBJECTIONS TO COMMUNAL
BEAR-RESISTANT DUMPSTERS**

◆ People worried about the noise

◆ They worried about smells

◆ They worried about property values

◆ They thought they dumpsters would
   be an eyesore.

◆ They were afraid they'd be
   hard to use and inconvenient

With all the preventative measures in place, the number of black bears destroyed dropped from four or five a year to just one in a two-year period.

Canmore has made huge strides, but is dealing with an ever-growing human population and ever-shrinking wildlife habitat, which inevitably puts pressures on both bears and people. The Canmore area is home to grizzly

RESULTS OF ALL THE PREVENTATIVE MEASURES

◆ The number of incidents and problems involving
   bears and trash dropped from 300 to zero

◆ The move cut the town's trash pick-up costs by
   44%—saving taxpayers over $160,000 a year

◆ The number of black bears destroyed dropped
   from 4 or 5 per year to just one in a 2-year period

town's trash pick-up costs by 44 percent—saving taxpayers over $160,000 a year.

Black bears are very adaptable, and quick learners, so when the bears could no longer get at the trash, they started going after backyard bird feeders and compost piles. Once bears have discovered how much easier it is to fatten up on a seemingly endless supply of high-calorie people food, it can be tough to persuade them they're better off sticking to nuts and berries. It's not because bears are lazy. It's because human garbage and food is such a dependable and concentrated source of easy-to-digest calories.

So in 2001 Canmore took one more step and banned the use of bird feeders from April to October while bears are active, and banned the outdoor composting of kitchen organic waste.

as well as black bears. There have been several grizzly incidents, including one human fatality, in the wildlife corridors that were designed to provide safe passage for bears and greenspace for people. The corridors also provide ample opportunity for people—especially mountain bikers and runners—and bears to quite literally run into each other. ❖

chapter 7

Gardens, Farms & Livestock

Avoiding Growing Pains

GARDENING IN BEAR COUNTRY

To a black bear, a garden is just a convenient collection of things that are good to eat. Black bears love tomatoes, squashes, melons, berries, early vegetables, sweet corn—especially when it hits the milk stage—and just about anything else that smells good.

One look at any popular gardening catalog is all it takes to confirm that protecting our gardens from all the critters that want to eat them is a daunting task, although few catalogs address what to do if you're trying to grow things in bear country. And some popular critter-repellants like pepper-based deer deterrents actually attract bears. Blood meal and fish fertilizer also smell like food to a hungry bear.

Tips for Planting a Garden

Plan It Locate your garden away from your home, and as far away as possible from natural cover, trails and obvious bear habitat.

Pick It Pick your produce as it ripens. Gardening books recommend picking produce in the morning when it's at its freshest, but leaving your ready-

SARA TUTTLE

to-be-harvested home-growns on the vine overnight is asking for a bear to beat you to them.

Fence It   If you have the room and your zoning or covenants permit it, installing an electric fence is a highly effective way to keep bears at bay. Many types are available, including portable and solar models; check out Chapter 8 for more information on choosing and installing an electric fence.

Flowers

Believe it or not, almost all flowers can attract bears. In the early spring green up, bears forage on forbs—tender young green plants. Once the plants bloom, bears switch over to eating the flowers, because they're nutritious and easy to digest. In fact, all herbivores "highgrade" plant parts looking for the best combination of nutrients and digestibility.

Rabbits, rodents, deer, elk and bears all enjoy grazing on tender vegetation and nutritious flower heads.

Fruits, Nuts & Berries

Bird nets might save your fruit trees from the starlings, but they won't do a thing to repel a bear. If you're putting in landscaping, and you long for fruit trees, locate them well away from your home, and be prepared to work hard protecting them. If you don't want to work that hard, or really don't want bears on your property, don't plant fruit, acorn or nut bearing trees or ornamental bushes that produce berries.

   If you have several fruit trees planted together, or a single large, valuable tree, electric fencing the area is the best way to keep the bears on the outside, longingly looking in. Just make sure there's nothing else for them to eat anywhere around. If you've already got lots of fruit trees, or have a small commercial orchard, continue reading.

Composting in Bear Country

When you're composting in bear country, think green. Grasses, leaves and vegetation should be the only things going into your compost pile during times of high bear activity. Keep your pile aerated and turned. An occasional sprinkle with lime will help mask odors and speed up the composting process.

Don't put fruit, kitchen waste, meats, dairy, oils, melon rinds or anything else with an odor in your compost pile. One Colorado gardener wrote to tell me she'd never had a problem with her compost until the night she added eggshells. The next morning her compost pile was strewn from one end of her yard to the other.

Indoor composting is now a real option; there are many ingenious indoor composters available that are odor-free and easy to use for kitchen scraps. Some of them are so nicely designed they can sit out on your counter. Others are big enough to put in the basement or garage.

ORCHARDS AND FARMS IN BEAR COUNTRY

In colonial times, in much of the eastern U.S., black bears were considered serious agricultural pests. They were often treated like coyotes with short tails and shot on sight. Today wildlife conservation has replaced wildlife extermination in much of North America, and bear populations in the eastern U.S. and elsewhere are returning to more natural levels.

Big time farmers and orchardists in bear country are undoubtedly already well-acquainted with their local wildlife agency, and hopefully up on all the latest methods of big-scale wildlife deterring. But many hobby farmers, folks who have a couple of acres of sweet corn or fruit trees and small commercial orchards, aren't prepared to deal with hungry bears. Bears will go after oats, barley, corn—especially at the milk stage—watermelon, peanuts, soybeans, berries and other crops, but they pose the biggest threat to fruit trees.

Bears are smart, but apparently not quite smart enough to understand that if they destroy the tree in their attempt to get at every piece of fruit, next year there will be no tree—and no fruit. A determined black bear can do permanent damage to fruit trees, breaking limbs or sometimes knocking down entire trees to get at the fruit.

We humans think of fruit as a low calorie, good-for-you-treat, but bears don't eat fruit by the piece. Just a dozen big ripe apples have over 1,000 calories. Most fruits are loaded with natural sugars; ingesting a lot of sugar during the late summer and fall gives a bear just the energy boost it needs to spend twenty hours a day foraging for food. An orchard filled with ripe fruit is a bear bonanza.

If you know there are bears in your area, you can be sure they'll follow their noses and show up around picking season. If you can't or don't want to fence your orchard, "Please Don't Pick the Fruit" signs won't help; your only practical defense is beating the bears to the bounty.

That means picking your fruit all at one time, before it starts to ripen enough to smell, and immediately picking up and removing any fruit that falls to the ground. Fruit continues to ripen after picking; in fact, most pear varieties won't ripen on the tree; they need to be picked and stored to finish the process. Store your fruit in a cool, bear-proof place.

"We have about eight acres of wild plums on our property. Last year I was really busy when they started to ripen. I remember it was a Wednesday when I noticed they were ready to pick. We planned to go out and pick everything Saturday, but by then three bears had

come through, and there wasn't a single plum left on those trees. I'm glad the bears got a good meal, but we learned our lesson. Pick 'em early if you want to keep them. With plums, it's better to pick them

An orchard full of apples is more temptation than a bear can resist.
National Park Service

before they're ripe anyway. They have more pectin then, and make better jam," says Melanie Hannafious, who also works at farm and feed supplier, Ranch-Way Feeds.

Don't dump fallen or buggy fruit near your orchard; it will just attract a variety of wildlife you don't want around, including elk, deer, coyotes, skunks, raccoons and orioles, as well as bears. Leaving it where it falls is like rolling out the red carpet and turning on a big neon "Forage Here" sign for the local wildlife.

Tom Beck tends a small orchard on his property in southwestern Colorado and says, "If you wait until the fruit is ripe, it's too late. I recommend picking a few days early, and letting the fruit finish ripening off the tree. I defy anyone to tell the difference between a tree-ripened plum and one picked seven days early and ripened off the tree. You need to pick all the fruit, and I do mean all; if you leave any fruit up in those hard to reach higher branches, the bears will damage or even knock down the tree trying to get at it."

With stone fruits, even a human's relatively poor-quality sniffer can detect fruit when it reaches the ripe state, so imagine how enticing it smells to a bear, with a nose that's one hundred times more sensitive than ours.

- Fence, pick early, pick entirely.
- Pick fruit seven days before you think it will be ripe.
- Store fruit in a cool, dry, bear-proof place to ripen up.
- Don't leave any fallen or buggy fruit on the ground or near your orchard.
- For a fool-proof solution, put in an electric fence.

Beck's Bits

"With my nectarines, I notice very little wildlife damage until the day I can smell the first fruit. By the next day I can have 25 to 30 percent damage," says Beck. "My biggest culprit is wasps, followed by birds, grey fox and raccoons. So pick early, and save yourself a lot of headaches."

Bear biologists must like growing things, because bear attack expert and author Steve Herrero tells this tale in his book, *Bear Attacks: Their Causes and Avoidance*. "I once picked almost the entire crop from our favorite prune-plum tree. The fruit left was at the ends of the highest branches and was the hardest to pick. We put

boards with nails sticking outward all around the trunk of the tree
and on the major limbs and left for a few days. When we returned,
the twenty-year-old prune-plum lay on the ground in a heap of
broken branches and limbs. Apparently the bear had not been able
to reach the fruit without knocking the tree down. Since then I've
tried to pick all ripe fruit before leaving."

How To Keep Your Corn

At 80 calories an ear, it's easy to understand why a field of ripening
corn is an animal magnet. Deer eat leaves as well as ears of corn.
Skunks pick off a lot of lower ears. Porcupines, deer, beaver, raccoons
and even coyotes all enjoy munching on corn. Black bears are attracted
to corn in the milk stage, and often flatten large circular areas, perhaps
giving rise to the theory that extraterrestrials have landed and made
off with a supply of one of our favorite summer foods.

   Electric fencing is the best way to keep bears out of fields. Use
single strand, baited polytape electric fencing. If you can't fence the
whole field, think like a bear and protect the areas closest to the
forest or greenbelt. You can use portable fencing to protect crops
before and at the milk stage.

   The next best way to keep bears away is to plant at least a mile
(1.6 km) from any forest cover; black bears don't like traveling long
distances in the open. You can
also put in mowed, open corridors around and in between
fields, and alternate row crops
to cut down on the appeal.

   Don't make the mistake of
thinking that feeding bears
somewhere else on your property will keep them away from
your orchard or feed plot.
Putting out food attracts bears

WHAT'S EATING THE CORN?

Entire cob missing > *bears*

Whole plants removed > *beavers*

Ears and silk nipped > *deer, coyotes*

Leaves eaten > *deer*

Stalks chewed and felled > *beaver, porcupine*

Lower ears eaten > *skunks*

Stalks pulled down, ears stripped, kernels chewed off
   small area > raccoons; large, circular area > bears

and other wildlife to the area. Once there, bears will generally investigate all other available food sources.

RAISING LIVESTOCK & PETS IN BEAR COUNTRY

Most black bears don't prey on livestock, but their habit of scavenging and taking advantage of food sources wherever they find them often gets bears blamed for deaths caused by other predators. In one Maine study, 57 percent of sheep losses attributed to bears were either fraudulent or undetermined.

But occasionally individual bears develop a taste for sheep, goats, chickens, turkeys, pigs, rabbits or newborn calves. Most losses are nursing females or newborns that are either penned up in a small area the bear can easily get into, or members of free ranging herds in remote and rugged terrain.

Once a bear starts preying on livestock, it can do a lot of damage. In most areas, property owners can obtain permits to destroy bears that are proven livestock killers. Tom Beck says swiftly dealing with a livestock-killer is the best way to keep other bears in the area from paying for one bruins' costly habit. The rules and regulations regarding when a bear suspected of preying on livestock can be destroyed, and by whom, vary. Check with your local Ag extension office or wildlife management agency for local guidelines.

The biggest mistake is to jump from bear feeding on carcass to bear having killed the animal without examining the carcass. Telltale bite and claw marks show up much better on the inside of the hide rather than the hairy side. This requires a semi-fresh carcass, a sharp knife and a strong stomach in the summer.

Beck's Bits

What's Eating the Livestock?

Bears are very opportunistic eaters, and will cheerfully scavenge another predator's leftovers, or lunch on an animal that's died of natural causes. Coming across a bear eating a sheep carcass is no guarantee the bear killed the sheep. It takes a forensic examination of the carcass itself and the inside of the hide, including bite or claw marks and other injuries or wound patterns, to determine what actually killed the animal.

Bears usually bite down on the top of the neck, or on small animals like lambs, across the back to break the spine. It's uncommon to see claw cuts through the hide for bears. Black bears don't swat or twist the head to break the neck. Bears don't like eating hair, and once past udders and livers will normally neatly skin out the carcass.

Mountain lions kill large prey like elk and horses by jumping onto the animal's back from behind and biting the neck. Lions kill by severing the spinal cord, twisting the neck to the side and snapping it, or biting down on the trachea in large animals. Mountain lions don't skin out a carcass the way bears do.

Coyotes attack the throat; they kill by strangulation of the windpipe rather than spinal injury.

Domestic and feral dogs attack the hindquarters, and usually make very messy kills. Dogs can do a tremendous amount of damage that other animals often get blamed for.

Predator Pets

Before you blame a bear for a livestock loss, consider this: the two most vicious killers of domestic livestock are domestic and feral dogs and cats. Cats prey on chickens, rabbits and other small birds and mammals, as well as being major killers of wildlife and wild birds. Domestic and feral dogs kill far more livestock than bears do. Dogs usually mutilate prey, and damage to the hindquarters and fore and rear flanks is typical. They often roam in packs, and can do a lot of damage once they begin to attack. Dogs also often harass and chase livestock, sometimes for hours. In many states dogs that are harassing or attacking wildlife or livestock can be shot on sight without a permit; check with your local authorities. Owners of dogs and cats that kill livestock can usually be sued for damages.

Think your pet could never turn killer? "Pet owners may not control their animals as much as they should because they are

The most vicious killers of domestic livestock aren't bears, lions, coyotes or wolves. Domestic and wild dogs and cats create the most carnage.

unaware of the threat that domestic dogs and cats pose to livestock and wildlife. Even seemingly harmless and friendly animals instinctually harass and kill wild species and livestock and it's important for members of human communities to understand the real danger of domestic pets running wild," points out APHIS, the U.S. Animal and Plant Health Inspection Service.

Tips for Safeguarding Livestock

Preventing problems is the best way to protect valuable livestock and domestic animals from bears and a host of other predators.

In years when drought, widespread fires, or early or late freezes decimate the bears' natural food sources, bears still have to eat to live. Hunger and the need to fatten up by any means possible before the winter can drive them to take risks they'd normally avoid. Bear "problems" of all varieties often escalate during years of food failure, so it pays to be extra vigilant when natural foods are scarce.

◆ Don't pasture animals in areas with heavy natural cover nearby, or next to travel corridors used by bears.

◆ Don't leave carcasses in fields, pastures or near buildings. Incinerating them completely is the most secure way to dispose of them. If you bury a carcass, it needs to be at least 8 feet (2.43 meters) underground. Portable electric fences have proved a reliable way to keep grizzly bears from feeding on cattle carcasses.

◆ Pen animals near or in the barn at night, especially pregnant females and those with young.

◆ Try to avoid birthing animals in the field. If there's no practical alternative, clean the area of all signs of birthing, including the afterbirth, which is highly attractive to bears, coyotes and other predators. I talked to one enterprising small rancher who collects the afterbirth from her llamas and stores it in the freezer until the morning of trash pick up. Portable electric fencing can be used during birthing season if animals must stay in the fields.

◆ Modifying or replacing existing fencing with high voltage (6,000 volts or greater) low impedance electric fencing around all animal enclosures is an almost sure cure. Small animals like chickens, turkeys and rabbits can be protected with electric fencing around pens. See Chapter 8 for all the details.

◆ Guard dogs may deter bears; trained bear dogs—not hunting hounds—can be used to work individual bears that have become a problem. See pages 141–147 for more on bear dogs.

◆ A radio, motion-sensitive lights or noisemakers might chase off a curious, inexperienced bear. But most predators adjust to "passive" controls like sirens, loud noises, alarms and flashing lights in a week or two, when they discover they're all bark and no bite.

Dogs That Chase Bears

Unless both dogs and people are specially trained in aversive conditioning techniques for bears, the results of chasing bears with hounds are pretty dismal. In Wisconsin, only one in five bears chased away eight times left the area for good. In Maine, over half the bears chased by hounds stayed within their home range.

Hounds typically tree bears, so there's no real consequence for the bear. Trained bear dogs harass the bear until it learns where it's welcome and where it's not. Montana's Wind River Bear Institute has an excellent track record using Karelian Bear Dogs to "recondition" grizzly bears as well as black bears, and teaches them to avoid people.

In many states and provinces the use of bear hounds is prohibited, licensed by law, or restricted to special seasons, so be sure to check with your local wildlife agency.

Dogs That Guard Flocks

Shepherds have used dogs to guard their flocks since Biblical times. Guard dogs need to be reared with the livestock in their charge in

Noisemakers and repellants that are all bark and no bite don't usually keep bears at bay for long.

order to bond with them; it's this bond that makes the dogs protective of their "family" and aggressive toward predators.

Guard dogs don't herd or chase sheep; they work independently of the shepherd and can be left alone with the flock. Most are large breeds, weighing over 75 pounds (34 kg) that are naturally wary of all intruders, and fierce and fearless when provoked. The Akbash and Great Pyrenees are the most popular, although Anatolian Shepherds, Komondors, Maremma and Shar Planinetz are also used. One or two guard dogs can protect about two hundred sheep, or 200 acres (80 hectares). Producers who graze very large herds on open range usually use three to five dogs. In Colorado 84 percent of the ranchers who used guard dogs gave them a good or excellent rating for protecting livestock; in just one year dogs reduced predation losses—due mostly to coyotes—by nearly $900,000.

This Great Pyrenees is moving his charges down from the high country near Durango, Colorado.
© Bryan Peterson

Guard Llamas and Donkeys

Llamas and donkeys have proved useful in protecting sheep from coyotes and wild dogs, but there's not much research on their effectiveness with bears. ❖

chapter 8

Shocking Solutions to Bear Conflicts
A Primer on Electric Fences

ELECTRIC FENCES MAKE FOR GOOD BEAR NEIGHBORS

An electric fence has the power to keep bears out of landfills, apiaries, cabins, campsites, campers, livestock enclosures, grain sheds and just about anywhere else you don't want bears to go.

Today there are permanent fencing systems powerful enough to successfully keep grizzly bears out of a landfill. There are portable electric fences that can be set up and functional in less than two hours, and solar-powered systems that can be installed anywhere there's enough sun to charge the batteries. There are even lightweight, battery-powered fences that weigh less than 4 pounds (1.8 kg) and cost under $300 USD that can protect a 30-foot x 30-foot (9.1-meter x 9.1-meter) campsite.

While some consider fencing a last resort, the State of Maryland—where bear-bashing of commercial beeyards has become a chronic problem—says electric fencing is the least expensive and most effective

One homeowner created an electric trash can corral that successfully keeps persistent black bears from raiding his garbage. He was even nice enough to warn the bears they're in for a shock if they go after the trash. © *Derek Reich*

97

way to solve most bear problems in bee yards. In fact, they think fencing works so well they'll loan fence chargers and fencing materials to harried bee keepers, and come out and help set them up. Twenty-five states and many provinces either loan fences or provide funding; many also provide onsite advice and hands-on assistance.

PERMANENT ELECTRIC FENCING

Once properly installed, a permanent electric fence can be left in place for years. Permanent fences require less maintenance and stand up under environmental stresses like snow loads better than portable fences. You can also tighten hi-tensile wire to 200 psi—when a bear pushes against the wire, the tension separates the bear's fur and the wire can deliver a shock right to the skin.

Permanent fencing makes sense for landfills, especially if bears are already conditioned to regard the area as a food source. Camps, feed storage sheds, livestock pens, small orchards and gardens, and cabins in areas with a long track record of bear-break-ins are also good candidates for a permanent electric fence.

PORTABLE ELECTRIC FENCES

Portable electric fences are great when you need temporary protection, like during lambing season. Or for apiaries that move hives to take advantage of pollination. Or even temporary back country camps. There are two main types of portable electric fencing designed to deter bears. One is a positive system, the other is an alternating positive/negative system.

A portable positive system normally consists of four strands of shock cord; 14 or 16 gauge wire stretched to 20 psi

Portable solar panels can power an electric fence just about anywhere there's sun. © *Patti Sowka*

of tension. This type of fence is most often used at apiaries, small camps and to fence off gardens or fruit trees.

A portable six-strand light gauge wire system can be used in areas without good grounding, like dry gravel. Install a wire mesh apron on extremely dry land, and spread calcium chloride around the fence to increase grounding during dry periods.

The Colorado Division of Wildlife has developed two designs for temporary electric fences. A 30-foot x 42-foot (9.1-meter x 12.8-meter) electric fence can hold 32 bee colonies and costs about $300 USD to install. You can make a temporary fence out of electro-plastic netting, electrified twine or hot tape attached to posts or trees. Costs range from $200 for hot tape to $750 USD for electroplastic netting. As usual, you get what you pay for.

HOW AN ELECTRIC FENCE WORKS

An electric fence acts like an open circuit, with repeating pulses of electricity produced by the energizer flowing through the charged wires of the fence. When something touches a charged wire, it grounds the fence, creating a closed circuit—and a shocking experience for whatever's on the other end of the wire.

How Much Voltage?

You can't have too much, only too little. Bears have heavy fur, very thick skin, a high tolerance for pain and heavy foot pads that minimize grounding. That's one reason Beck prefers an alternating ground wire configuration. Because they have big thick fur coats and insulating layers of fat, the latest recommendations suggest a minimum of 6,000 volts to effectively shock a black bear.

Many state, local and provincial agencies will help landowners design and even install an electric fence. Some even lend out portable fences for free.
© Patti Sowka

Components of an Electric Fence

Beck's Bits

In very dry parts of western North America you can improve the ground by building a small dike around the grounding rod—as if it were a small tree—and periodically dumping in ten gallons of water to keep soil moisture up. You'll be able to literally hear the difference in the battery charger sound as the water penetrates.

◆ An energizer operated by a solar module, a battery or plugged into a 110-volt outlet delivers the power.

◆ Live wire or wires of high tensile steel carry the pulses around the area being protected; 11 – 14 gauge wire with a minimum tensile strength of 200,000 psi and a minimum breaking strength of 1,800 pounds is recommended.

◆ Fencing posts made of treated wood, cedar, steel or fiberglass.

◆ High quality fence chargers. Use a 110-volt outlet or 12-volt deep-cycle marine batteries connected to a high-output fence charger approved by UL or the Canadian Standards Association (CSA). Maryland suggests using RV batteries, because they're designed for continuous operation and suffer no ill effects from being repeatedly run down and recharged.

◆ A grounding system that starts at the energizer, with low-resistance ground rods which go along the fenced area

◆ Insulation to protect the live wire from accidental contact with the ground, which would short it out and "turn off" the fence.

◆ Tension springs on long stretches limit the mechanical tension in the wires, which contract when air temperature drops.

◆ Lightning protectors to protect your investment from lightning strikes and induction from power lines.

INSTALLING A PERMANENT ELECTRIC FENCE

Here's how the State of New Jersey recommends installing a permanent electric fence:

◆ Drive the corner posts and remove grass and weeds in an 18-inch (46-cm) strip along the fence line.

◆ Spray the cleared area with a herbicide to prevent re-growth; don't spray wider than 18 inches (46 cm) because the bear will be better grounded if it's standing on grass.

- Use four strands of polywire or electronet at 4, 16, 26 and 36 inches (10, 40, 66 and 91 cm) above the ground. Stretch the wires to eliminate sagging. Use stones or weights to keep the wires at the correct heights when going over low areas.
- Leave extra wire at the knot so it can be wrapped around the lower wire to complete the circuit
- Use a minimum voltage output of 6,000 volts. Verify your volt output with a voltmeter.
- Locate the fence posts every 12 to 15 feet (3.65 to 4.57 meters) along the fence line, and install the insulators and wires. Wires have to be able to slide freely through insulators on fence posts.
- Put your battery in a water-tight container inside your enclosure, and energize all the wires.
- Every half-mile (.80 km) of fence line, drive four to six ground rods 5 to 7 feet (1.5 to 2.1 meters) deep into moist soil. In very

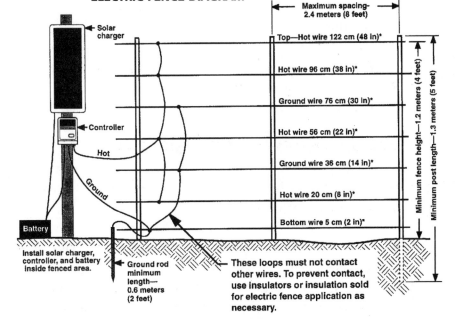

ELECTRIC FENCE DIAGRAM

Although this information was created for electric fencing on National Forest lands, the information is helpful for homeowners wishing to deter predators on private property.

Source: U.S. Forest Service "Tech Tips" report on electric fence systems.

* Height above ground; distance between wires may vary from 6 to 10 inches.

dry, sandy soil or on rocky ground, grounding can be increased by laying grounded chicken wire around the outside perimeter of the electric fence—the predator will be standing on metal when it touches the hot wire.

BAITING THE FENCE

It's generally not smart to lure wildlife to places you want them to stay away from. But if you know bears in the area are likely to come around, baiting increases the odds the bear's sensitive nose, lips or tongue will come in direct contact with the hot wire and the resulting shock will send the bear on its way. If you decide to bait, try raw bacon dipped in honey or molasses, aluminum foil strips smeared with peanut butter or tins of salmon or tuna with a hole punched in them.

> "Electric circuits and fencing designs for repelling black bears have continually improved over the years to the point where I now regard properly installed and maintained electric fencing to be a highly effective black or grizzly bear deterrent."
>
> STEVE HERRERO,
> *BEAR ATTACKS: THEIR CAUSES AND AVOIDANCE*

MAINTENANCE

Anything that comes in contact with a charged wire can create a partially or completely closed circuit, including fallen trees or branches, blowing vegetation, or other animals like raccoons or deer. Routine maintenance is the key to keeping an electric fence in top shape, because if a downed tree branch closes a circuit, the fence is rendered powerless until the branch is removed and the circuit is open again. For the best performance, somebody should walk the fence line every day or two.

Beck's Bits

Never, never leave up an uncharged fence. This totally negates the value of the fence. If the bear gets through and doesn't get shocked, it will then challenge the fence, even if it's recharged.

◆ Grass or shrubs touching the wires draw down voltage; keep grass cut low under the bottom wire.
◆ Make sure the wires are tight, and batteries are charged. DC chargers (6- and 12-volt) need their batteries recharged every two to four weeks.

- Use at least a 70 amp-hour battery.
- The fence charger should always be on. Check voltage weekly with a voltmeter. You should have at least 3,000 volts at the furthest distance from the charger. Always recharge during the day, so the fence is at maximum output at night, when bears are most likely to come calling.
- Marine battery terminals and lead-composition eyelets resist corrosion. Keep your battery and fence charger dry and corrosion free. Disconnect lower wires if they're covered by snow.

GATES

Gates should be electrified, well-insulated and practical—they can range from single strands of electrified wire with gate handles to electrified panel or tubular gates. Some landfills install automatically closing gates to prevent wily bears from following vehicles into the landfill. Others find they can leave gates open during the day, as long as they're closed and fully electrified at night.

HUMAN SAFETY

Whatever you do, don't make the mistake one of our neighbors did and wire straight into the household current instead of using a fence charger. Households use continuous alternating current (AC) to power everything from lights to power tools, and it is always on. If an electric fence is plugged into an outlet, when someone gets zapped their muscles will contract and only partially release—making it very hard to let go, and pretty easy to get hurt.

Electric fencing combines high voltage with low amperage in a pulsating charge at 60 – 65 pulses a minute. When someone gets shocked, there's an involuntary muscle contraction. The pulsating charge gives the person ¾ of a second to let go of the wire.

Getting zapped by an electric fence doesn't do any permanent damage to bears or people. But it's highly unpleasant, so put up a

CHECK YOUR JOULES
Voltage is only part of the electric fence story. The joules rating on your energizer tells you the amount of energy the fence actually delivers. It takes a big jolt to shock a bear painfully enough to teach it to avoid the fence in the future. Check the specifications on the unit for the joules rating. You need at least 0.7 joules delivered, based on your local moisture conditions. With joules, it isn't really the more the merrier, because the higher the joule output, the greater the danger to people accidentally contacting the fence.

warning sign. In some municipalities, electric fences are illegal within city or township limits; be sure to check with your home-

> **WARNING:**
> **ELECTRIC FENCE IN USE**

owners association or local government before installing one.

HOW TO GET FENCED

Many state and provincial agencies have diagrams, installation instructions and more on their Web sites. The folks at Premier Sheep are regarded as world leaders in electric fencing. You'll find a wealth of information and just about anything you could possibly want to order on their Web site at *www.premiersheep.com*, including a handy chart that shows you what kind of fence to install based on what you're trying to protect. ❖

KID-PROOFING YOUR FENCE

People with kids who help tend the critters are often nervous about putting in an electric fence, and small children who get themselves tangled up in a fence can get a serious shock. One way to electrify a pen without electrifying a kid is to use wooden posts for your fence posts; this allows a 4-inch (10-cm) separation between the inside wire and the outside wire. Use regular barbed-wire on the "outside" of the fence, at 12-inch (30-cm) spacing. Use the electric wire on the "inside" of the fence, also at 12-inch (30-cm) spacing, but set in between the barbed-wire. Your outside barbed wire will be at 12, 24, 36 and 48 inches (30, 50, 61, 91 and 122 cm); your inside electric wire will be at 6, 18, 30 and 42 inches (15, 46, 76 and 107 cm). A child will encounter the barbed wire first; a predator will have to squeeze between the barbed wire, which puts its nose right in line with the hot wire. Install an electric cut-off switch at the gate to the pen or field, so when someone enters they can turn the power off.

— *Tom Beck*

Florida's Threatened Bears

Working Together for a Sunnier Future

How can a state with 34.5 million acres (13.9 million hectares) and fewer than 3,200 black bears have bear problems?

It's easy. Just take a population growing by over 300,000 people a year, subtract over 7,000 acres (2,830 hectares) a year lost to development, add thousands of miles of highway criss-crossing all the remaining bear habitat, and stir gently. Add 2.5 million tourists and visitors each year, and you've got a recipe for trouble.

The 1,000 plus people a day who move to Florida expect a lot of things: sunshine and citrus. Beaches and tropical storms. Alligators and bugs the size of birds. They don't expect black bears.

A century ago over 10,000 black bears may have roamed throughout the state, but by the 1960s decades of unregulated and illegal hunting and human encroachment had decimated the bear population, and landed Florida's

> *"Conflicts between humans and bears have escalated in central Florida over the past five years. The scope and magnitude of these conflicts extend beyond the responsibilities and capabilities of any one agency; handling these problems requires cooperation among multiple agencies and organizations."*
>
> CAROLYN SEKERAK,
> WILDLIFE BIOLOGIST – OCALA
> NATIONAL FOREST

unique subspecies of black bear on the state's threatened and endangered list.

Hunting bears ended in 1994, but "progress" marches relentlessly on. One of the results of so much development is that the eight or so areas of mostly public lands that are home to Florida's remaining bears have become land islands, surrounded by human populations that

Two Florida black bear cubs in their den. *Photo: Florida Fish & Wildlife Conservation Commission (FFWCC)*

A collared sow on a Florida trail. *Photo: FFWCC*

number in the millions, and grow and spread faster than kudzu.

But in those protected areas where lush habitat remains, Florida's bears live large. In fact, in central Florida's Ocala National Forest there's at least one bear per square mile.

Ocala National Forest is ideal bear habitat, with highly productive scrub that produces a dependable bumper crop of acorns and palmetto berries and thick, dense sand pine forests that make great bear cover. With an average annual rainfall of over 55 inches (140 cm) a year, food is so abundant that, except for pregnant females, many of Florida's bears don't bother denning up for the "winter."

It's such a benign climate that Florida bears are the octogenarians of the bear world, often living several decades in the wild. On average, Florida males live from 15 to 25 years, females live up to 30 years; considerably longer than many of their eastern and western relatives.

At one time Ocala National Forest was in the middle of nowhere. Today the surrounding area is one of the fastest growing in the nation, with over eight million people living within a one-hour drive, and six major highways slicing through Ocala's 389,000 acres (157,000 hectares). No wonder Florida is also the bear road-kill capital of the U.S.

Now rural lands that were once used for timber, ranching and growing citrus are being transformed into residential communities and ranchettes that often back up to large tracts of federal and state owned lands. It's a classic wildland/urban interface situation, with tremendous potential for bears and people to come into frequent contact with each other.

The home of Walt Disney World is just one example of how bears and people are rubbing elbows. Orlando has acre upon acre of gated communities almost literally carved out of the swamps and wildlands. Plenty of community greenspace and homes with rivers and swamps in their backyards create ample corridors for bears to travel. But most of those corridors lead bears to people. So it's not uncommon for a suburban soccer mom to come home, hop out of her minivan and discover a bear in her garage, digging into the birdseed, rummaging through the refrigerator, or enjoying a nice bag of dog chow.

Human-bear conflicts have risen from one in 1978 to over 1,300 in 2002. In just six months from July – December 2000, staff from the Florida Fish and Wildlife Conservation Commission spent 300 person-days responding to bear-related calls. In 2001 Ocala National Forest started to get reports of bears destroying campsites, raiding dumpsters and bluff-charging picnickers.

One thing Florida has in common with the rest of North America: about half of the calls coming in are about bears getting into the garbage. A phone tracking study revealed that most of the people calling about bears were angry, upset or afraid, and thought bears were dangerous.

All the various agencies responsible for the wildlife and wild lands of Florida decided they had to find ways to make people want to get along with their furry native Floridian neighbors. They all cooperated, and came up with a wide-ranging collection of tactics all designed to get people informed, involved and interested.

THE FLORIDA BLACK BEAR FESTIVAL

The first Saturday in October the little town of Umatilla, population 2,400, braces for the invasion of up to ten thousand bear people. It's an invasion they welcome with open arms. Because the more people show up, the more people go home with a better understanding of how to get along with the state's bears—and why they should want to.

SARA TUTTLE

The Umatilla Bear Festival was the brain child of the Florida chapter of Defenders of Wildlife, but its success depends on a diverse group of organizations and agencies that put aside political and territorial issues to work together to make life better for Florida's bears.

The coalition includes the Ocala National Forest, the City of Umatilla, the Umatilla Chamber of Commerce, the USDA Forest Service, the Florida Fish and Wildlife Conservation Commission, Defenders of Wildlife, the Florida Chapter of the Sierra Club, the Wildlife Foundation of Florida and Walkabout Adventures.

Each partner has a representative that serves on the festival's executive committee.

Together they're responsible for planning the activities and logistics, getting funding, attracting and approving vendors, and promoting the festival to the general public. All decisions are made through joint approval.

It sounds like a time-eating bureaucratic nightmare, but according to the parties involved, most of the work gets done through e-mails and phone calls, with little infighting or turf-protecting.

The festival is a free, one-day event that takes up the entire City Park in downtown Umatilla. There are seminars, field trips, stage shows, booths selling honey and other natural products and all sorts of engaging activities cleverly designed to help people better understand bears. Festival coordinator Sherre Dabanion estimates that over 50,000 people have attended the festival since it first debuted in 1999.

A family activities pavilion staffed by environmental educators offers hands-on games and crafts that teach about bears and conservation. A teacher's resource center provides educational materials for teachers and parents. A life-size maze guides people through the life of a bear. There's an ABC's of bears scavenger hunt, a scent identification activity and a local author's corner.

Interactive exhibits and presentations teach campers and hikers how to travel safely in bear country. Homeowners learn how to avoid bear conflicts, and the "Ask a Biologist" booth is a favorite place for the curious to get their bear questions answered by an expert.

Free shuttle buses whisk people off to field trips into bear country hosted by the U.S. Forest Service that give people a hands-on learning experience with the type of work the Florida Fish and Wildlife Conservation Commission does with bears.

Florida Black Bear Festivals attract over 10,000 people every year.
Left: courtesy of the Florida Black Bear Festival. Above: U.S. Forest Service

Left to right: Checking out a bear-resistant dumpster; using a bear skull to teach kids the bear facts; Smokey the Bear is always a big hit at the Florida Black Bear Festival. *Photos: U.S. Forest Service*

Local businesses and corporations contribute funding and advertising, and underwrite the costs of the popular Black Bear Activity Guides they hand out.

The Umatilla Chamber of Commerce helps recruit local school clubs, civic groups, businesses and individual volunteers that are the operational backbone of the festival. Newspapers, magazines and radio give the festival plenty of free publicity.

"I want people to understand why protecting bear habitat is just as important for humans who want to preserve their quality of life. I personally doubt that nothing-but-shopping-malls is quality of life," said Jim Fowler, host of Mutual of Omaha's Wild Kingdom, who's been a popular attraction at the festival.

BEAR AWARE TEAM FOR HIRE

Florida has an unusual group of bear agents who are trained and contracted by the Florida Fish and Wildlife Conservation Commission, but are not state employees. When bear complaints come in, a bear agent who's paid by-the-call goes out to evaluate the incident and make recommendations to prevent any further problems. Since it's against state law to feed bears, once the agent tells the harried home or business owner how to correct the situation, they have to comply or risk being ticketed. Agents are also trained to trap bears that need aversive conditioning, work them and release them on site, or if absolutely necessary, relocate them. Agents don't destroy problem bears; only a biologist can make that call.

Florida's innovative curriculum integrates bear facts into lessons on everything from math to language arts, and includes hands-on field trips to bring the lessons to life. *Photo: U.S. Forest Service*

FLORIDA BLACK BEARS GO TO SCHOOL

Thanks to a partnership between the Florida Fish and Wildlife Conservation Commission and Defenders of Wildlife, Florida school kids in the 3rd to 8th grades have a chance to learn about bears while they study reading, language arts, history, math, geography, social studies, and the arts and sciences. Teachers attend a training session to get acquainted with the Sunshine State Standards-based curriculum, and get teachers' notebooks packed with activities and information about how to use bear behavior and biology to bring lessons to life. ❖

"This unit favorably impacted my students' learning throughout the year. I was surprised in the spring at how far-reaching this experience had been. We were studying line graphs, a very difficult and abstract concept for 4th graders, when one of my students suddenly exclaimed, "I get it! It's like the bear graphs! You know, how many more are killed on the roads every year!"

"My students live in bear country, and through my teaching and their experiences at the Florida Black Bear Festival and school workshops, they've learned the importance of respecting wildlife and incidentally, the importance of preserving their own quality of life.

"At school we use the black bear curriculum to apply academic skills, both basic and problem-solving, to students' lives outside of school. One student in particular used his love of bears to get further involved in our community; he interviewed community members, and gave speeches and presentations for other groups. This trip and curriculum has far reaching influence on our students, their parents and our community."

Patsy Stine — 4th Grade Teacher, Seminole Springs Elementary School

chapter 9

Give Bears a Brake

Safe Driving in Bear Country

In the U.S. collisions with wildlife kill over 200 people, injure 29,000 more and do a billion dollars in vehicle property damage every year. Every year hundreds of black bears die on our roads.

When you're driving through heavily wooded areas or on roads with wildlife crossing signs, do yourself and the bears and other wildlife a big favor, and slow down. If you're in a hurry, easing up on the accelerator will improve your chances of arriving alive and undented. Take your time and you might spot a bear or other wildlife.

Most bears avoid roadways during daylight hours, but are quick to feed on the tasty grasses growing in the right of way, or cross roads to get where they're going between dusk and dawn. If you're driving at night in bear country, it's tough to spot a black bear on a black road.

WHY DO BEARS CROSS THE ROAD?

Most of the time, because they have to. Humans build roads to create the easiest ways for people to get from here to there.

Bears have to get from here to there, too, often many times a month if the road they're crossing bisects their home range. The drive to find food overrides a bear's natural desire to avoid places with a human imprint. A black bear's territory can range from 5 to 100 square miles (13 to 260 sq km) or more; it's not unusual

When cars and bears collide, everyone loses.
Photos: U.S. Forest Service

111

DON'T COMMIT

BEARICIDE

Slow down.

Save a bear's life.

And maybe your own.

Lake Tahoe bear crossing sign. © Ann Bryant

for a bear to travel 5 to 15 miles (13 to 39 km) a day looking for food. It's hard to travel across 15 square miles (39 sq km) in much of North America without crossing a road.

Bears have been using their own roadway system for years; well-worn game trails that take their four-footed travelers to all the best spots in their territory to forage, find a mate, take a nap or den up for the winter. Sometimes the deadliest spots on a highway can be easily identified by tracking animal highway deaths, which are often concentrated where game trails and asphalt intersect.

In 2004, after five years of meticulous record-keeping by the BEAR League proved that bears were regularly being run over on the California side of Lake Tahoe, the California Department of Transportation installed fifteen bear crossing signs on killer highways. Sister-state Nevada had installed similar signs with much success in 2000, after a mother bear and her two cubs were killed on a busy highway in the fall of 1999. All told, nineteen road signs went up warning motorists they were driving in bear country.

Unfortunately, the signs on the California side were mounted on simple break-away wooden posts. All but one were soon swiped by folks wielding chainsaws in the night who apparently thought they'd look better in their dens than on the streets doing their job protecting motorists and bears.

While signs were posted, the vehicular bearicide rate along the deadliest stretch of road on the North Shore of Lake Tahoe dropped to zero. The BEAR League's Ann Bryant speculates the signs make people slow down in hopes of seeing a bear, and slowing down helps them avoid a collision. CALTRAN says they'll replace the stolen signs with ones on steel posts that should defeat the chain saw gangs.

Some places are building wildlife underpasses, overpasses or land bridges—tunnels, culverts and earthen bridges that offer animals safe passage under or over the highway. Other methods of trying to keep animals off the highway include fencing and strategically placed vegetation designed to funnel animals to safe crossing points and keep them off the roads.

Floridians travel an estimated quarter-million miles (400,000 km) a day—twice as many miles as back in the '70s. Roads criss-cross the state, and travel through all five core areas for black bears. Since 1976, 84 percent of the 1,337 known bear deaths in the state resulted from motor vehicle collisions; half the fatalities have been on roads that slice through Ocala National Forest, particularly busy State Highways 40 and 19.

CRITTER CROSSINGS

University of Florida scientist Daniel Smith worked with the Florida Department of Transportation to develop a computer-based model that identifies ecological hotspots—sections of road where high quality habitat, vehicles and vulnerable species collide. Wildlife corridors, road kill sites and other key factors were all fed into a computer. Monitoring 290 of the worst spots for two years proved that animals were using them as frequently as the model predicted—with deadly results.

Underpasses are now being installed at dozens of the deadliest locations to help everything from Florida's endangered panthers and threatened black bears to species like turtles safely cross the road. In Wekiva State Park, hidden cameras show that when the new underpass was first opened, bears tried to find a break in the fence that funnels them to the underpass, but once they discover that the underpass makes it safe to cross the road, they head right for it.

The computer program Smith developed is reportedly adaptable and easy to use, and works on an area as big as a state or province, or as small as a single intersection.

Overpasses like this one spanning the Trans-Canada highway in Banff *(lower photo)* appeal to species like deer, elk and moose that prefer to stay out in the open. Underpasses *(top photo)* are often the safe passage of choice for predators and other animals that prefer to travel under cover. As a general rule, the bigger the tunnel, culvert or underpass, the more comfortable large animals like bears are using it.
© *Susan Hagood, The Humane Society of the United States*

There are hopes it will be able to help guide conservation strategies across the continent.

Florida put in a state road wildlife underpass on busy SR 46, the state's deadliest road for bears, in late 1996. Between November 1996 and December 1999, the underpass was used by 48 Florida black bears, 78 coyotes, 119 bobcats, 154 white-tailed deer, 14 dogs and eight trespassing humans. By the time you're reading this, there should be a new dual purpose land bridge south of Ocala that's designed to be used by people during the day and wildlife at night. Since their research shows that underpasses work for bears, the state is also considering retrofitting the worst bear hotspots with underpasses or other structural solutions.

Highway underpasses were a new concept in the U.S. just ten years ago; the latest $217 billion Transportation Equity Act has now made them a national consideration.

FENCING BEARS OUT

Over 14,000 vehicles speed down the Trans-Canada Highway right through the heart of Banff every day; the Trans-Can is the major east-west highway in Canada, and one of the deadliest wildlife highways in North America. Parks Canada has put in a variety of fencing, wildlife underpasses and overpasses in busy Banff National Park. Two 164-foot (50-meter) wide overpasses are the first of their size and scope in North America. Cattle grates—called Texas gates in Canada—were put in where fencing intersects roads leading to the highway.

Measuring performance along three four-lane sections from 1981 through 1999 showed that fencing reduced vehicle collisions

SURE-FIRE SLOWDOWN

In 1976–1977 we installed several underpasses on the interstate as part of a deer-vehicle accident research project. We also tried signs, animated signs and overhead lighting. We discovered the best way to reduce collisions was to slow down traffic, and the best way to slow down traffic was to leave dead deer along the shoulder. Motorists would see the carcass and slow down, and stay slowed down. If bear activity in an area is highly seasonal, leaving the carcasses along the road for several days might slow down traffic during a key period. Unfortunately, I think locals become habituated to anything left up permanently, but signs can still be useful in tourist country.   — Tom Beck

with ungulates—deer, elk and sheep—by more than 95 percent, and with all wildlife by more than 80 percent. However, half the black bears killed during the study period died along fenced sections of the highway; apparently bears could easily climb the fence. As far as human safety goes, 63 percent of the collisions occurring along unfenced stretches of highway involved wildlife; along the fenced stretches, the rate dropped to one in ten.

THE RIGHT-OF-WAY BUFFET

Highway departments often plant grasses and forbs in the right-of-way and in median strips that unintentionally attract many animals, including bears. In some parts of the East they plant clover, because it's low growing and cuts down on mowing costs. It also cuts down on bears, because clover is highly attractive to bears and other wildlife. The Colorado Department of Transportation worked with the Division of Wildlife and decided to plant less appealing greenery in the right of way.

In any language, the message is the same—for your sake and theirs, please don't approach bears.
© *John E. Marriott; Sign posted at Banff National Park, Canada*

WHAT TO DO IF YOU HIT A BEAR

If you hit a bear, first make sure the people involved are okay, get your car off the road and call 911. Then check on the bear. If it's dead, and you think it was part of a family group—it's a cub, or you saw cubs before the collision—the mother will attempt to come back and remove it, even if it's dead. If it's a mother bear, the cubs will stay with her body for quite awhile, so it's important to get the remains out of the road to keep from adding to the body count.

If the bear is injured, but still alive, no matter how badly you feel, don't approach the bear. Call 911 and ask them to notify the local wildlife authorities. In some situations an injured bear may be taken to a rehabilitator; if cubs are involved and too young to be on their own, they'll be captured, if possible, and taken along. Don't try to help the bear yourself; injured animals are often in great pain and shock, and will

This little cub was one of the 10 to 20 bears killed in vehicle collisions each year in Yosemite.
Photo: Jeffrey Trust, 2003; National Park Service

lash out at anything that comes near. Even an injured bear is strong and powerful, and can do serious damage. ❖

THE TWO MILLION DOLLAR LICENSE PLATE

Florida's drivers have raised over two million dollars to help bears and other wildlife. The special license plate costs $17 more than a standard plate; fifteen of those dollars

go to the Wildlife Foundation of Florida, which doles out the money for species and habitat research, watchable wildlife initiatives, and educational and conservation programs, with a focus on projects involving Florida black bears. The Florida Fish and Wildlife Conservation Commission, Defenders of Wildlife and the Wildlife Foundation of Florida all worked together to get the 10,000 petition signatures and $30,000 application fee necessary to get the proposal before the Florida legislature, which authorized the plate in 1998. Since then over 46,000 plates have been issued, and the amount of money raised has gone up every year since the plate was introduced. The adaptable black bear is found in many different habitats throughout Florida, so preserving and improving habitat for bears helps many other species as well, including people.

Durango, Colorado

Bear Smart Durango

Bear Smart Durango is undoubtedly one of the best-looking bear education and preparedness campaigns out there. That's because it's the brain child of nationally known commercial illustrator Bryan Peterson, who dreamed since he was a young boy of drawing the wildlife of the West. In 1996 he left his big-city agency job behind, and followed his dreams to Durango. Today Bryan Peterson is doing a lot more for bears than just drawing them.

Durango is a small community tucked into southwestern Colorado's Four Corners region near the rugged San Juan Mountains. The Bear Smart program borrowed its name and much of its philosophy from Canada's Bear Smart Program, minus the extensive audit and certification process Canada has in place.

Durango, population 15,000 and growing, is smack in the middle of some of the state's best bear habitat. The city is surrounded by oak brush, and there's a state wildlife area just

> *"You find bears in town because that's where there's a lot of food. Unfortunately that's also where there are a lot of people. We're focusing on education and awareness— hence a brochure, Web site, city bear video, media campaign, Bear Week and Bear Beer."*
>
> BRYAN PETERSON, PRESIDENT
> BEAR SMART DURANGO

west of town. And like so many other cities of all sizes, the growing population is migrating to the outskirts of town, right into the heart of the bears' favorite fall feeding grounds.

All it took was one particularly bad natural food year in 2001 for Durango's bear problems to start growing faster than the housing developments.

Peterson had gotten involved with La Plata County's wildlife shortly

Durango backyard bears. © *Warren Holland*

RESIDENT COMPLAINT No: 38

My neighbor is feeding bears dog food. What can I do?

PAID FOR BY THE LA PLATA COUNTY ANIMAL DAMAGE ADVISORY COMMITTEE

BEAR SMART

BE SMART ABOUT BEARS. GO TO WWW.BEARSMARTDURANGO.ORG

RESIDENT COMPLAINT No: 13

A bear knocked our garbage can over at 6 a.m. What can we do?

PAID FOR BY THE LA PLATA COUNTY ANIMAL DAMAGE ADVISORY COMMITTEE

BEAR SMART

BE SMART ABOUT BEARS. GO TO WWW.BEARSMARTDURANGO.ORG

after moving out, and soon was relocating beavers for the wildlife committee, and rubbing elbows with one of the region's more famous citizens, retired bear biologist Tom Beck. Beck's philosophy, forged from decades of working with bears and people for the Colorado Division of Wildlife, is both simple and powerfully persuasive. He believes that people who choose to live in bear country have a responsibility to adapt and adjust to the bears, and create solutions, not problems. It was a philosophy that made sense to Peterson.

Peterson arranged a "Living with Bears" panel presentation for the Animal Damage Advisory Committee of La Plata County. The event scored a big bulls-eye with many, including city officials grappling with an ever growing number of human-bear conflicts.

A series of Bears and Trash Roundtables followed, with the facilitated meetings bringing together representatives from Durango's waste disposal providers, the city and county, law enforcement, the Division of Wildlife, the USDA, Animal Control, the Forest Service, the Bureau of Land Management, Durango Public Works and concerned citizens.

After throwing out lots of ideas, everyone agreed on one thing: the public needed more education and information. Somewhere along the way Bear Smart Durango was born.

Soon the fledgling group had nearly 150 volunteers who all wanted to help. Everyone at the roundtables wanted to know more about what the citizens thought about the bears before they decided what to do. So Peterson and the group drafted a Bear Smart Citizens survey, the Division of Wildlife picked up the tab for printing and the city mailed it out as an insert in utility bills.

SARA TUTTLE

◆ 22% of residents responded, a rate that's practically unheard of in surveys. "People here care about bears," said Peterson. "They think it's important to resolve conflicts."

◆ 90% said neighborhood trash cans were "always" or "sometimes" a problem.

◆ One-third were willing to pay for the additional cost of a bear-proof can.

◆ 20% each said intruding bears were either "no problem" or a "major problem."

◆ 60% said bears were a "minor problem."

◆ 61% were willing to change their habits to avoid issues

◆ 42% supported citations for offenders

Most frequent comment: **"Durango's bears have a people problem."**

Unlike some places where cities have passed legislation mandating bear-proof trash, outlawing and enforcing the feeding or attracting of wild animals and levying fines, Durango's efforts are still both voluntary and largely grass roots, with growing support from the city, the media, the Division of Wildlife and Durango's citizens.

Bear Smart Durango focuses on education and awareness. They have a stylish and comprehensive Web site, where you can find an answer to just about any black bear question, plus a brochure they hand out to residents and a media advertising campaign. The *Durango Herald* offers a Bear Tracker line so people can call in bear sightings. Bear-resistant trash cans are available from the city for $150, although few residents have purchased them. Peterson is lobbying for a "pay as you go" plan where residents who want a bear-resistant container can pay it off by adding a dollar or two to their utility bill every month.

Some of the city's parks are switching from standard trash containers to bear-resistant ones, thanks to plenty of gentle nudging and reams of information comparing options, prices and performance provided by Bear Smart Durango.

"It's an evolutionary process," says Bryan. We've accomplished a lot, but we've just scratched the surface, and we've run into some roadblocks along the way.

"Some people in Durango love their bears to death. Most people like to see bears; many don't mind them in their yards, as long as they don't do too much damage. It's hard for people to understand that their neighbors may not feel the same way they do—and if bears cause

The next generation learns all about bears.
© Bryan Peterson

Photos & Beer Labels: Bryan Peterson

problems, they could be sentencing *their* bear to a possible demise.

"Right now I know of at least five people—including friends of mine—who are intentionally feeding bears, which is illegal in Colorado. But the ordinances are meaningless if they're not enforced, and down here the Division has such a full plate that, somewhat understandably, handing out tickets for having bird feeders out, or even garbage overflowing, is a low priority.

"But I know we're making progress—there's an awareness of bears, and of our responsibilities as residents of bear country—that was nonexistent a few years ago. People want to do the right thing, I think," Peterson said.

BE BEAR SMART WEEK

The second week of August is Be Bear Smart Week in Durango—a week of events designed to raise public awareness and spur public action to reduce human-bear conflicts, sponsored by Bear Smart Durango, the Division of Wildlife, the Animal Damage Advisory Committee of La Plata County, and the City of Durango, and supported by dozens of local businesses and residents. Representatives appear on local television and radio programs, the *Durango Herald* runs articles and the library and local bookstores feature bear books. The City Bear Video that Bear Smart Durango helped produce runs on local cable, and Tom Beck appears on local cable TV and often presents his popular slide program on black bears. The Division of Wildlife displays bear information, the city displays bear-resistant trash cans, and Ska Brewery, a local micro-brewer, displays—and sells—three popular bruin brews, with some of the proceeds going to the BSD Program. ❖

> "I was in the supermarket, half listening to a conversation in the next aisle over. One woman was inviting the other over at 9:00 p.m. to see the bears, and explained that every night they put out popcorn, spaghetti and other treats. The bears showed up just like clockwork, and the neighbors turned out to watch. I couldn't believe what I was hearing. They thought it was 'neat' to feed these bears. I left the supermarket thinking 'That's it! Something else needs to be done about this. People are just not getting it.'"
>
> *BRYAN PETERSON, PRESIDENT – BEAR SMART DURANGO*

chapter 10

Come Get Your Bear

Relocating Bears

From Florida to British Columbia, "***Come Get Your Bear***" is a common cry. When people are frightened, anxious or nervous about bears, they just want "someone" to make the problem go away. Many people think a quick, easy solution is to move the bear "somewhere it can't get into any trouble."

On the surface, it seems like a great idea. Trap the offending bear. Move it somewhere there aren't any people. Give the bear a second chance. Solve the problem. Make both people and bears happy. But bear managers have learned the hard way that bears have the homing instincts of pigeons and the persistence of a four-year-old determined to get into the cookie jar.

At one time relocating bears used to be a much more widely accepted—although probably not any more effective—approach to managing human-bear conflicts than it is today. Today there are precious few places where there are no people. And most of those precious places with no people and good habitat are already home to plenty of bears.

The majority of experts now agree, and research studies confirm, that relocation is at best a temporary and generally ineffective way to resolve human-bear conflicts.

So why do agencies still relocate bears? For some, established policy gives them little choice—it's either move the bear, or kill the bear, and most

Relocated bears seldom live happily every after.
© Derek Reich

people who've chosen wildlife management as a career hate to needlessly kill animals. And no matter how big of a problem a bear's behavior is causing, killing it often stirs up a hornet's nest of negative publicity and a flood of hate mail from concerned citizens.

Tell someone a bear will be moved, and they heave a sigh of relief. Their problem goes away, and they imagine the bear will live happily ever after out in the Disney version of the woods "where it belongs." They're relieved because they don't want the bear to die. But all too often, sooner or later that's exactly what happens.

One Bear's Tale

Imagine being lured into a nice cozy space that smells like it's full of food. Then next thing you know a gate slams down, and you can't get out. Pretty soon a bunch of loud two-legged creatures show up and you get jabbed with something really sharp. While you're knocked out they take blood and hair samples, pull a tooth so they can find out how old you are and staple tags to your ears.

When you wake up you're bumping along in the back of a noisy truck. When you're finally turned loose, you're yelled at and hit with something that hurts and makes a lot of noise. You can't wait to get away, but when you stop running, you have no idea where you are. And the bears in your new neighborhood aren't happy to see you.

You try to stay out of fights, but you can't find much to eat, and you don't know all the local food sources. The resident bears make your life miserable. You're hungry, uncomfortable and far from home.

You hit the road, following your nose and using that built-in radar that most animals from lost house cats to parrots seem to have.

But now it's hunting season, and people wearing orange want to turn you into a rug. At one busy highway, you just miss being hit by a speeding pickup truck. You see another bear lying in the ditch on the side of the road that wasn't so lucky.

When you finally make it back home, you stop by your favorite haunts, and sure enough, the nice folks on the corner have filled up their bird feeders again. And something sure smells yummy inside that screened in porch.

You haven't been eating very well, so you're really hungry. You clean out the bird feeders and push against the door.

It's unlocked; in seconds you're inside, where you find a bag of dog food that makes up for all those calories you've been missing. You're half way through the feast when the owners come home.

For some reason they start screaming. You run right through the screen, but next thing you know the humans in the green shirts are back, and they track you down.

They look at your ear tags, and shake their heads. The last thing you hear is the sound of the gun that ends your life.

The hard truth is that relocating a bear long distances is expensive, time consuming and often traumatic for both bear and people. Even worse, simply moving the bear usually doesn't solve the problem for either the people or the bear.

If garbage, bird seed, pet food or human foods attracted a bear, moving that bear only makes room for another one to discover the bounty. Moving a bear to solve a problem that's been created by human carelessness or indifference is like passing a disease along to someone else, and thinking it's been cured because you don't feel bad anymore.

When bears are moved, their behavior patterns move with them. Bears that have come to rely on human food sources often end up in conflicts with people in their new territories. Even if they don't, they're likely to have plenty of problems of their own.

It's hard work being a bear. If there aren't abundant and easy to find natural food sources, a strange bear in a strange land can literally starve to death. And relocated bears sometimes have bear problems themselves when the resident bears react badly to having a new competitor for food, denning space, and mates dropped into their turf. A relocated bear might even be killed by a dominant bear already occupying the territory.

Waiting for release or execution. © *Derek Reich*

When bears follow their instincts and try to return home, they often have to cross roads, and are frequently hit by cars. They're also more vulnerable to hunters and poachers. If they do make it back, they often resume searching for human foods. And if they're recaptured again for coming into conflict with people, it's usually the end of the road.

In British Columbia, they've given up on relocating black bears long distances in hopes of giving them a fresh start in life. The British Columbia Ministry of the Environment studied the issue and decided that the low success rate combined with the high cost in dollars and time made it impractical to move black bears any distance. So each year approximately 900 black bears and 50 grizzly bears lose their lives as a direct result of conflicts between people and bears.

In those rare areas where there's good available habitat and few people, moving bears can work, and can even help reestablish bear populations. But places like that are few and far between these days.

Wildlife management agencies don't manage wildlife, they manage people. They also juggle complex responsibilities and answer to many masters. The fact that the public thinks moving bears solves conflicts and expects them to come get the bear and take it away makes it harder for agencies to try different approaches. Public opinion can be a powerful force for change; many of the programs that have been most successful at reducing human-bear conflicts were first developed after ordinary people became outraged at a particular incident and demanded agencies and municipalities find other ways to solve human-bear conflicts.

Regardless of whether or not an individual bear might be willing and able to stay put in its new home, relocation as a management practice can never eliminate human-bear conflicts. There's no substitute for developing ways for people and bears to peacefully share space, and preventing the conflicts that result in bears being moved in the first place.

A VICIOUS CYCLE

"Some states think trap and relocate works. I do not feel it works very well as we have a lot of return bears. Where can I take a bear where there is good habitat, good forage, no homes within 10 miles (16 km), and no other dominant bears which may kill subadults? If we jump right into trap-and-relocate and the property owner doesn't change the habits that attracted the bear in the first place—garbage, unlocked doors and windows, bird feeders—another bear will show up and they'll ask us to trap that bear. It becomes an endless cycle. Where and when does it end? People need to take responsibility for where they choose to live. The general public believes that once we trap and move a bear it lives happily ever after. I do not believe that is the case. The majority of relocated bears get into trouble again and return to the area in which they were trapped and are then euthanized."

LAURIE SMITH, ANIMAL OFFICER
THE TOWN OF SNOWMASS VILLAGE, COLORADO

A NOTE TO BEAR PROFESSIONALS

Relocation is a complex and controversial topic. As long as the public thinks the bear is going to live happily ever after, from a public relations point of view it's a safe solution. No one can fault you for trying. And out of sight, out of mind. If the bear messes up again, it will be someone else's problem.

But that doesn't make most wildlife managers feel any better about relocating their bears. Most know it's just postponing the inevitable. From a practical and effective point of view, overall statistics are pretty grim, with up to 80 percent of relocations failing—from the bear's point of view—for one reason or another.

Years with an unusual number of human-bear conflicts are often also years with natural food shortages—times when a late spring freeze or a hot, dry summer causes major food sources, like berries or nuts that bears depend on, to fail. A bear moved from one food-short area to another is at a double disadvantage. It's unfamiliar with the new territory, and there's not much food to be had. Bears roaming around looking for food and trying to avoid encounters with other bears are more vulnerable to road accidents and hunting, and more likely to encounter human places. Since coming into conflict with people while trying to find food was most likely what got the bear moved in the first place, odds are good it will approach people again.

A 1986 study by Lynn Rogers found that relocating subadult males (under two years old) has the highest probability of success, presumably because they are young, impressionable and already looking for new digs, as long as suitable habitat is available and it's free of big adult males. Still, over 80 percent of them moved under 40 miles (64 km) returned to their old haunts. Success rates went up with the miles, but 48 percent of bears moved between 40 and 80 miles (64 and 128 km) returned, and 20 percent of bears moved between 137 and 168 miles (220 and 270 km) still made it back.

In reality, most agencies have a

"We believe that if we have to move a bear, we've failed."

BILL STIVER, WILDLIFE BIOLOGIST – GREAT SMOKY MOUNTAINS NATIONAL PARK

PERCENTAGE OF RETURNING BEARS (> Two Years Old)

SOURCE: Lynn Rogers, 1986 (Translocation of Black Bears)

	8 - 63 km	64 - 119 km	120 - 219 km	220 - 271 km
	5-39 miles	40 - 74 miles	75 - 137 miles	138 - 170 miles

"It's not very pretty to trap a bear, tranquilize him, and drag him out of the trap and shoot him. It's the absolute worse thing I have to do, and I hate it. We don't want to be the executioner."

KEVIN WRIGHT, COLORADO DISTRICT WILDLIFE MANAGER – ASPEN/SNOWMASS

tough time moving bears far enough away to give them a good chance of surviving. City, county, state, federal, provincial and agency guidelines get in the way, and in most parts of the continent, the number of wide open spaces available to move bears has shrunk dramatically in even the twenty plus years since Rogers' study.

Yosemite National Park made a total of 124 relocations between 1989 and 1993. Bears must be relocated within park boundaries, which limited the distance they could be moved. Approximately 80 percent of the relocations failed, with the bears eventually resuming their problem behavior and being recaptured in developed areas in the years following their release.

Driving a bear long distances to its new home takes a lot of time, energy and gas. For that same investment in time and money, you can aversively condition the bear. At the very least you could try a technique designed to teach the bear to avoid the scene of its "crime," called hard release.

ABOUT HARD RELEASE

Hard release is an evolving technique that some bear experts and bear biologists feel is one of the most promising tools for reeducating bears. It teaches the bear to associate the release site with bad things, so it won't want to come back. Typically the bear is trapped, worked up, and allowed to recover completely from the anesthesia, so it's alert and fully conscious before it's released. As soon as the bear exits the trap, it's yelled at, pelted with bean bag rounds or rubber bullets, chased by trained bear dogs or otherwise made miserable until it is well away from the release site and back somewhere it is safe for the bear to be. At that point it's important for all harassment to instantly stop, so the bear is rewarded—by being left in peace—for heading back into the forest.

Hard release appears to be very effective at teaching the bear to avoid the capture/release site like the plague. So if you're moving a bear for any reason to an area you hope will be its new home, the release should be as gentle and non-traumatic as possible. Some experts advise opening the trap door while the bear is still anesthetized, then backing off well out of sight to a place where you can still watch over the bear and make sure it wakes up and safely leaves the area. Harassing the bear or chasing it away from the trap tells the bear it's not in a safe place—and can send it fleeing right back to where you moved it from.

A FED BEAR IS A DEAD BEAR

We've all heard that phrase; it always sounded like nagging to me. On August 15, 2005 I learned what it means.

At 6:45 a.m. I received a call that a large bear had been trapped at the house where a break in had occurred the night before. I proceeded to the location, notified DOW, arranged for security to close off the area and waited for wildlife officers to arrive. I spent the next several hours with this magnificent creature. At times he would stand quietly, other times sleep peacefully. Most often he reminded me of my old dog waiting for me at home.

Not once in that time did he try to escape. If you approached within 20 feet he would stand and begin clacking his teeth, then expel air in a loud hissing sound, and moan. All were sounds of nervousness and fright, as we learned in our volunteer training.

It's no longer practical to relocate bears. There is no longer anywhere to take them. You either relocate them to be a problem in another community or they just return and continue to cause problems.

As the wildlife officer approached the cage [to shoot the bear] I began crying so hard it was difficult to take pictures. I've been a hunter all my life so I didn't understand the emotion I was feeling. I looked over at my wife and she was crying also. The wildlife officer looked at me with tears in his eyes and said, "This is the part of my job I hate." He turned out to be a very healthy bear in the prime of his life.

This is the part of his job I hate also.

— JIM TIFFIN, CDOW BEAR AWARE VOLUNTEER

© Jim Tiffin

NOTE: Jim is spearheading the newly organized Bear Aware team in Crystal Lakes, a large subdivision north of Fort Collins, Colorado. The education, community involvement, and use of deterrents and aversive conditioning now being employed came too late to save this bear, but hopefully will help future generations of bears and people learn to get along.

"Relocating a bear is at best a tactic to buy time to remove attractants. This is not to be confused with on-site releases, which constitute the most effective bear-shepherding tool we've got—you catch a bear where it is getting into trouble, hold it a while, then set up the trap so the bear can get to cover quickly—but will also know exactly where it is. Having this chance to associate this experience with the place can teach a bear in one go-round that this is a place to avoid. You can't get those immediate results most of the time with other methods. It's basically saying to the bear, see this? This is wrong. See those trees? You go to those trees and stay out of here and we leave you alone. Pretty nifty, and it has also been shown at Great Smoky Mountains National Park to lead to less mortality than other methods," says Anne Braaten, bear biologist for the National Park Service's North Cascades complex.

NOT SO HARD RELEASE

Great Smoky's bear biologists believe the experience of being trapped, handled, transported, poked and prodded and otherwise subjected to a big overdose of people is enough to traumatize the average bear. The key is releasing the bear back at the scene where it was trapped, and making sure it's fully conscious before it's released. Even so, they're now experimenting with adding aversive conditioning when the bear is released at the trap site as an added inducement to persuade the bear to beat it back to the woods and avoid people places in the future. For more on Great Smoky's innovative bear management programs, keep reading. ❖

BECK ON MOVING BEARS

"In my opinion, relocating adult bears of either sex is a big waste of time and effort.

"Moving subadult males will likely solve the immediate nuisance crisis, but you should expect high mortality. Subadult males don't know where they were yesterday, or where they're going tomorrow. So when you move one, it isn't a big deal. He is still pretty clueless. He will sometimes return, more often wander a new way, and wind up more vulnerable to hunting and accidents—but these are characteristics you would find in a subadult male that was not moved. Moving subadult females makes sense those few times when there is vacant habitat available.

"I believe negative conditioning AT THE SITE of trapping may convince the bear that free lunch isn't free. There is a cost; make it pricey enough and natural foraging starts to look better. In my opinion it holds the best promise for improving trapping/relocating results."

Great Smoky Mountains National Park

Creative New Solutions to Old Problems

A lot of bears…a lot of people…a lot of garbage. It's a lethal combination.

"If we get into a situation where we have to move a bear we've failed somewhere—we haven't been proactive enough, maybe a dumpster is broken, or we haven't kept the campground clean enough," explained Bill Stiver, a wildlife biologist for Great Smoky Mountains National Park. That philosophy has been the cornerstone of the park's bear management program since Stiver first went to work for supervising biologist Kim Delozier in 1988 as an eager grad student. Today he has nearly two decades of bear experience, and the park has an enviable track record for cleaning up bear problems.

With nearly ten million visitors a year, Great Smoky Mountains is America's most popular national park. Its rolling mountains, lush valleys and expansive views are within a one day drive of two-thirds of the population of the United States.

It's one of the few national parks with no entrance fee, so it has a very high percentage of day visitors who drop in to see the sights, have a picnic and move on. They come to see masses of pink azaleas in the spring, wildflowers in the summer and spectacular foliage in the fall. They come to hike part of the Appalachian Trail and brave the circular drive that rings historic Cade's Cove. And they come to see the bears.

The park's 521,000 acres (210,000 hectares) are home to between 1,600 and 2,000 black bears. That's about two bears for every square mile (2.6 sq km) of park, one of the highest bear densities east of the Rockies. The park is surrounded on three sides by national forests, giving bears even more roaming room, but on the Tennessee side it's bordered by the city of Gatlinburg, and encroaching civilization.

Historically Great Smoky has also been home to lots of human-bear conflicts. Millions of visitors who don't venture past parking lots and picnic grounds give the bears plenty of opportunity to become overly comfortable with people. Human-habituated bears—and other wildlife—are a common problem in

> *"It would be easy to manage the bears. All you'd have to do is keep out the people."*
>
> BILL STIVER, WILDLIFE BIOLOGIST—GREAT SMOKY MOUNTAINS NATIONAL PARK

As part of the park's education for visitors, Wildlife Technician Chuck Hester gives a tranquilized "nuisance" bear a work-up, while teaching the crowd how they can help keep bears wild and out of trouble.
Photo: GSMNP

many parks and protected natural areas throughout North America.

Bears that learn a steady stream of people means a steady stream of food sometimes graduate from night-time raids on picnic grounds to panhandling by the side of the road. The resultant bear-jams of gapers and gawkers snarl traffic and create situations that are potentially dangerous for both bears and people.

Several research studies show that roadside beggar bears are four times as likely to die a premature death than wild bears. They live high on an energy-packed diet of human garbage, and die before their time. Because they hang around roads, they're more likely to be hit and killed by a car. If they leave the park, their familiarity with humans and the fact that they connect people with food makes them easy pickings for poachers, and more likely to be killed by hunters. And garbage bears are the most likely candidates to graduate from nuisance to menace, and earn themselves a one-way trip to the great garbage dump in the sky.

No entry fees mean no entry stations where smiling park employees can hand out literature to a captive audience. That makes it tough for park staff to get the word out to visitors about the bears.

"Even if we were able to reach 90 percent of the people and teach them everything they need to know about getting along with bears, we'd still be left with a million people who don't know. And it only takes a few people to cause a big problem. Educating people about bears is a huge challenge here," says Stiver.

Under Delozier's guidance, Stiver, a steady stream of eager summer interns and a staff of seasonal biotechs have studied the park's crafty, panhandling, picnic-grounds raiding, dumpster-diving bears, and over the past decade have devised some solutions that are remarkably successful.

In the early 1990s when Stiver joined the staff, the park had hundreds of bear-resistant, "mailbox-style" garbage cans; as many as ten were lined up in the more popular picnic areas. But picnickers typically used only the first two or three; when they were full they'd leave their garbage outside, or on the picnic tables. The maintenance crew went off duty at 3:30 p.m.;

in the summer people picnicked until dusk, and picnic grounds were often occupied until dark. When the last car pulled out of the parking lot, the bears took over.

One of the worst sites for bear problems was the Chimneys Picnic area, which over the years had developed a widespread reputation as a place you could take your family any time during the summer and see a bear. People arrived in the late afternoon, set up lawn chairs, put out chicken or watermelon or something else the bears wouldn't be able to resist, and sat back and waited for the nightly bear show to begin.

During the three years between 1988 and 1990 the park handled twenty-four individual problem bears at Chimneys, did thirty-five relocations (some bears got more than one trip to Cherokee National Forest) and three chronic bears that became overly aggressive had to be killed. "Our job is to protect the resources. We believe if we're killing bears and moving bears, we're not doing our job right," Stiver explained. "We've failed."

They went to work analyzing the problems, and coming up with solutions. One of the first things Delozier and his crew did was replace all the old garbage cans throughout the park with big, bear-resistant dumpsters that hold more trash. Although they have occasional problems with latching and other mechanical and human malfunctions, the move from cans to dumpsters made it much easier for

people to stash their trash, and much harder for the bears to get at it.

But people will be people, and bears will be bears, and switching to dumpsters didn't make all the problems go away.

It seemed logical to the wildlife staff that one of the problems was that the maintenance crew went off duty at 3:30, several hours before the picnic areas closed at sunset. So for two years a night-roaming bear squad of biologists, interns and biotechs cruised the park, taking pictures of all the trash that was left all over, and

The bear in the culvert trap is on his way back to the capture site to be released. The bear on the operating table was rescued as an injured cub, and rehabbed at the Appalachian Bear Center. After a final hip repair, the bear was successfully returned to the park in 2005.
Photos: Emily Guss, GSMNP

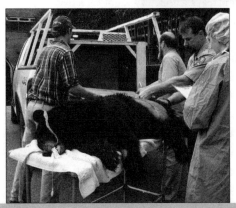

sending them to the head of the janitorial staff.

The bear facts were overwhelming; after studying the evidence, the maintenance staff volunteered to pitch in and change their hours; they now work from 1:00 p.m. to 9:30 p.m. And the three most problematic picnic areas close at 8:00 p.m. between May 1 and August 31 in order to give the staff enough time to visit all of them and make sure all the garbage is where it belongs before the sun goes down and the bears come out.

The park also installed fiberglass signs on every picnic table, with the message that hot dogs, fried chicken and watermelon rinds are some of the most lethal substances to bears, and asking people to stash their trash.

If rangers or staff find food, coolers, packs or something else out in the open, they confiscate it and leave a courtesy tag with a bear message in its place. Sheepish people must go to the ranger station to pick up their belongings—and listen to a friendly chat about the bears. Chronic offenders get ticketed and fined.

Even with all the changes, many bears still viewed the picnic grounds as bear fill-up stations. Until 1991 their bear management strategy was to trap, tag and relocate problem bears. But the large percentage of repeat relocations and outright failures convinced Kim Delozier there had to be a better way.

He believed if they could intervene while bears were hitting the trash at night, before they lost their wariness of people and became day active, they'd have the best chance of breaking them of their bad habits, and saving lives.

So he organized a team of interns to patrol picnic areas and campgrounds after dark, and set traps for bears on the prowl for garbage. Captured bears were typically taken to park headquarters for ear-tagging, a thorough medical exam and a lip and flank or groin tattoo.

After their ordeal the majority of bears were taken back to the place they were captured and released, rather than relocated. Stiver credits this innovative technique with teaching the bears to associate picnic areas or campgrounds with negative experiences instead of easy meals.

Since the program began, a remarkable 73 percent of the bears they've captured and released at the site mended their ways, and didn't need to be relocated.

Delozier cautions that one key to success is nipping problems in the bud. "It's a

SARA TUTTLE

lot easier to teach a young kid that stealing pencils is bad than to wait until he's graduated to breaking into homes. We're very proactive with our bears, and try to catch them at the stealing pencils phase," he explained.

Before the new program, at the Chimneys Picnic area they'd done thirty-five relocations in just three years. Between 1991 and 2004 the staff handled forty-three individual bears at Chimneys, capturing and releasing them on-site fifty-nine times. During those fourteen years they relocated just sixteen bears they couldn't reeducate, the vast majority of them during just one year when the park had a massive food failure.

Of course, some bears refuse to learn. And sometimes, despite one of the most proactive bear programs on the continent, the park can't intervene quickly enough. Relocation then becomes the last life-saving option for bears that graduate to brazen daytime raids and walkabouts in developed areas. Delozier says they have the highest success rate with young, impressionable bears—subadults they can relocate at least 40 miles (64 km) to an area with good food sources and a relatively low bear density. Bears relocated to the national forest go with a "Bear Back" guarantee—if the

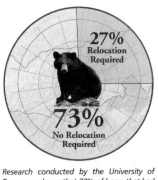

SUCCESS OF ON-SITE RELEASE OF NUISANCE BLACK BEARS

27% Relocation Required

73% No Relocation Required

Research conducted by the University of Tennessee shows that 73% of bears that had on-site workups and releases did not require relocation from the site for at least one year.
Source: GSMNP

bear gets into trouble in its new home, the park will respond. So far they've only had to reclaim one offender.

The park used to have persistent bear problems in backcountry campsites. It was tough for campers to follow the rules and hang their food, because the trees grow tall in this lushly vegetated park, and often the first limb is 60 feet (18 meters) off the ground—well out of range of even the best throwing arm. The park installed metal poles and food storage lockers at some sites, but they didn't work well—backpackers had a tough time balancing their packs

So far the bear's haven't defeated Great Smoky's clever pack hanging system. Happy Hanging!
GSMNP/USFS/Leave No Trace

on top of the poles, and the bears quickly learned to shimmy up them. The food storage lockers turned into back country garbage bins, creating more problems than they solved.

The staff studied possible solutions, and eventually adapted a food cable storage system that was designed in Banff National Park in Canada, and in use in Olympic National Park in Washington. The ingenious system can keep up to four food packs suspended out of a bear's reach between two trees. Stiver says the key to success is making sure the first pulley is out of a bear's considerable reach.

In one shelter along the highly traveled Appalachian Trail, where the trees were too small to install the cable system, the park flew in telephone poles and sunk them into the ground. All the AT shelters are now in the process of being remodeled. Gone are the chain link enclosures originally built to protect hikers from the bears that frequented the cross-country trail's pit stops.

"We're not going to cater to sloppy campers. People need to clean up their acts," says Stiver. ❖

Camper cages like this fenced enclosure along the Appalachian Trail are gone now, because too many hikers tempted bears to approach with treats so they could take photos like this one. *Photo: GSMNP*

IN BRIEF

◆ Replaced capture-and-relocate with capture-and-release-on-the-spot and aversive conditioning, reducing the number of problem bears relocated by 73 percent.

◆ Replaced 32-gallon "mail box" bear-resistant garbage cans with bear-resistant dumpsters.

◆ Changed the closing time for three problem picnic areas from sunset to 8:00 p.m. from May to September.

◆ The maintenance staff switched their hours from 7:00 – 3:30 p.m. to 1:00 – 9:30 p.m.

◆ Installed picnic-table signs and stepped up visitor education.

◆ Volunteers, interns and staff patrol picnic areas and campgrounds, making sure they're clean.

◆ Provided a unique food storage cable system in the back country pulley system.

◆ Temporarily close campgrounds, backcountry campsites and picnic areas if they're having active bear problems.

◆ Removed chain-link enclosures that gave hikers license to be careless with food and garbage.

Gatlinburg, Tennessee

Bear Town, U.S.A.

The city of Gatlinburg is the eastern gateway to the most visited national park in America, Great Smoky Mountains. Black bears are one of the most enduring and recognized symbols of the Smokies, and a big tourist draw.

Just a few years ago it was possible to walk Gatlinburg's back alleys any night of the week—and often during the day—and use up a roll of film taking pictures of all the bears rummaging through open dumpsters, unsecured garbage and grease and scraps thrown out by local restaurants. On a typical day, the city's 40,000 visitors, and local residents and businesses generate 56 tons of garbage.

Today Gatlinburg could serve as a model for gateway cities everywhere, thanks to an innovative program of cooperation between the city, Great Smoky Mountains National Park, and the Tennessee Wildlife Resources Agency (TWRA).

Gatlinburg city officials had wrestled with the issue of what to do about bears for years, but the few resolutions they created had been voted down by a city council nervous about offending residents and tourists alike.

Gatlinburg, then and now, permits hunting within the extensive city limits. In 1997 a late freeze caused a massive food failure in the area, and even more bears than usual came to town looking for food. Several bears were shot as they pawed through dumpsters or foraged in alleys, and suddenly the state wildlife agency was flooded with letters and phone calls from citizens, landowners and even tourists, all shocked and disgusted both by the number of bears (370) that were killed that year and the manner in which some of them

SARA TUTTLE

met their fate. The media had a field day, and editorials, news stories and features kept the topic on the front burner.

Public opinion was clearly in favor of finding a solution people and bears could live with, and early in 1998 a joint committee with representatives from the city, the park, the TWRA and the private sector buckled down and came up with a better way to deal with Gatlinburg's growing bear problems.

They agreed to tackle the root of the problem—the trash—instead of focusing on the symptoms—the human-bear conflicts, and crafted a broad-ranging ordinance that made it illegal to intentionally or unintentionally feed bears, and required most residents and all businesses that produce food in any form to bear-proof their trash receptacles, complete with a $500 per day fine for violations.

Enforcing the regulations proved to be even more challenging than creating them. So the TWRA, Great Smoky Natural History Association and the city of Gatlinburg teamed up once again, and agreed to jointly fund and hire a "bear warden" to professionally monitor and manage the bears, identify and correct situations that attract bears, provide the public and the city with technical guidance and assistance, take on the enormous and ongoing task of public education, and enforce the ordinances and laws.

The first bear warden was TWRA wildlife officer and bear researcher, David Brandenburg. "It's hard to blame the bears," he says. "There are over 500 dumpsters in the city, plus thousands of residential containers. If you're a hungry bear, there are thousands of places to get an easy meal. If they're defeated by one dumpster, bears are so smart they just go to plan B, or C. I don't think we'll get this licked until at least 90 percent of the dumpsters are in compliance."

Right now he estimates about a third of the businesses and residences are in full compliance with the trash laws. Even so, he says the situation is much improved from twenty years ago, when trash and garbage lay in open piles in all the alleys. The city is now a safer place for people and bears, and there are far fewer human-bear conflicts.

"We're moving in the right direction," he says. "It's not an easy problem to solve. It's not going to be fixed overnight. Right now we're talking to the city about stepping up enforcement, and making sure all the city's own dumpsters are in full compliance."

Brandenburg did such a good job he got promoted, and is now the regional biologist for Region 4, overseeing bears and other wildlife in twenty-one counties. But another officer has stepped up to take on the broad ranging responsibilities. Brandenburg hopes the city of Gatlinburg will continue to move forward, and that one day other cities will point to it as positive proof that even the worst human-bear conflicts and problems can be solved when humans show as much ingenuity and perseverance as the bears. ❖

chapter 11

Aversive Conditioning
Bear Behavior Modification School

If relocating bears generally doesn't work, and destroying individual bears doesn't do much to improve the long-range outlook for human-bear coexistence, what other options are there?

There's growing support among bear professionals for a variety of innovative techniques that can teach bears to avoid people and people places, for their own good as well as ours.

Aversive or negative conditioning is based on a simple principle: that if bears are smart enough to learn from positive experiences, they must be smart enough to learn from negative ones as well. When a bear raids a garbage can, makes off with a bird feeder or dives into a dumpster and comes up with a bag full of goodies, and nothing bad happens, it learns that human places are safe and easy places to forage.

Aversive conditioning techniques are designed to teach the bear to associate its undesirable behavior with a negative experience instead of a positive one. When reaching for the bird feeder earns the bear a face-full of bear spray and a rubber buckshot pain-in-the-butt instead of several pounds of nutritious sunflower seeds, it's likely to steer clear of bird feeders in the future.

When a bear crosses the line established by a community, a responder

A Karelian Bear Dog preparing to shepherd a bear back to the forest. The dog will reward the bear by immediately leaving it alone when it's safely back on its own turf. *Photo: Rocky Spencer, Washington Dept. of Fish and Wildlife*

WHAT'S FOR BREAKFAST?

In Lake Tahoe a bear walked through a family's open screen door, sat down at the breakfast table and stared longingly at a big plate of bacon. Instead of running or screaming, someone swatted the bear on the nose with a spoon, and it ran away.

KELLY ST. JOHN
SAN FRANCISCO CHRONICLE
AUGUST 2004

© Ann Bryant, The BEAR League

TWO-YEAR OLD TAKES ON BEAR

A harried mother in Lake Tahoe left a plate of freshly-frosted cupcakes on a table in front of an open screen door facing the forest. Lured by the irresistible smells, a three-year-old bear came out of the forest and into the house, his bear brain focused on only one thing: cupcakes. The woman panicked, picked up her baby and ran out the front door, then realized she'd left her two-year-old sitting on the floor in between the bear and the object of his desire. She crept back inside in time to see her son stand up, shake his finger at the bear and yell, "No bear, those are MY cupcakes." The bear turned tail and fled back into the forest.

---

professionally trained in aversive conditioning first uses body language bears understand and a tone of voice that lets the bear know it's not welcome.

If the bear doesn't leave, it then gets the equivalent of a spanking—a rubber bullet or beanbag fired from a shotgun in the butt or a shot of bear spray in the face, for example, delivered aggressively, usually accompanied by a lot of yelling and aggressive body postures.

The principle is based on the idea that people can communicate with bears in a language they understand—body language. Fighting is not a commonly accepted way to solve problems in black bear society. In fact, a bear in the wild will do just about anything to avoid getting into paw-to-paw combat with another bear—especially one it thinks could kick its butt.

The techniques have been used very successfully in many parts of the western U.S. and Canada, including Mammoth Lakes, California; Lake Tahoe Basin; Whistler, British Columbia; Yosemite National Park; and Stehekin Valley, Washington. Properly employed aversive conditioning appears to work well with at least three out of four bears. Some groups report even better results.

"Bears do not understand English or French, but they do understand a language of dominance and submission. By posturing or faking the bear into believing the human is in control of the situation, the wildlife manager can assert his dominance, and become

© *Paul Conrad* / The Aspen Times

Beck's Bits

In my opinion, I believe negative conditioning at the scene of the "crime" holds the most promise for bears.

BEAR PERSUASION

"Generally people don't behave appropriately in the presence of front-country or urban black bears. It's not appropriate for bears to enter people's homes or vehicles or come too close to their backyards, or from the bear's point of view, "human territory." When we allow bears to cross the line, we create the potential for conflict. Don't act passively with a front-country black bear. Shoo it away in a persuasive manner, by banging pots and yelling from a safe distance. If you're not comfortable, or are unable to do so safely, call a local wildlife manager for assistance. If a grizzly bear enters a residential area, call for help."

SYLVIA DOLSON, GET BEAR SMART SOCIETY

the alpha bear—the one calling the shots," says Syliva Dolson, executive director of Whistler's Get Bear Smart Society, and author of the *Non-Lethal Black Bear Management Guidebook*.

WHAT'S A BEAR'S LIFE WORTH?

Solving problems one bear at a time can be expensive and time intensive, but it stacks the odds for long-term survival in the bear's favor, and teaches bears to avoid human places. There's also high hope that aversive conditioning can break the chain of bears teaching other bears to visit human food sources. When the bear being conditioned is a female, she'll hopefully pass her new-found distaste for human places along to her cubs, instead of her mental map to all the best spots to find garbage or other human-provided treats.

YOUR OPINION COUNTS

Agencies set management policies, but public opinion is a lot more important than the public generally realizes. When people pressure agencies to solve conflicts by moving or destroying bears, it makes it politically more difficult for the agency to try other methods. When people make it known they don't want bears moved or destroyed except as a last resort, it's easier for managers to go to bat for bears, and get the funding they need to try other approaches. ❖

TAKING BACK THE 'HOOD

"BEAR League teams camp out in the area, and we scare the living hell out of the bears— we chase them, shoot at 'em with paintball pellets, harass them until they're terrified. As soon as they leave the neighborhood and cross the border into the wilderness we reward them by instantly leaving them alone."

ANN BRYANT, THE BEAR LEAGUE

BEAR "ABUSE"

Yosemite issues media alerts when rangers are actively engaged in negative conditioning. Even so, tourists who see them chasing bears, firing at them with guns loaded with annoying-but-harmless bean bag rounds, assaulting them with bright lights and loud noises and otherwise trying to teach them to associate their undesirable behavior with unpleasant consequences are often outraged, and frequently call to complain about "bear abuse."

Wind River Bear Institute, Florence, Montana

Life-Saving Lessons for Bears

The "Partners in Life" Bear Shepherding® program is based on a simple yet eye-opening belief: that both bears and humans can learn to act in ways that reduce conflicts. And that once conflicts are reduced, people and bears are better able to peacefully share space. Bear Shepherding involves teaching bears to recognize and avoid humans and our boundaries, and teaching people to prevent situations that cause bear conflicts.

Pioneered by experienced bear biologist and bear-conflict specialist Carrie Hunt, the revolutionary program uses a variety of aversive and positive conditioning techniques, and employs both highly trained Karelian Bear Dogs and bear-savvy people to teach bears their life-saving lessons.

When Hunt was developing the basic methods that form the backbone of bear shepherding she worked with a seriously habituated, slightly food-conditioned female grizzly

"We believe this program has changed the way we manage 'nuisance' bears in Montana and believe that the methodology has far reaching implications that will change the way other species of 'problem' wildlife are managed throughout Montana and perhaps the world."

PATRICK J. GRAHAM
DIRECTOR, MONTANA FISH AND
WILDLIFE (2000)

bear in Yellowstone National Park who'd become enough of a "nuisance" she was slated for destruction. Hunt and the dogs worked the bear for a month in 1986, and two weeks in 1987. The bear lived conflict-free for fifteen more years and successfully raised four litters of cubs.

Karelian Bear Dogs getting ready to work.
© *Wind River Bear Institute (WRBI)*

Karelian Bear Dogs shepherding a grizzly bear out of harm's way. © WRBI

She was killed in an auto accident in 2000, but the lessons she taught Hunt live on.

A wealth of research supports the principle that bears learn and retain things in much the same way dogs and horses remember lessons learned in obedience school. Hunt uses how bears naturally learn in the wild, and bear-to-bear relationships and hierarchies to structure lessons that bears can absorb and retain.

Bear shepherding doesn't try to teach bears to fear people, but rather to fear choosing to approach people or human-associated areas like campgrounds and neighborhoods. Bears get a clear message that if they choose to come into the presence of humans, things will go badly; if they choose to leave, things will instantly get better.

It's not only bears that go to conflict-avoidance school. Because bear-shepherding is very hands-on and one-on-one, the humans involved are well aware of what's going on, and required to do their part in reducing potential conflicts by removing attractants and preventing situations that lead to conflicts.

Hunt says that improper aversive conditioning or hazing can have the opposite effect on bears. For example, if a bear is repeatedly shot with rubber bullets while it's up a tree or hurt by humans while it's in a trap, it learns it can't leave when confronted by people.

SARA TUTTLE

The dogs are used, almost always on leashes, to chase bears raiding camps, hanging out by roadsides, or hanging around homes back into the cover of the forest. When the bear responds and leaves the area, the chasing stops.

Sometimes bears that repeatedly enter campgrounds, approach hikers, or harass home-owners are lured into baited culvert traps, and then "hard released." That means when the trap opens and the bear gets several feet away, the Wind River team opens fire, using non-lethal weapons that were originally developed for use in riot control situations like rubber bullets, bean bag rounds and noisy cracker shots.

When the bear streaks for cover, Carrie and the handlers pursue it with the dogs until it clears the area and is safely back in the woods. As soon as the bear is back where it belongs, all harassment stops. Bears are very smart. For most bears, it's lesson learned.

After ten years of field work in Montana, Wind River's track record is a perfect zero—no bears injured, no dogs or humans injured, no bear aggression.

Wind River's "Partners in Life" Program and Bear Shepherding protocols have now been formally sanctioned by all of the national parks with grizzly bear populations in the U.S. north-west, as well as in contiguous parks and habitat in Canada. National parks in Montana and Washington have written Wind River's pro-gram and Bear Shepherding protocols into their formal bear management plans, and five of seven grizzly and black bear managers outside the parks in both states are now the enthusiastic and proud owners of Karelian Bear Dogs bred and placed with them by the Institute.

Recently Wind River has worked with bears in southwestern Alberta and Japan, and will soon be taking bears to school in Alaska,

Hunt's bear dogs come from Karelia, a region along the Finland-Russia border, where they're renowned for their hunting and guarding skills, and undergo hundreds of hours of training to hone their natural instincts. *Left*: A WRBI teams shepherds a bear away from human property. *Right*: Karelian Bear Dog puppies © *WRBI*

Wisconsin, the Apostle Islands and Columbia, South America. There is even talk of the Department of the Interior funding floating Bear Shepherding teams in key national parks and areas where the grizzly bear may be delisted from Endangered Species status.

Wind River has a success rate in the 90th percentile, making bear shepherding paws down the most successful way to deal with problem bears. But working bears one at a time takes an enormous amount of time, resources and money. That may be one reason bear shepherding has been more widely used on grizzly bears, listed as endangered and threatened in the lower 48 states, although the techniques have been used with equal success on black bears.

Most wildlife management agencies are in a constant budget crunch, and agency contracts provide only a small portion of Wind River's operating budget. Since 1999 the Wendy P. McCaw foundation has provided the majority of the underwriting for the Wind River Bear Institute; without their commitment and generous support, Hunt says Wind River wouldn't be able to operate.

The Institute offers a variety of classes, seminars and workshops for bear managers to show them how—with or without dogs—they can manage human-bear conflicts without moving or destroying bears. For more info, visit *www.wrbi.com*. ❖

An interagency team of biologists from Montana Fish, Wildlife and Parks, Glacier National Park and Wind River at work in Glacier. © *WRBI*

"I have been involved in bear management in Glacier National Park for 15 years and have found Carrie's work to be the most innovative and effective approach to resolving bear-people conflicts. Carrie's efforts have produced tangible improvements in conflict situations, and her approach to bear-human conflict resolution has gained wide acceptance among park staff." STEVE GNIADEK, WILDLIFE BIOLOGIST – GLACIER NATIONAL PARK

Stehekin Valley, Washington

The Human Bear Shepherds of the North Cascades

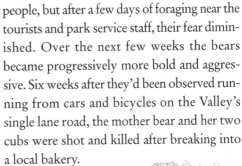

The remote Stehekin Valley in Washington's Lake Chelan National Recreation Area in the heart of the North Cascades Range is accessible only by small aircraft, boats and determined hikers. The valley's black bears live in splendid isolation, sharing space with about two hundred year-round and seasonal residents, and assorted tourists and visitors.

As long as there's ample snow or rain, the lush valley produces a bear buffet of serviceberries, huckleberries and bear berries. Kokanee salmon abound in the Stehekin River watershed, and plenty of ants provide the bears with plenty of protein. An apple orchard that's a National Historic site has been providing people—and bears—with crisp Washington apples for many years.

During 1998 a severe drought brought an increasing number of black bears into the valley in search of food. Anne Braaten, the bear management biologist for the North Cascades National Park Service Complex, tells the story of one female bear with two cubs that is "all too typical."

When the bears first showed up in mid-July, they were very wary of people, but after a few days of foraging near the tourists and park service staff, their fear diminished. Over the next few weeks the bears became progressively more bold and aggressive. Six weeks after they'd been observed running from cars and bicycles on the Valley's single lane road, the mother bear and her two cubs were shot and killed after breaking into a local bakery.

Eight more bears were shot in the lower valley that year as well: one

SARA TUTTLE

because of problem behavior; the others were hunting mortalities on the periphery of the orchard. All the dead bears, as well as several more that apparently survived, had learned to tolerate people while foraging at the orchard.

In July of 2000 the Wind River Bear Institute was asked to evaluate the bear problems in the valley, and recommend a solution. Director Carrie Hunt identified the apple orchard as the behavioral "nursery" for most human-bear conflicts. There were low numbers of people participating in low-key activities, and mostly ignoring the bears—which taught the bears it was okay to be around people while they were foraging for food.

In poor food years, up to a dozen black bears fed in the orchard. Most days the NPS orchardist was there throughout the day, joined periodically by residents and visitors who came to pick apples and tourists who arrived in the afternoon for brief tours. Hunt figured out that the bears learned habituation first from the solitary orchardist; then quickly graduated to ignoring the tourists.

She developed a shepherding strategy that used people instead of bear dogs to get the message across. Any bear showing itself away from cover would be "shepherded" back out

A trained Karelian Bear Dog waits patiently to go to work. Trained people did most of the follow-up shepherding in Stehekin.
Photo: Anne Braaten, National Park Service

of sight by people yelling, and firing loud but essentially harmless riot rounds of rubber bullets, bean bags and noise makers. The bears well away from human activity at the far end of the orchard would be left alone to feed as long as they didn't move away from cover.

In the summer of 2002 there was another natural food shortage, and Braaten and the NPS staff had their first real opportunity to test the bear shepherding strategy. They followed Hunt's strategy, and shepherded every bear exhibiting habituated behavior in the orchard and elsewhere in the valley. Bears that moved quickly into cover on detecting people were left alone.

While Braaten says that one year does not a study make, she is proud of the fact that the bear mortality in 2002 was zero. No bears had to be destroyed. And no bears using the orchard came into conflict with people elsewhere in the Valley—a real first, according to Braaten.

As an added bonus, the NPS staff and private residents are now working together to improve human-bear relations in the Valley. Plans are underway to have a week-long, community-based bear shepherding workshop that would give the residents the same background and training as the rangers and NPS staff, and allow Wind River to work with private landowners as well.

"I'm really hopeful the workshop will further unite the community. Because of the effectiveness we've seen when bear shepherding is applied, and the failures when it isn't—like when a bear was killed at a very bear-unsecure house in the valley last fall," Braaten says.

"Ideally, I'd love to have a couple of 'bear rangers' with a couple of Karelian Bear Dogs," she continued, "but lack of funding prevents it. Our rangers have all been trained, and the State Wildlife folks are always willing to come and help us bear shepherd."

Discussions are underway about the possibility of using electric fencing to keep the bears out of the orchard; ironically one of the issues is what the bears will do when they're cut off from such a popular and dependable feeding ground. There are salmon runs nearby, and fall berries, but it's hard not to worry about what will happen if the bears decide to investigate people's homes to see if they're a good alternative food source.

The community workshop will teach people what to do if bears denied apples head for the village under the mistaken impression that people's homes might make a dandy substitute for the orchard.

Braaten has her fingers crossed that through a combination of prevention and persuasion they've found a livable solution that will help the people and the bears of the Stehekin Valley peacefully coexist. ❖

Foraging bears have damaged many of the trees in this historic apple orchard.

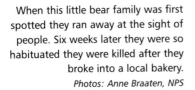

When this little bear family was first spotted they ran away at the sight of people. Six weeks later they were so habituated they were killed after they broke into a local bakery.
Photos: Anne Braaten, NPS

Ursinomorphizing
Taking Advantage of How Bears View People

by Anne Braaten

People's projecting human attributes to other species is anthropomorphizing—it is logical that since bears can only know their own behavioral expectations and thought processes, they view the world through an "ursinomorphizing" filter: they appear to respond to humans much as they would other bears. The "natural" response is to give us wide berth, as though we were dominant bears.

What they learn from us is how much leeway we'll give them. If they challenge us by showing themselves to us (leave cover in proximity to people), and people allow them to do so, they have just learned that they can be in proximity to people. From there they ramp up their testing of people until they learn they can really push us around. This can happen in the course of a day or two. And this is where they wind up dead. One thing people miss is how big a deal it is for a bear to show itself to someone it presumably would think was a dominant individual, albeit a different species. Subordinate bears give wide berth to dominant bears, and won't show themselves if they can avoid it.

I ask people to try to look at the world through a bear's eyes, as a good shepherd tries to do with his or her charges. Bears live in an intrinsically social system where they move around each other as the social ladder dictates. They are also out there making a living on the best of whatever they can find. If they find your food, your pet's food, your horse's feed, the bird feeder, the garbage can—they are doing what bears do: finding the calories they need to live not just through the summer, but also through a winter of not eating.

Being good shepherds of bears involves making these things unavailable to bears, but it goes even further than that. It also involves learning enough to know that it's okay to be "top dog" to a bear. It doesn't "insult" a bear to be put in its place; this happens to them most days with other bears, already.

Not letting a bear graze in your front yard isn't "harrassing" it; it is merely asserting your personal space, something bears totally understand. You don't have to like bears to do these things; understanding these simple principles can help keep them out of your way, as well as saving their lives.

chapter 12

The Backyard Guide to Bear Behavior Modification

Discouraging Bears From Your Backyard

The use of pyrotechnics, rubber buckshot, trained dogs, culvert traps and other tools are best left to professionals or trained volunteers. But there are some do-it-yourself techniques that can help you chase an unwelcome bear away, and deterrents that might persuade it not to come back.

An ounce of prevention is worth a pound of bear spray. The best way to deal with bear conflicts is to prevent them from happening by making sure bears aren't attracted to your home, yard, car or neighborhood.

Whatever the reason, there may come a day when you need a good way to convince a bear to leave you alone. When a bear comes too close for comfort, or behaves in ways we wouldn't tolerate from another person, the normal human reaction is to freeze, retreat to the house and wait for the bear to go away.

Bear behavior experts say that's sending the bear the wrong message. Instead of standing wide-eyed at the window watching a bear paw through your trash or bash your bird feeder—or even worse, running for your camera or calling your neighbors to come watch—you need to let the bear know you want it to leave right now.

First, make sure the bear isn't cornered and has a safe escape route, and that when it leaves it won't be headed into your neighbor's yard where a birthday party for a dozen kids is in full swing.

© Paul Conrad / The Aspen Times

149

Then simply look directly at the bear. In this situation direct eye contact is a powerful and simple way to send the bear a clear message that this is your territory, and you want it to leave. According to Sylvia Dolson, executive director of the Be Bear Smart Society in British Columbia, the stare-down works on all but the most habituated of bears.

If the bear just ignores you, keep staring and start making lots of noise. Yell, bang pots and pans or throw small rocks in the direction of the bear.

Don't approach the bear. If you have bear spray and the bear's within 30 feet and the wind isn't blowing in your face, spray the bear while you're yelling "GET OUT OF HERE, BEAR!" Dolson says a super-soaker filled with water and a touch of vinegar can also work—bears dislike getting blasted in the face with water.

Once the bear leaves, try to figure out what attracted it in the first place. Bears have been attracted to homes by insects nesting in the walls, bags of pet food and bird seed, smoke houses, barbecue grills, garage freezers and a host of other things less obvious than an overflowing garbage can or dangling bird feeder. Make sure you remove everything that might be remotely attractive enough to bring the bear back again for another look. Err on the side of caution.

Favorite Excuses for Bear "Problems"

"But we had a lid on the trash can."

"We didn't know bears could open doors."

"Our neighbors are slobs."

"We thought the ice cream would be safe in the garage freezer."

"We forgot to tell our company not to leave food out."

"We forgot to...bring in the bird feeder, lock the windows, scrub the barbeque, pick the fruit, take the picnic stuff out of the backseat..."

"The people who used to live here fed the bears."

WHEN TO CALL FOR HELP

Simply having a bear in your neighborhood isn't necessarily a reason to sound an alarm. If you live in bear country, you and the bears are sharing space. Your job is to make sure the bear doesn't find any reason to linger at your place.

So if a bear passes through your property on its way to somewhere else, make a note of the day, time and anything distinctive about the bear; there's no need to yell for help.

If a bear is wandering around your deck or house in broad daylight, testing your doors and windows to see if you've left anything unlocked, or is very aggressive to people, it's time to call your local wildlife agency or bear response group and report it. Even if the bear finds nothing at your place, it may keep exploring the neighborhood until it finds a home where the owners have been less vigilant. Unless the bear has injured someone, you can request they use non-lethal means to deal with the bear.

The trap Colorado Division of Wildlife Officer Claire Solohub is demonstrating was designed by Tom Beck and Jack Beach to avoid injury to bears and be easier for humans to handle. It's also proved to be very efficient in terms of capture. *Photo: Lisa Evans, Colorado Division of Wildlife*

WHAT HAPPENS TO THE BEAR?

The fate of the bear all depends on what the bear has done, if it's been in trouble before, what local, state, provincial or federal policies prevail, and the community's general tolerance level for bears. There are places where all a bear has to do is enter someone's yard and the police come out firing. There are other areas where bear activity is both expected and frequent, and anything short of a bear literally breaking into a home through a locked door or window, or physically hurting someone is treated with a liberal dose of homeowner education, and, if possible, a course of aversive conditioning for the bear.

BEAR DETERRENTS

Using bear deterrents may stop a bear from doing damage to your home or property, but it's no substitute for doing everything you can to prevent conflicts. Here's a roundup of the most popular and reasonably effective ways to keep bears out of places it's not safe for bears to be.

Electric Fencing

Electric fences are one of the most fool-proof ways to keep out bears and other predators. Electric fencing is available in permanent and portable models, at prices that start under $300 USD. For more info see Chapter 8.

Bear Unwelcome Mats

A corner view of a bear unwelcome mat. Sharp nails or screws correctly set into sturdy plywood create a great "bear-ier" when mats are securely installed in front of accessible doors and windows.

Bear unwelcome mats are half or full sheets of sturdy plywood with screws or nails sticking up every couple of inches. Properly constructed, they cause instant pain if a bear attempts to walk over the mat to reach a door or window, but do no permanent damage.

Bear unwelcome mats for black bears have been adapted from similar devices that have been used successfully in Alaska, where they're usually meant to deter grizzly bears. Grizzlies have heavier paw pads than black bears, so don't copy an unwelcome mat designed for a grizz. For black bears, the nails or screws should stick out of the board no more than ½ to ¾ inch (20 to 30 mm). The objective is to cause the bear enough pain to abandon its approach, not to cripple or injure it.

The Lake Tahoe BEAR League swears by galvanized roofing nails, because they have big heads that don't bend or twist under the weight of a bear paw. Others prefer carpet tack strips because they're wickedly sharp, evenly spaced and easy to work with. Beck likes dry-wall screws, because they're very sharp and easier to use than nails.

If you're thinking about trying an unwelcome mat, be sure to check with your local authorities and homeowner's association to make sure they're permitted in your area.

How To Install An Unwelcome Mat   It's important that the mat fully covers the entire area in front of the doors or windows where the bear is trying to gain entry. If it's on a deck, screw or tack it down so the bear can't shove it out of the way.

If it's on the ground, pound two 18-inch sections of rebar in each corner facing out so the bear can't flip the mat over or shove it out of the way, or drill holes in the front two corners and pound in long spikes with sturdy heads. Your objective is to "nail down" the mat so the bear can't move it.

Cautions: Pets, other wildlife and small children can't read—be sure you've thought about who or what might drop by before you roll out the unwelcome mat. You can install a filament line with bells or noisemakers a foot or so in front of the mat and about a foot off the ground to warn off people and pets.

Unwelcome mats are commonly used when people don't have to get in and out all the time—at vacation homes, for instance, or intermittently used campers or mobile homes. They can also be used as a temporary, short-term measure to deter a specific bear from returning.

Lights and Sirens

Motion-activated lights, loud sirens and sprinklers may temporarily deter a bear, but if nothing else happens to reinforce the experience, there's evidence the bear will eventually learn to ignore them. If you're in the midst of a conflict with a specific bear, automatic noise making devices like the Critter Gitter can alert you that something is in your yard, and give you time to take action. They're not

DETER, NOT DISABLE
Unwelcome mats are meant to deter, not disable. You don't want an injured, extremely irritable bear limping around the neighborhood. Follow directions, and make sure nails, screws or tacks don't stick out more than ½" to ¾".

a substitute for thoroughly bear-proofing your place, or installing a more permanent repellent, like an electric fence.

Noisemakers

Air horns, sirens, whistles and other loud, high-pitched noisemakers may startle a bear enough to chase it off. Air horns can be found in the handy travel size as well as a countertop model in the boating supplies sections of discount and sporting goods stores for under ten bucks.

Barking Dogs

An authoritatively barking dog may convince a bear that pickings will be easier elsewhere. At the very least, the barking lets you know something is in the area. Many people have asked if a motion-activated recording of a barking dog will work. Answer: I don't know; I can't find anyone who's tried this.

Super-Soakers and Garden Hoses

A blast in the face from a high pressure hose or Super-Soaker filled with water and a touch of vinegar can deter a bear. For extra success, accompany the spraying with a lot of yelling and hollering.

Bear Spray

See Chapter 18 for all about bear spray. If you use bear spray offensively—to chase a bear away—don't chase the bear. Make sure the wind is at your back and that you can spray from a safe place, and a safe distance.

Pine Sol & Ammonia

The strong smell of ammonia-based cleaners like Pine Sol irritates a bear's sensitive mucous membranes. In Lake Tahoe they've had success saturating areas like window sills or sometimes walls with Pine Sol. This is a treatment that needs to be frequently repeated to remain effective.

Straight ammonia is a powerful irritant; as such, it's best used to create an odor barrier, not as a weapon. An ammonia bath is a great way to disinfect garbage cans, scrub down barbeque grills, or spray down tents. Or leave an ammonia-soaked sponge "sachet" in a bucket with a lid you've poked holes in.

Don't use ammonia in an application where it could end up in a bear's eyes—like in a squirt gun, or in a water balloon that may burst under pressure and splash up into a bear's eyes, temporarily or even permanently blinding it.

Rattlesnake Cans

This one comes from Lake Tahoe, where the bears apparently don't know there are no rattlesnakes. Take a clean, empty can, add enough small pebbles or pennies to produce a rattling sound when the can is disturbed, and string the cans on wire about three feet off the ground, at bear shoulder height. When the bear passes under the wire the cans rattle—and rattle the bear.

Radios

I know at least one instance where someone installed a "guard radio" inside her chicken coop tuned not to music, but to talk radio. Apparently bears are not attracted to Dr. Laura. And for those of you with chickens—it didn't seem to bother the birds any. They kept on laying eggs right on schedule. ❖

When you meet a bear in your yard, you're dominant.

When you meet a bear in his "yard," he's dominant.

We teach people how to take back their territory.

The bears need to respect us. And we need to respect bears.

ANN BRYANT
THE BEAR LEAGUE

Colorado Division of Wildlife

Neighborhood Watch for Bears

Lisa Evans, the education and outreach coordinator for the Northeast Region of the Colorado Division of Wildlife, went to a monthly staff meeting one day during the very busy bear season of 1998 to offer to train dispatchers on how to better deal with bear calls.

Colorado is divided into districts, with wildlife officers responsible for all wildlife issues in their territories. The district wildlife managers at the staff meeting thought the dispatchers were well trained, but soon ideas were flowing on other ways to improve human-bear relations.

"They felt like all they did all summer long was handle bear calls—and even worse, that they weren't really being effective at getting people to change their habits," said Evans, whose own background includes nearly a decade as a District Wildlife Manager.

Eventually they came up with the idea of starting a bear volunteer program built around the premise that people might be more willing to listen to their neighbors than to the government. The Division of Wildlife already had a strong volunteer program. Why not recruit people who were interested in bears?

And that's how Colorado's Bear Aware program got started. Bear Aware is a kind of a Neighborhood Watch program for bears, with team members helping people understand what to do to avoid conflicts with bears, and how to handle any that do develop.

To date over 300 volunteers have gone through Bear Aware training; team members have put in more than 7,600 hours acting as a liaison between their neighbors, the Division, and Colorado's 10,000 to 12,000 black bears.

SARA TUTTLE

Every spring before the bears wake up the Bear Aware regional teams across the state go through an intensive, one-day training with biologists, officers, staff and other experts. They trade tips and share success stories, and get an annual refresher course on bear behavior and biology.

Then, decked out in Bear Aware golf shirts and ball caps, armed with notebooks, report forms, slide shows, bear kits and a library full of literature, posters, videos, Power Point presentations, brochures, handouts and giveaways like bear paw magnets and key chains, the teams set out to help people learn to get along with bears.

In the beginning, some District Wildlife Managers were reluctant to get involved. Some thought the program implied they couldn't handle bear issues in their district. Others were concerned that volunteers might not get the message right. But as the program got underway, good news started flowing in from the field, with officers reporting that calls and conflicts were dropping in areas where the bear volunteers were active.

Every year the program spreads and expands, with more volunteers taking on more responsibilities, and more communities coming on board as word travels that having Bear Aware volunteers in your area lightens the load for the officers, and helps make the world a better place for people and bears.

My husband Cory Phillips and I consider

Bear Aware volunteer Gail Marshall talks with people about getting the summer off to a beary-good start at Silverthorne's annual Safe Summer Kickoff. © *Mark Hamschmidt, Silverthorne Police Dept.*

ourselves pretty active volunteers—in 2005 we spent over 200 hours on bears—but our dedication pales in comparison to some of the "Super Volunteers," like Summit County's Gail Marshall and team, who've built floats, donned bear costumes, marched in parades and talked to thousands of people about what they can do to prevent human-bear conflicts, and Estes Park's Jim Boyd, whose enthusiasm and dedication are so boundless, he cheerfully tells 911 to call him any hour of the day or night with bear emergencies.

WHAT BEAR AWARE TEAMS DO

◆ Serve as the neighborhood resource on how to prevent bear conflicts.

◆ Respond on non-emergency bear calls:

bears in the trash, bears in the bird feeders, neighbors feeding bears, etc.

◆ Reach out to neighbors and members of the community; going out on a bear call at midnight holds a certain adventurous appeal, but prevention is the name of the game. Volunteers attend homeowner association meetings, write articles for newsletters, give talks at schools and other organizations, staff booths at county and local fairs and festivals, call on new neighbors, and generally do whatever they can to get the word out on how people can peacefully coexist with bears.

◆ Many volunteers work closely with their district wildlife managers, responding to routine calls and doing interventions in situations where people are clearly causing problems. Officers and people both agree that talking to a friendly, knowledgeable fellow citizen can be less intimidating than talking to someone wearing a bullet-proof vest and packing a gun who can write you a ticket.

◆ Some regions have also enlisted the aid of high school students working on community service projects.

◆ In some busy bear areas, there are designated Lead Volunteers, so the officer can make one call, and the lead person will either handle it or assign it to the closest team member.

"The Division's volunteer program and the Bear Aware program in particular make my job easier and more enjoyable. It is so nice to know that citizens of Colorado care about the wildlife of the state and their neighbors. All too often when a customer service rep or an officer talks with a person, the CDOW is seen as 'big brother,' or the government telling someone what to do. I think

CDOW Bear Aware volunteer Gail Marshall (in the camo) gets lots of help from folks of all ages in Summit County who regularly pitch in to help people learn to get along with bears. You gotta really believe in what you're doing to wear a bear suit in July.
Photo: Carol Christiansen

the option of neighbors chatting brings folks together and is less threatening. It's a win-win situation for everyone," says District Wildlife Manager Aimee Ryel, one of the DWMs we work with closely.

Of course, there are always folks who just don't want to change. Volunteers don't write tickets or get involved in law enforcement, so when friendly explanations and advice don't do the trick, teams get their officers involved. Intentionally or unintentionally feeding big game is illegal in Colorado so if all else fails, people and businesses can be fined daily until the situation is remedied.

Not all human-bear conflicts have happy endings. Sometimes, despite everyone's best efforts, bears that have been taught the lethal lesson that people-equal-food just can't be saved.

But all agree that since the Bear Aware program got started, there are fewer unhappy endings for bears and people.

TEAMING UP FOR BEARS

Estes Park, the gateway to Rocky Mountain National Park, is home to black bears, legendary herds of elk, and even bigger herds of tourists and big-city transplants.

"We have a lot of retirees and transplants who have moved to Estes Park from places like Chicago where there are no bear or elk. They come out here on vacation and think it's Nirvana. Then they move out, and they've barely unpacked before the elk have ripped up all their ornamental trees and shrubs, and the bears have ripped into their garbage," explains experienced District Wildlife Manager Rick Spowart.

"It's usually the people who are the problem, not the bears," chimes in Jim Boyd, who's been a Bear Aware Volunteer in Spowart's district for so long that some of the frig magnets he gives out with his name and phone number have been passed down to two or three different home owners.

"Jim is a godsend," says Spowart. "He has a real passion for bears, he's very good with people, and has an endless supply of patience. I've got a very busy district; if I can get good volunteers, I'm in much better shape. A lot of people don't trust the government, but they trust Jim.

"No matter what people have done to create the situation—leave windows and doors open, leave food in their cars, or store garbage or birdseed where it's easy to get at— they want us to come and trap the bear, instead of locking up their

Magnet from the Colorado Division of

place, or getting bear-resistant garbage cans. I tell people, 'I'm not going to move a bear because it's getting into your garbage. I'll let you off with a warning ticket if you promise you'll get a bear-resistant garbage can and remove all your attractants.'

"We also have people who deliberately feed bears. One guy I've been working with claimed he wasn't feeding them, but he'd given them all names. And then one of his neighbors ratted him out and showed us a picture of a bear with its face buried in a big can of beans this guy was holding," Spowart continued.

"People think it's cute until the bear breaks into their house because one day there was no food, or it just wanted more. That's what happened to this guy—one of his 'pet' bears finally broke into his home and did quite a bit of damage. When one of his next-door neighbors had a bear try to break into her bed-

room, she told the guy if she had another incident, she was going to sue him.

"Three years ago we had a horrible problem with bears breaking into the subdivision where Jim and his family live. Most of those folks are wildlife lovers, but they don't know how to coexist with wildlife. They didn't want the bears killed, so for a long time, no one told anyone, even Jim, about the break-ins. But finally the situation got out of control, and the story came out. Jim called a community meeting, and that was the turning point. People finally seemed to 'get it,' and started taking responsibility for preventing conflicts.

"Today our problems are way down. Jim's a neighbor talking to neighbors, and it works." ❖

DWM Aimee Ryel, the author Linda Masterson, Education Coordinator Lisa Evans, and Cory Phillips planning a Bear Aware event. *Photo: Phil Accetturo, Colorado Division of Wildlife*

chapter 13

Vacationing in Bear Country

How to be Welcome in Bear Country | Photographing Bears

HOW NOT TO BE A TOURON

You gleefully stuff your bags with everything you might possibly need, stop the mail and the newspaper, empty the frig, lock your doors and hit the road, wondering what you've forgotten this time. You're finally on vacation.

Most of us look forward to escaping from our every day lives and every day responsibilities, so it's easy to understand why many people don't give much thought to the new responsibilities awaiting them if they're vacationing in bear country.

Perhaps that's why so many folks who live year-round in the places others come to visit think that one of the most important essentials many tourists routinely forget to pack is their brain. That mindset might account for bumper stickers reading: "If it's tourist season, how come we can't shoot them?" and "Relocate tourists, not bears."

When my husband and I lived in Chicago we fled to the mountains and forests at every possible opportunity. We thought we were responsible guests, but I'm sure we did things then we'd never dream of doing now. That's because now we live in one of those places other people come to vacation. And we finally

Not so cute when you know how much damage bears do to cars (a.k.a. rolling pantries) each year. Or how many bears die in pursuit of human food.

Harlan Kredit, 1976; National Park Service

161

understand why the locals have a love/hate relationship with the hands that feed them.

In 2004 over 275 million people visited National Parks and forests in the U.S. and many millions more headed off to Canada's National and Provincial Parks. Millions more own or rent second homes in the countless communities lining what's referred to as the urban-wildland interface—the areas where civilization and nature collide, with results that are often fatal to the wildlife, plants and other natural wonders people come to enjoy.

Ten million people visit Great Smoky Mountains National Park each year. Over three million visit Yellowstone. Two million visit Canada's Jasper National Park. Banff hosts 60,000 visitors a day.

Most people arrive with only the sketchiest knowledge of the place they've come to explore and enjoy. But everyone wants to go home with a suitcase stuffed full of memories. If that means they have to leave out a few goodies to lure a bear into photo range, or hop out of the car so the kids can get a better view, what's the harm in that? And if they forget to lock up their cooler for the night or scrape off the barbeque grill, or they're too tired to clean up after their party on

TOURIST + MORON

= TOURON

a person who's oblivious to who or what their behavior hurts because their brains are on vacation

the deck, what's the worst thing that can happen? You can always buy another cooler.

But you can't buy another bear. Eventually tourists go home. But the problems they helped create remain behind. And there's a good chance that bear they photographed pawing through the trash or eating the donuts they left out will ultimately pay for the free meal with its life.

Multiply one "I forgot," or "I didn't know," or "What bears?"

by millions, and you get an idea of how all those little mistakes can add up to big trouble—for people and bears.

But you don't have to be a touron. You can be part of the solution, instead of part of the problem. Just follow some basic Do's and Don'ts, and you'll be a welcome visitor in bear country.

HOW TO BE WELCOME IN BEAR COUNTRY

- Do read up on your destination, and know before you go if you're going to be visiting bear country.
- Do remember the place you're vacationing is someone else's home. Think about how you expect your guests to behave. Respect the animals, wildlife and people who live there.
- Do repeat to yourself over and over: bears are wild animals that deserve my respect. They're not cuddly teddies or ferocious killers. My job as a guest in bear country is not to make the bear's job of earning a living any harder.
- Do remember that what's trash to you could be food to bears. Bears are attracted to just about anything that smells…it doesn't have to smell good.
- Do close and lock all accessible windows and doors at night, and whenever you leave your temporary home, and close any curtains or shutters that provide a bear's-eye view.
- Do keep trash, coolers, beverages, pet food and other supplies inside.
- Do pack as many unscented toiletries, shampoos and lotions as you can find, and bring along or buy a box of freezer-weight plastic bags—they'll come in handy for double bagging stuff.
- Do read and pay attention to any literature on living with the local wildlife—it's there for a good reason.
- Do stash your trash in a bear-resistant container, and take an extra ten seconds to make sure it's securely latched. If none are

"Take only photos, Leave only footprints… not beer cans, bags of chips or cookies."

A tourist got out of a running car to take a picture of a bear. The bear got into the car to get the food left on the seat and jostled the gear shift. The car drove off with the bear inside.

CHUCK BARTLEBAUGH,
CENTER FOR WILDLIFE
INFORMATION

available, take trash back to where you're staying, and keep it inside until you can safely get rid of it.

◆ Do make sure everyone in your group knows what to do in bear country. This includes all children old enough to walk and talk. Kids can be a great conscience. When you're too tired to clean up the yard, a kid will pipe up and say, "But Mom, what about the bears?"

◆ Do clean out your car every night, and lock the doors before you turn in. And remember to check in the glove compartment and under seats for crumbs, leftovers and empty cans, bottles and packages.

◆ Do speak up if you see someone else being careless, and leaving trash or food out where bears can get it.

◆ Do your part to be a good guest in bear country, and you could save a bear's life.

THINGS TO AVOID IN BEAR COUNTRY

◆ Don't think, "It won't happen to us." That's what everyone who's ever had an unpleasant bear incident thought.

◆ Don't use air fresheners in cars or near open windows in homes. They smell yummy to bears.

◆ Don't do something stupid just because someone else is doing it. As your Mom used to say, "If all your friends jumped off a cliff, would you jump off after them?"

◆ Don't leave food, beverages, gum, containers, coolers, picnic baskets, toiletries, bug spray, sun tan lotion or packaging in a vehicle overnight.

◆ Don't leave your doors and windows open or unlocked when you're not there.

◆ Don't stand on the deck taking pictures of the bear rummaging through the trash you forgot to bring inside. Yell, throw something, make lots of noise and try to chase it away.

◆ Don't ignore trail and area closures. If an area is closed because of recent bear activity, you could be risking your life and a bear's if you insist on hiking anyway.

♦ Don't feed the wildlife. Some snack foods have so much sodium and other preservatives they are literally lethal to small mammals. And associating people with food often has lethal consequences for bears.

♦ Don't use food to try and attract a bear so you can get a better picture.

♦ Don't approach bears for any reason. It's stressful for them and could be dangerous—even deadly—for you.

♦ Don't assume a bear is tame, just because it's hanging around by the road or doesn't run away when it sees you. There are no tame wild bears.

♦ Don't party into the wee hours and then leave all your trash out on the deck when you hit the sack.

♦ Don't put out trash the night before pick up.

When bears come begging, just say "No."   *R.. Robinson; NPS*

Yogi Bear sign at the west entrance to Yellowstone.
William S. Keller, 1961;
National Park Service

CAPTURING ONE PERFECT BEAR PHOTO
by professional photographer Bill Lea *www.BillLea.com*

Photographing bears always requires a lot of time, the best equipment and a great deal of luck. I had wanted to capture a brown-colored black bear mother and her cub on film with just the right look on their faces for years. I had spent countless hours in the woods with nothing to show for my efforts.

Needless to say, when I came across this black bear with her little brown cub I was excited about the possibilities. Yet I knew it wouldn't be easy to capture that one perfect bear photo. Using a long telephoto lens so I could keep a safe distance between us meant I would have very little depth of field. I knew they would have to get into a position where they were in nearly the same plane of focus. It was also overcast, which is what I needed in order to avoid the contrasting light of bright sunlight and dark shadows in the woods.

These conditions, however, meant I would be using a slow shutter speed. So, I needed the bears very close to each other, holding nearly perfectly still, and situated in a setting with no distractions with just the perfect look that would reflect their personalities. I knew the likelihood of this happening was slim, but after hours of waiting and a lot of luck, the mother bear approached the cub from behind and stood still for just a split second while her cub looked up. I fired off two shots and one turned out just as I had hoped.

I may spend another ten years in the woods photographing and never again have such an opportunity.

© Bill Lea

Photographing black bears is about as challenging as any kind of wildlife photography I ever do.

PROFESSIONAL WILDLIFE PHOTOGRAPHER BILL LEA

PHOTOGRAPHING BEARS:
SMILE AND SAY "BUFFALO BERRIES"

Taking great photos of wild bears is a challenge; it can be equally frustrating for professionals and hobbyists. Learning and following the rules for bear-smart photography can make snapping pictures in bear country more fun and less dangerous, for you and the bears.

Be A Bear-Smart Shutterbug

A researcher in Great Smoky Mountains National Park once photographed a woman trying to sit her child on a bear's back so she could take a photo.

And they say people are smarter than bears.

◆ Remember that even in national parks, bears are wild animals. Don't make the mistake of thinking a roadside black bear is "tame" and it's okay to get out of your car and approach. Bear experts say the kindest thing you can do is honk your horn, try to get the bear to leave, and keep driving. Most roadside bears lead unnaturally short lives. Stopping to photograph them just gets them more habituated to humans.

◆ Use your car as a blind. In many situations you can remain invisible and non-threatening if you stay in your car. Talk to the rangers or locals about good places to observe wildlife, and be prepared to get there early in the morning or in late afternoon/early evening, and be patient.

◆ Invest in a good telephoto lens, and photograph bears from a safe distance. A safe distance is one where your presence doesn't change the bear's behavior in any way. "Most people don't know how to read the signals bears give. For example, even a slight yawn is a sign of stress and conveys a need for the photographer to step back," says well-known wildlife photographer Bill Lea.

◆ If you approach too closely and the bear runs away, you might be chasing it off an important food source it worked hard to find.

◆ Avoid newborn or young animals, including bear cubs. Mom is around, and she's not happy you're there.

◆ Avoid bear dens. A hibernating bear can be up and moving in seconds. Imagine what kind of mood you'd be in if you were rudely awakened by some smelly stranger in the middle of a great dream.

◆ Watch other people in the area—are they acting in ways that put you—or the bears—at risk? If they're acting foolishly, leave. And if you can, report them to the authorities.

"I was just trying to get a better shot"

Trying to get just a little closer, or entice a bear to "perform" for the camera puts you and the bear in danger. Every year bears are destroyed because people created situations that triggered the bear's defensive responses. You don't really want to go home and show off the photo of the bear you got killed, do you? If you'll invest in a camera with a good telephoto lens, and avoid these common photography pitfalls, you'll get better pictures and take fewer risks.

Your car makes a great photo blind, as photographer Jim Barry discovered when snapping this photo in Hemlock Farms, Pennsylvania. Luckily he was driving slowly enough nobody got hurt when the family of bears decided to cross the road.

◆ Work in pairs; photography is a hobby it's easy to get lost in. One person can keep an eye on the lens, while the other keeps an eye on the big picture.

◆ Don't get out of your car and approach wildlife. You have no way of knowing when you've crossed the line and invaded an individual bear's comfort zone. Some bears appear to be comfortable letting people get within a few dozen yards. Others bristle if you're a football field away. And bears aren't robots—a bear's reaction on any particular day will depend on what it was doing when you interrupted it. Getting too close can make the bear defensive—and suddenly a bear that was just minding its own business becomes an aggressive bear encounter statistic because you had to get just a little closer.

These are not "roadside bears," just bears trying to get from here to there. That's why it was okay for Jim to stop and take this picture. Kudos to Jim for staying in his car.
© Jim Barry

Writer Tom Stienstra, who's covered Yosemite for years for the *San Francisco Chronicle*, wrote of seeing experienced campers on their last night leave out an open tub of butter on a picnic table to entice a bear into camp, impress the family and get pictures. He wrote, "Hey, if you were a bear, what would you rather eat? Grass, ants, termites and bugs under rocks or a tub of butter?"

◆ Never deliberately sneak up on or surprise a bear. Many bear attacks have resulted from sudden encounters that trigger a bear's defensive instincts.

◆ Don't surround, crowd, chase or follow a bear. If a bear can't run away, it's probably going to fight back. You don't want to trigger the "fight-or-flight response" in a bear.

◆ Don't try to get an animal to pose for you, or move to a different location so you can get a better shot.

◆ Never use food to try to entice a bear to approach you. All it takes is one handout for a bear to start associating people with food. And many people have been nipped, bit, scratched and cuffed by bears that are still hungry when the goodies are gone.

HOW DO THE PROS GET SUCH GREAT SHOTS?

A professional photographer might spend several days, or even weeks trying to capture that one perfect photo, and sometimes still go home without it. That's why they're professional photographers. I love taking pictures, and I've gotten some good ones with my trusty Olympus. But I'm no pro. When I want a spectacular photo, I stop by a gift shop and buy some postcards. The lighting and composition is perfect, and they fit nicely in a photo album.

Pros use appropriate telephoto lenses—in the 600 mm range—and other equipment that the average amateur wouldn't want to invest in, or lug around. One good lens can cost more than $8,000 and weigh over thirteen pounds.

Many spectacular wildlife photos are taken at zoos, game farms and other private wildlife sanctuaries. Pros often get their best shots of large animals like bears in controlled wildlife management areas with special access permits. Few photographers have the intestinal fortitude to take close-ups of a wild grizzly bear's tonsils. ❖

The Lake Tahoe BEAR League

PAWS to the Rescue

In the fall of 1998 a mother bear and one of her two young cubs were mistakenly trapped and killed in the small community of Homewood, in the Lake Tahoe Basin. The trapper had been called in by a tourist who'd gotten a permit from the California Department of Fish and Game (CDFG) to kill a large male bear that had tried to get at some garbage in the cellar of the cabin he was renting.

But instead of the big male, the trap attracted a small female bear and her two cubs. According to neighbors interviewed at the time, the bear family had been passing through the little community tucked between Lake Tahoe and the surrounding forest since emerging from their den in the spring. The trio had never created any kind of problem.

Even though the trapper had already killed the mother bear and one cub and taken their bodies to the town dump, he told local wildlife rehabilitator and neighborhood resident Ann Bryant the bears would

be relocated. Later the CDFG warden who'd issued the permit told the press the trapper had lied to "soften the blow" and make it easier on the residents, because "relocation doesn't work well."

The warden told the *Sacramento Bee* that even though they lied to the neighbors, they always tell the person who calls and asks for the permit the truth. "I always tell them if the bears are caught, they're going to be destroyed, we're going to kill them. That forces them to make a choice."

The person who called for the permit was a tourist from Pasadena who'd rented the cabin, further infuriating the locals. "We live with bears up here, and it's really not fair for

SARA TUTTLE

a visitor to make a decision like that," resident Sally Hobson told the reporter.

The widely publicized incident galvanized the community into action; dozens of people called Bryant wanting to know what they could do to help. And that was the beginning of the BEAR League.

Today Ann Bryant, a once shy and reclusive wildlife rehabilitator, is the executive director of the BEAR League, which has over 900 dues-paying members. She writes a regular column for the local newspaper, and her calendar is jammed with speaking engagements, presentations and workshops. Bryant and between 150 and 200 trained volunteers work with the police force, area residents and businesses, and the bears to promote ways that bears and people can peacefully share space in one of the most beautiful places on earth.

Volunteers live throughout the Nevada/ California Tahoe Basin; when a call comes in to their popular bear line (530-525-PAWS) a captain is called; then a volunteer who lives near the incident is sent out to assess the situation, educate the residents, and employ aversive conditioning techniques if the bear is still there—or plan a big surprise for the next time the bear comes back.

The BEAR League's unique alliance with the police force has worked out well for all parties. The BEAR League provides the police department with rubber buckshot, cracker shells and other aversive conditioning tools that aren't covered by a budget designed to protect people, not bears. In turn the police happily call the BEAR League with any kind of bear emergency, from a home break-in to a bear that's been injured or killed on the highway.

"Our volunteers go through formal training every year. They're registered with the police department, issued badges and wear special vests that identify them as BEAR League volunteers. As far as I know we're the only organization that has this magnitude of trained volunteers who respond 24 hours a day," says Bryant. "The nearest CDFG person is 50 miles (over 80 km) away, and department policy is no strikes—if they come out on a bear call, and the person requests that the bear be killed, by law the bear has to be destroyed. We want

Curious Lake Tahoe bears.
© Ann Bryant

to get the calls so we can respond in a non-lethal way."

In 2005 BEAR League volunteers went through two days of training, which included hands-on sessions with Mammoth, California aversive conditioning expert Steve Searles and renowned bear researcher Lynn Rogers.

"Our goal, our mission, the whole reason behind the BEAR League is that we believe in educating people on how to properly respect living and vacationing in bear territory. Our house is our den; our yard is our territory, and we need to defend that. When we're in the woods, we're in the bear's territory, and we need to respect that," explained Bryant.

The BEAR League uses a combination of outreach, education and hands-on bear-proofing help for people and re-education—aversive conditioning—for bears. If they have a particularly serious case, they use a special indelible dye in the paint balls, so they'll easily be able to tell if a particular bear returns; otherwise the pellets use a biodegradable vegetable dye.

Bryant says they've had tremendous success working with their marked bears. Teams camp out all night if necessary at the scene of the problem, and wait for the bear to pay another visit. When it does, they pelt it with paintball pellets, yell, fire their air horns and harass the bear until it's very happy to escape back to the forest. "We harass them relentlessly." Bryant says. "It's for their own good. They need to learn to avoid people's homes if they're going to survive."

Although much of the publicity they've received over the years has been centered on the more glamorous aversive conditioning efforts, the backbone of the organization is unrelenting

BEAR League members Cheryl Millham, Gail Turle and Ann Bryant install bear crossing signs with the help of Nevada Department of Transportation.
Photo: Tahoe Tribune

Bear Education Aversion Response

The BEAR League is a volunteer, community-based, not-for-profit organization in the Lake Tahoe Basin, Truckee, and beyond, committed to keeping bears safe and wild in their natural habitat. Lake Tahoe straddles the borders of California and Nevada. There are an estimated 25,000 – 30,000 black bears in California, and about 200 in neighboring Nevada.

© Ann Bryant

public education—a never ending task in a place where tourists and part-time residents greatly outnumber locals.

The BEAR League prints and distributes brochures, posters and bumper stickers by the thousands. They've created public service announcements that run before movies in the local theaters. Ann Bryant and other members give countless presentations to schools, community groups, homeowners' associations and local organizations. The group maintains a high public profile, part of their belief that

education and awareness are the two most potent weapons in the battle to save bears. PBS recently spent a week with BEAR League founder Ann Bryant, filming the group's story for National Geographic and Animal Planet.

The BEAR League also works with local and county governments to try to enact bear-friendly ordinances; although it is illegal to feed or attract bears in California, the state ordinance isn't regularly enforced. Today there are tough ordinances in all the counties ringing Lake Tahoe that are in bear country. For the complete Placer County ordinance, visit *www.savebears.org.*

Like so many grass-roots organizations, the BEAR League is a powerful testament to all the good that can come out of people working together to solve problems. ❖

NO STRIKES AND YOU'RE OUT

One hundred black bears in California were killed under depredation permits in 2004. Permits are easy to obtain if the property owner can demonstrate damage to property caused by bears, and wants the bear destroyed. The California Department of Fish and Game (CDFG) says they always provide information and education about how to avoid bear encounters, but by law if a property owner insists on getting a permit, they have to issue it. Agency policy is that nuisance bears are destroyed; there are no second chances or relocation option. The BEAR League in conjunction with California's Twelve Tribal Councils has twice collected over 10,000 signatures petitioning the CDFG to implement a non-lethal bear management policy.

Hitting the Trail

Hiking, Running & Riding in Bear Country

WHY HIKE IN BEAR COUNTRY?

My husband and I are experienced day hikers; over the past twenty years we've put on thousands of miles hiking in national forests, national parks, wilderness areas and other places bears call home. If you like to hike, it's hard to avoid hiking in bear country, unless you're partial to the high desert, city parks or paved nature trails.

Why do we do it? Because there's nothing like the feeling that comes over you when the sounds of civilization are replaced by the chattering of squirrels, the calls of birds and the occasional mysterious rustle in the bushes.

Not knowing for sure what's around the next bend in the trail or what's making that noise in the bushes is part of the adventure. In the back of my mind, I know there's a chance I could get stung or bitten or twist an ankle, or even have an unpleasant encounter with wildlife that's bigger than I am.

But there's also a chance I could see a spotted fawn frolicking in a wildflower-filled meadow, hear the bugling of a bull elk in rut, spot a golden eagle soaring overhead or, if I'm very lucky, watch a black bear industriously digging grubs out of a rotting log.

For us, the potential rewards far outweigh the potential risks. But that's a personal decision every hiker has to

What's the best thing to bring along on a hike in bear country? *Your brain.*

How can I absolutely, positively guarantee nothing bad will happen if I go hiking in bear country? *Stay home.*

Do bear bells repel bears? *Probably not, but they're pretty sure to repel your fellow hikers.*

Is it dangerous to hike in bear country? *Statistically, it's a lot more dangerous to get in your car and drive to the trailhead.*

What should I do if I meet a bear? *Keep reading.*

175

make for himself. You have to come to terms with that slight element of danger if you're going to spend time in the woods. As elsewhere in life, there are no guarantees.

WHAT DO WE DO WHEN WE SEE A BEAR?

We consider ourselves very, very lucky. Over the years we've seen many black bears, and a few grizzlies. Sometimes we've been able to sit still and watch a bear through our binoculars without bothering it. Other times we've simply gone our separate ways; we knew the bear was there, and the bear knew we were there, and we mutually agreed to avoid each other. Although there are cases of hikers who haven't been so lucky, we've never even come close to having a bear conflict out day hiking.

BEFORE YOU HIT THE TRAIL

If you're hiking in an unfamiliar area, find out whether or not there are bears around, what species, and if there have been any recent problems. If you're hiking in a state or provincial park or a national park or forest, a phone call to the visitors' center or office will usually get you all the information you need. If you arrive at a trailhead and see "Bear Frequenting the Area" signs, bear-resistant storage lockers, or other evidence that bears are regular visitors, you'll know you need to take extra precautions—for your sake and the bears'.

In many popular parks the resident bears have learned that ice chests, bags and boxes have fun food surprises inside. In some areas there are regulations prohibiting leaving food or other things that might attract a bear's attention in your vehicle overnight. Ignoring regulations can result in hefty fines, or having your food or vehicle impounded.

Nighttime photo of a bear licking the food lockers at Yosemite. *Photo: DNC Parks & Resorts in Yosemite, Inc.*

And getting fined will be the least of your problems if a determined bear discovers goodies in your car. In Yosemite National Park bears sometimes pop out windows, peel off doors and remove back seats to get into trunks. During 1998, when the park had an unusual number of bear problems, the park garage repaired an average of four vehicles a day that had been damaged by bears.

Even if there are no mandatory food storage regulations, play it safe and don't leave things like coolers, grocery sacks, beverages or anything else resembling food, even empty packaging, out where a bear could see or smell it.

Bears are attracted to just about anything that smells—even dirty diapers. Wildlife officers use vanilla air freshener to bait live traps. Lock up your air fresheners, scented toiletries and sunscreens, and anything else with an odor, with your food.

ON THE TRAIL

If you absolutely, positively don't want to see a bear, even at a distance, there are some precautions you can take that will decrease the odds of encountering one.

Read the Information Board Yes, really. Sometimes trails, campgrounds or back country campsites are closed because of bear activity in the area. Warning signs should be taken seriously—they're a strong indication of recent bear activity. Do yourself and the bears a favor, and don't ignore them.

Hike Mid-Day Avoid hiking in the early morning or near dusk, and don't even think about hiking at night. Those are the times when most wildlife, including bears, is most active. Hike in the middle of the day, and most of the wildlife you see will be other hikers.

Hike in Groups The more the merrier. Lots of people

Bears don't like crashing through the bushes any more than people do, and are often found on trails, especially early in the morning, near dusk and at night.

make lots of noise, and wild creatures get plenty of warning the woods are being invaded.

Make Noise If you talk loudly, sing and occasionally clap your hands or blow your whistle, you can be pretty sure anything within range will skedaddle.

Pay Attention If you're hiking in rough terrain, it's easy to focus on the trail instead of the woods around you. If you really have to concentrate on your footing, make it a habit to stop every five or ten minutes and look around. As an extra bonus, you'll probably enjoy the hike more when you make time to look at something other than the rocks beneath your feet.

Avoid Food Sources and Travel Corridors Berry patches in the late summer, dense cover, streams, and edge zones where forest meets meadow are all good places to encounter bears and other wildlife.

Double Bag Your Food If you're going to be out for several hours and you're packing lunch, snacks, sunscreen, lip balm or anything else with an odor, seal it in double plastic freezer bags. You can use the empty freezer bags to pack out your trash.

Trail closure and warning signs are there to protect both hikers and bears. Ignore them and you put both bears and yourself at risk. © Cory Phillips

Stay Away from Carcasses Unless the carcass has already been reduced to a pile of bones, something is probably nearby keeping an eye on it—and you. A carcass cached under a pile of brush is more likely to belong to a mountain lion or a grizzly bear than a black bear; in any case, hanging around could cause the rightful owner to abandon its hard-earned meal. It could also put you in danger, as grizzlies and lions will often defend their food. So avoid the urge to play CSI and discover the cause of death. Keep on hiking and leave dinner to whatever it belongs to.

Don't Hike at Night This sounds painfully obvious, but the popularity of personal headlamps would indicate plenty of people hike in the dark. If you're coming back or heading out after sundown, be aware that bears, mountain lions, deer, elk, bobcats, and many other species of wildlife also use people trails at night. Wild animals don't need headlamps to see in the dark; bears have much better night vision than you do. And it's hard to see a black bear at night.

Hiking with Dogs Most experts recommend leaving your dog at home, and national parks in the U.S. prohibit dogs on trails. Regulations vary in Canada, but even where dogs are allowed, they have to be on a short leash. If you do hike with your dog, it should be on a sturdy, short leash at all times. More than one canine off-leash trail adventure has ended badly when the dog startles a bear and starts to bark or even attacks. When the bear takes a swat in self-defense or extreme irrita-

Always hike with your dogs on leashes. © *Linda Masterson*

tion, the dog turns tail and runs back to its master…often bringing a now very aggravated bear along with it.

Hiking with Kids Kids have a tendency to want to escape from their parents, whether they're in a shopping mall or out in the woods. And people who'd never let their children roam through the suburbs alone don't pay much attention when they run ahead of them down the trail, or lag behind. So practice making a kid sandwich— adults are the bread, kids are the filling. The filling has to stay between the bread at all times. That way, in the unlikely event you

As the Dukart family demonstrates, make a kid sandwich when you hike with children— adults are the bread, kids are the filling. No fair for the filling to run away from the bread.

encounter a mountain lion, bear, rattlesnake or anything else, everyone will be together, and you'll be able to focus on how to respond, instead of worrying about where your children are.

Experts also recommend teaching kids not to squeal, shriek or make other noises that could make them sound like prey, and not to run under any circumstances. If everyone carries a whistle you'll all have an easy way to call for help.

KNOW WHEN TO PLAY IT SAFE

We often hike at dawn and dusk, near wildlife corridors like stream beds and meadow edges. Sometimes we'll go an hour or more without uttering a word. That's because one of the reasons we hike is to see wildlife—and you can't have everything. If you follow all the bear precautions, chances are you'll never see any bears—or anything else.

But we don't take unnecessary risks. We follow the rules when circumstances dictate that avoidance is the smart choice. If we're hiking with the wind in our face and the trail twists and turns along a stream bed and through berry patches, we become very talkative.

We stop and clap our hands before we round a bend. Sometimes when the hairs on the backs of our necks stand up and we get that funny feeling, we even turn around.

We also take extra precautions in the late summer and fall, when bears don't think about much of anything except eating twenty hours a day, and are more likely to be so food-absorbed they don't notice you coming. As the long winter's fast draws closer, bears are also less likely to give ground if they've found a good food source.

MOUNTAIN BIKING

Mountain bikes are quiet and fast; you can cover a lot of ground in a short time. Riding a mountain bike on trails increases the possibility you'll surprise a bear. Bears don't like to be surprised, and may react badly to suddenly finding you on top of them. Bicyclists may be especially vulnerable in areas where there are "roadside bears." Some cyclists attach a can with pebbles to their bikes, or add bells or other noisemakers. If you're biking in bear country, it's smart to avoid dawn or dusk rides, and to travel at speeds that allow you to keep an eye on your surroundings. Bike with a friend; you'll make more noise, and have someone available to help in an emergency. Carry bear spray and a small, portable air horn. And bike with identification…just in case.

JOGGING

Joggers are even more preoccupied with watching the trail than hikers, and have an alarming tendency to jog at dawn and dusk when bears and other wildlife are most active. After years of talking to people who run in the woods, I've given up the idea they can be persuaded to stop. So how about a compromise? You don't want to zone out in bear country, so leave your personal portable sound system at home. If you're going to jog in the early morning or evening, avoid roads and trails that go through dense cover, or where

Some bears that are startled by fast-traveling joggers and bikers run away. Some don't.

there are frequent bear sightings. If you can, jog with a friend and periodically make some noise—give a nice war whoop, sing a few bars or blow your whistle. Carry bear spray and a small, portable air horn. Tuck an ID card in your pocket…just in case. Tying bear bells into your shoes is annoying, but not effective.

HORSEBACK RIDING

Horses, llamas, donkeys and other livestock seem to set off the bear's early warning detection system. Most bears associate livestock with people, and give the whole party a wide berth. According to Steve Herrero's research, no one has ever been injured by a bear attacking a horseback rider, although several people have been injured when their horse sniffed out a bear and bolted or bucked. If you're heading out for an overnight pack trip, see the chapter on camping, and treat your stock feed just as you would your own. ❖

A backpacker hiking in the Inyo National Forest in California was bitten on the shoulder by a black bear. According to a spokeswoman for the forest, the bear was attracted because the hiker hadn't properly stored his food in a bear-resistant food canister. The man escaped with nothing more than a bruised shoulder. The bear got the death penalty.

KELLY ST. JOHN
*SAN FRANCISCO
CHRONICLE*
AUGUST 2004

NATIONAL BEAR AWARE TRAILS PROGRAM

The Center for Wildlife Information offers a free, interactive national field program designed to teach kids of all ages how to hike safely and smartly in bear, mountain lion and rattlesnake country. Trained instructors work with groups to teach them everything from how to recognize bear sign to how to hang a pack.

If your group is interested in participating, visit the Web site at *www.bebearaware.org* and click on *Educating Youth*.

chapter 15

Camping in Bear Country
Front-Country and Backcountry Guidelines

Hot dogs roasting over an open fire. Chicken, fish or burgers sizzling on the grill. Gooey marshmallows sticking to your fingers. Coolers full of beer, pop, watermelon and potato salad. Plenty of chips, cookies, and snacks. Sunscreen, lip balm, shampoo, deodorant, insect repellant, moisturizing lotion. Welcome to the bountiful bear buffet served up at the average front-country campground.

We may go camping to get away from it all, but many folks bring their pantries with them. The average drive-in camper shows up in the bear's back yard toting enough calories to put the average bear into a food coma. Combine plenty of available food with an endless supply of calorie-laden garbage, and it's easy to see why bears are attracted to campgrounds.

A tent full of food, beverages and scented soaps, shampoos and lotions is a powerful invitation for bears to drop by. © Bill Lea

The majority of bear incidents that occur out in the woods happen in campgrounds, picnic areas and parking lots—places where the resident bears expect to find plenty of tasty treats.

Whether you're camping in a drive-to, developed campground, a hike-in back country camp or just pitching your tent in a nice spot in the middle of nowhere, some common-sense precautions can help keep your camp bear-free.

DO YOUR CAMPING HOMEWORK

Precautions that might be more than adequate if you're front country camping in an area where bears are few and far between may prove woefully inadequate—or even illegal—in a region like the Sierra Nevada Mountains, where bears excel at filching provisions. A few minutes visiting the Web site, dropping in to the visitor's center or talking to the campground host can save you and the bears a lot of trouble.

CLEAN UP YOUR ACT

The single most important thing you can do when camping in bear country is to keep a clean camp. Leaving food, trash or other things with odors in the open is asking for bear trouble. Depending on local regulations, store food in the trunk of your car, hang it in a tree in a plastic bag or stuff sack, lock it in a bear-resistant locker or use a bear-resistant food canister.

Don't bury or burn garbage or trash. Burning actually makes trash more attractive, because the food molecules and odors intensify and disperse on the wind.

If bear-resistant garbage cans or dumpsters are available, use them—and make sure they're properly closed and latched when you're through. Don't leave trash outside a dumpster. If it's over-

Experience has taught this bear that getting food from people is a picnic.
© Nelson Kenter

flowing or broken, double bag your trash and stash it in your trunk.

Pack a can of Lysol. Or mix up a concoction of 50 percent ammonia and 50 percent water, and then spray down your picnic table, the outside of your tent, even your backpack or day pack frequently. Don't use bear spray as a repellent; it's designed for bear encounters.

Declare your tent a food-free zone. There are few things more startling than being woken up in the middle of the night by a bear licking the remnants of a chocolate bar off your face. Don't eat in your tent or sleeping bag, and store food and all scented toiletries as far away from your tent as possible. You might know your avocado-honey shampoo only smells good enough to eat, but a bear doesn't. Food or other attractants have been involved in the vast majority of cases when a black bear has entered someone's tent.

Store the clothes you cook in along with your food, and wear clean clothes to go to sleep. Clean up yourself with unscented soap while you're at it; there's evidence overly-ripe human smells may attract bears. Don't turn in with so much as a breath mint or a tube of toothpaste in your tent.

A bear-smart camper takes the time to stash her trash in one of the bear-resistant containers at Valecito Reservoir near Durango, Colorado. © *Tom Beck*

Cooking grease, dishwashing liquid, and liquid used to cook or boil food all smell great to a bear. Bring something to collect grease, double bag it and pack it out.

Filter food particles out of the dishwater—use a tea strainer or a small piece of window screening—and dispose of them with your garbage. Dump the remaining dishwashing and cooking liquid well away and downwind of your sleeping and cooking areas.

I encourage people to store food in a lockable metal container, which is what I do at all my car-accessible camps. This works great to defeat raccoons as well. I use a military surplus metal box—the kind commonly used by river runners because they're also waterproof. They're relatively inexpensive and very effective. They're small enough to be easily handled by one person, and will fit neatly in most cars and trucks. The main source of failure is operator error—forgetting to lock the lids on every night.

Beck's Bits

Burn off any food residue on your grill or stove and thoroughly incinerate any grease or food particles. And at the request of numerous harried campground hosts, please don't leave your trash piled in your fire ring. It's not going to magically incinerate itself, or hop into the dumpster.

A bear cleaning up after a sloppy camper.
© Nelson Kenter

Don't sleep where you cook. If you pitch your tent right in front of the fire you're cooking on, guess what your tent will smell like? Follow safe camping and cooking guidelines. No matter how bad the weather, never cook in your tent.

Hide your cooler. Experienced bears love coolers; just pop off the top and dig in. You can't bear proof a cooler. No matter how badly you want a frosty nightcap, lock it up in your trunk. Don't leave empty cans or bottles in your tent or out in the open. If you don't have a trunk, cover your cooler with a blanket. Remember to read up on local regulations—in places like Yosemite National Park, you'll be ticketed if you leave anything that looks or smells like food in your vehicle overnight.

Clean up your car. Reducing clutter in your car lessens the chance a bear will think there's something in there worth ripping off the door to get. It will also give you a chance to find any food, wrap-

NO INDEPENDENCE DAY FOR ONE BEAR

In 2004 during the busy Fourth of July weekend, Idaho Conservation Officers Charlie Anderson and Clark Shackleford responded to calls about a black bear making brazen daylight raids on National Forest Service campgrounds at Teardrop Lake. It turned out this particular bear had been trapped in early June near the Jenny Lake campground in Grand Teton National Park, where it had discovered that wherever humans could be found, so could improperly stored food and garbage. It took the officers exactly half an hour to lure the bear into a baited trap. There was no Independence Day celebration for the bear. IDFG Protocol prohibited them from releasing it again, so they had to kill it.

pers or packages that have disappeared under a seat or gotten stuck to the carpeting. If you have a child's car seat, this is a good time to get out the Lysol and give it a good wipe down.

Use a flashlight at night and make some noise if nature calls or you're coming back to camp after dark; there's much less of a chance you'll startle a bear if it can clearly see you coming.

HARD FACTS ABOUT HARD-SIDED CAMPERS

It's a pretty simple matter for a determined bear to break into the average camper or trailer. Resist the urge to leave the windows open when you leave for the day. Store food out of sight, and don't leave coolers, grocery bags or picnic baskets in plain view. Don't leave pet food, food bowls or trash bags outside.

The number one source of food odors wafting out of hard-sided campers is the exhaust system over the stove that often vents outside. The filters, fan and exhaust ducts collect grease, moisture, dust and odors. The whole area should be regularly cleaned with a heavy-duty, ammonia-based cleaner.

Enticing odors waft out of a camper's exhaust system unless it's kept scrupulously clean. © *Tim Halvorson*

"I have seen many unoccupied, empty, locked up trailers broken into by bears at the exhaust duct. This area is a real odor magnet, and a place that's easily forgotten when it's clean up time," says Tom Beck, who's an avid camper.

"PICK-A-NICKS"

Like Yogi and Boo Boo, some bears that routinely see humans have developed a nose for a well-stuffed pick-a-nick basket. Stay close to your food, don't feed anything that comes begging, and clean up thoroughly when you're done. Even if you don't have any problems, leaving a

mess can attract a bear to the area, and create a problem for the next picnicker, as well as the bears.

WHY CAN'T WE FEED THE BEARS?

There are always people who think it's either cute or harmless to deliberately leave food out for the bears. For some, waiting for the bears to show up is the evening entertainment. Others want a photo to take back to the folks at home, or a story to swap around the campfire. Some think it's a less wasteful way of taking out the garbage. Others truly seem to think the bears are starving, and Twinkies and fried chicken will save them.

"The bears are already used to it," you reason. "One more hunk of watermelon won't make any difference. And I want the kids to see a bear."

Bears that learn to associate people with food are much more likely than bears that retain their natural wariness of the human race to end up damaging property, harassing people, breaking into tents, cabins, campers or cars, or even injuring someone. Bears that engage in that kind of behavior often enough often end up dead.

Unless you want the kids to see a bear being trapped, shot and killed, please, please, please, don't feed the bears.

"Preparation and adequate planning is the best way to respect the bears you'll encounter in the wilderness. Bears are amazing, especially in their diligence to get your food. I respect them enough to not even try to outsmart them—instead, I carry a bear-proof canister whenever I'm on a wilderness patrol."

CALDER REID
WILDERNESS MANAGER –
MOUNT WHITNEY REGION,
INYO NATIONAL FOREST

Yosemite bears have learned to recognize grocery sacks, food and coolers, even when you try to hide them under a blanket.
Photo: DNC Parks & Resorts at Yosemite, Inc.

BACKPACKING AND BACKCOUNTRY CAMPING

When you're carrying literally everything you need to survive in your pack, you don't want to lose it to a hungry bear. And you don't want to take a chance of getting hurt defending it, either.

Selecting a Site

Try to arrive at your campsite before dark, so you can pick out a good spot to hang your packs if there aren't bear boxes or other systems available, and you're not using a bear-resistant canister.

No matter how tired you are, if you're in grizzly country and your chosen site shows signs of a recent bear visit—there's trash strewn around from the slobs who came before you, or fresh bear scat or tracks—leave, even if it means camping somewhere you're not supposed to be. When you get back to the trailhead, report the site to a ranger or someone in authority.

If you know there are only black bears in the area, it's still recommended you choose another site if you can. If you can't, you'll need to take every possible precaution—and accept that there's a good probability you'll have a midnight visitor.

Try to avoid pitching your tent near berry patches, stream corridors, trails or dense cover. The farther out in the open you are, the less likely it is that a black bear will come into camp.

As this old postcard shows, bears have been going camping for a long time. In addition to all the bear no-nos like unsecured food and cans of scented hair spray that lured these bears into camp, these folks have also pitched their tent much too close to the shoreline.

Smart Planning

Trees for hanging food and packs should be at least 100 yards (91 meters) downwind of your camp. If there are no trees, and you don't have a bear canister, double or triple bag everything (of course

BEAR BREWSKIS

Workers at the Baker
Lake Resort 80 miles
northwest of Seattle
discovered a two-year
old black bear passed
out one morning when
they arrived for work.
The camp host
discovered some
campers had left out
coolers, and the bear
had broken into them,
opened the cans with
his teeth, and started
guzzling. The bear tried
a Busch, but apparently
preferred local brew
Rainier. He gulped
down 36 cans before
passing out.

USA TODAY, AUGUST 2004

you've packed a variety of freezer bags) and leave the bags on the ground at least 100 yards (91 meters) downwind of your camp. When you go home, buy a bear canister.

Your cooking area should also be at least 100 yards (91 meters) downwind—your sleeping area, cooking area and hanging trees should form a nice little triangle.

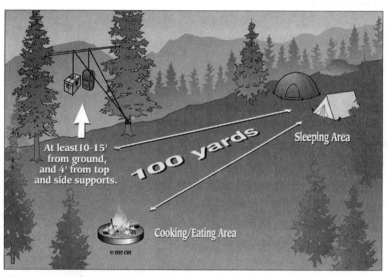

How to set up a bear-smart campsite. *Courtesy of Center for Wildlife Information*

Backpacking with Bears

Many areas with heavy bear activity require backpackers to use bear-resistant canisters, and often provide them free or for a nominal fee. They can also be bought or sometimes rented at outdoor stores. The canisters are cylindrical, so bears can't get their paws on a seam, lid or latch. And the newest ones are lighter, roomier and easier to pack. It's recommended you hang them if you can; if you can't, they can be left on the ground in the open, well away from your tent.

Pack toiletries in plastic bags as well. You'll have less trash to worry about, and you can use the empties to secure things you need to pack out. Think nutrition and weight when you're packing—freeze dried foods are light, easy to pack and relatively odor free. Leave the aged salami at home.

Make sure your packs aren't in a location where the wind will blow smoke and yummy cooking smells in their direction—even today's ballistic fabrics absorb smoke and odors, and you don't want your pack to smell like dinner.

When you're done for the day, pack up all your food, toiletries, trash, the clothes you cooked in, pots, pans and anything else that might remotely have an odor, and hang your pack at least 10 feet (3 meters) off the ground, and 4 feet (1.2 meters) out from the trunk of the tree.

Bear-resistant canister.
Courtesy of Backpacker's Cache
www.backpackerscache.com

If you're going to burn any trash or bits of food, you need to completely incinerate them. If you're not, they should be packed in plastic bags and stored with your food. Some people who don't like the idea of their food rubbing elbows with their trash bring a separate stuff sack for garbage.

WHEN BEARS GO CAMPING

If a black bear comes into your camp, picnic ground or other developed area, do the bear and all the campers who will come after you a favor, and do everything you can to drive it off.

Don't toss it food or stand around taking pictures, no matter how "tame" it seems. Wild black bears are never "tame." Certain individual bears just learn to overcome their natural distrust of humans because they think they'll get a big food reward, and no punishment.

Round up your fellow campers, make lots of noise, bang pots and pans, blow whistles, air horns and car horns, and try to convince the bear it's not welcome. Don't crowd the bear, and make sure it has an open escape route. Don't force the bear to go through people to get away, or someone could get hurt.

Beck's Bits

Most people never really think about soap, toothpaste, bug spray, deodorant, shampoo and the like. I myself prefer Dr. Bronner's Peppermint Soap as an all-purpose soap/shampoo, but I leave it at home in bear habitat. It's curiosity about out-of-the-ordinary odors that brings bears shuffling in.

After it's gone, try to determine what attracted the bear in the first place, and make sure the attractants are removed, so if the bear comes back, it won't find anything worth the trouble.

If it's a chronic situation with another camper or the campground in general, and if they're not willing to clean up their act, report the problem to the campground hosts or area management. Looking the other way could get somebody hurt—campers, bears or both.

Report encounters to the local authorities; they may want to close a campground or trail if there are a lot of reports from one area.

HELP, THERE'S A BEAR IN MY TENT

If you wake up and hear something snuffling outside your tent, start talking in a firm monotone so whatever it is knows there's a person inside the big nylon mushroom.

Curious or human-food-conditioned bears sometimes bite or claw the outside of a tent. Noted bear attack expert Steve Herrero surmises they may be test-biting to see if something yummy is inside, and says he avoids sleeping next to the tent wall.

Turn on your flashlight or lantern, and get your bear spray

Grizzly bears love to check out tents too. © *Derek Reich*

ready. If the bear starts ripping through your tent, prepare to defend yourself. If you're woken up by a bear already inside your tent, fight back with anything handy. And start yelling; many a campground bear has been driven off by a posse of campers with pots and pans.

GOING TENTLESS

Experts strongly recommend you don't sleep out under the stars in bear country. In many areas, it's illegal, and you'll get a ticket, so if you're determined to go tentless, check local regulations first.

There are numerous instances of both black and grizzly bears investigating a sleeping bag, and licking, nipping or biting the big object in the cocoon. It would be simple for a bear to mistake something big lying quietly on the ground for carrion—an easy, protein and fat packed meal. Enjoy your dinner under the Big Dipper, (away from your tent) but don't take a chance on becoming dinner for something else. Sleep inside.

Steve Herrero says, "Sleeping under the stars is one of my favorite things to do while camping, but I choose areas in which to do this carefully. My data strongly suggests that people sleeping without tents were more likely to be injured, even killed, than were people who slept in tents."

What's a good place? Herrero says to choose an open area, well away from trees, big rocks, bushes and other landscape features that would make good cover for a bear. Above treeline is okay, as long as you're not in grizzly country. If you're in grizzly country, there is no good place to sleep under the stars. ❖

I was once on a river trip in Idaho with thirteen other people. The second night out we had a great sand beach, so no one put up a tent. One idiot had kept two trout and put them in a 5-gallon bucket in the kitchen area. I usually wake up first, and when I was putting coffee on I noticed the fish were gone from the bucket. When the morning light got better the bear tracks shone like neon strobes. The bear had walked within a foot of every one of us, checking us all out. That night, everyone was in a tent. Even me.

Beck's Bits

The Bear Essentials When Camping

- ◆ Keep your camp so clean your mom would be proud
- ◆ Safely stash food and trash
- ◆ Wipe down picnic tables
- ◆ Burn food off stoves, barbeques and grills
- ◆ Avoid scented toiletries and cosmetics
- ◆ Don't leave anything in your tent that attracts bears
- ◆ Don't sleep with snacks

FOODS

Fresh foods

Frozen foods

Canned foods

Packaged foods

Dried fruits and nuts

Bottled or canned pop, including diet pop and flavored water

Beer, wine, energy drinks

Coffee

Gum, candy, trail mix, snacks, energy bars

Grease

Pet food and treats

Grain and horse feed

Items that Attract Bears

NON-FOOD ITEMS

Scented toiletries like shampoo, sunscreen, hand lotion

Toothpaste, deodorant, cosmetics

Insect repellant

Scented candles

Air fresheners

All garbage and trash

Packaging, wrappers, empty cans

Dishwater and cooking water

Spices and seasonings

Rubber, vinyl, many chemicals

Petroleum products, especially lantern fuel and propane

Motor oil

Cedar and aromatic woods

Yosemite National Park

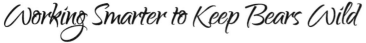

The legendary bears of Yosemite are the Einsteins of the bear world. If "ways to get your paws on people food" was a category on *Jeopardy*, they'd walk away with the jackpot every time.

You can't hide food from a Yosemite bear. The overly bright bruins recognize ice chests, grocery bags, picnic baskets and other food related supplies—even when they're hidden under blankets. Bears sidle into campgrounds and quickly make off with packs left unattended, and have broken into countless cars for as little as a stick of gum in the glove compartment, an empty soda can or a discarded candy bar wrapper. They've paddled out to rafts and swum back to shore with the

> "*Each year black bears are killed in Yosemite as a direct result of human carelessness and improper food storage. Some call it a 'bear problem,' but bears are not to blame.*"
>
> YOSEMITE NATIONAL PARK
> WEB SITE

rafters' provisions, and pawed through climber's bags in search of treats. Between 1989 and 2002 there were over 9,300 bear incidents reported at Yosemite National Park, and well over a million dollars in property damage.

Yosemite encompasses an area about the size of the state of Rhode Island, straddling both sides of the rugged Sierra Nevada range in central California. The broad Yosemite Valley is a veritable Eden for bears, with nutritious natural foods available during virtually every month of bear activity.

EVERYTHING SMELLS GOOD TO A BEAR

A bear in Yosemite National Park broke into a van that contained no food or beverages...it was attracted by a can of cherry car freshener and a tube of Neosporin antibiotic ointment.

Photo: DNC Parks & Resorts at Yosemite, Inc.

There have been human-bear clashes in the awe-inspiring Yosemite Valley ever since the first European settlers arrived back in 1855. Those early pioneers quickly exterminated the grizzly bear, but black bears were seen as less threatening, and allowed to remain. In 1864 fear that the valley was being overdeveloped led to Yosemite and the Mariposa Grove of Big Trees becoming the first natural protected areas in the United States.

In those early days of the park, pit dumps were the popular and practical way to dispose of garbage and food waste. By the 1930s as many as 60 bears roamed throughout the valley.

In an attempt to draw bears away from the developing east end of the valley, artificial feeding areas were established in 1937 in the valley's western portion, as well as in other less-developed areas of the park. The feeding sites quickly became major tourist attractions, as people came to watch the bears chow down as much as 60 tons of human food scraps every year.

By the 1940s biologists and park managers began to suspect that artificial feeding was changing the very nature of Yosemite's bears. The last dump was closed in 1971.

But the bears weren't willing to kick their habit cold turkey. Bears used to fattening up on human food turned to raiding campsites and breaking into vehicles in search of the food they'd come to depend on.

In 1975 Yosemite implemented what is today one of the oldest and most comprehensive bear management programs in the national park system. Over the years Yosemite has tried just about everything to reduce conflicts and keep bears wild, but until recently the Yosemite Valley remained the SuperBowl of bear problems.

Yosemite Valley's 7 square miles (18 sq km) represent less than one percent of the total area of the park, but are home to nearly half of the park's 1,948 campsites and most of the 1,600 lodging units. Almost all of the 3.5 to 4 million people who visit the park every year use the valley, staying in accommodations that range from rustic tent camps to the posh and historic Ahwahnee Hotel, and frequenting the dozens of restaurants and food courts.

One of the most dependable byproducts of tons of people is tons of garbage. It's no wonder that on average six out of ten bear

This bear is down in the dumps because somebody forgot to close and latch this bear-resistant dumpster.
Photo: Jeffrey Trust; National Park Service

incidents occur in the valley, the vast majority in campgrounds and parking lots. A comprehensive study done in 2000 traced three out of four incidents directly to human error—usually improperly stored food or garbage.

In 1998, the high-water year for human-bear conflicts, bears broke into over a thousand vehicles, and did over $630,000 in property damage. Several food-conditioned bears became so aggressive they were destroyed. Human-bear conflicts in Yosemite had reached the crisis intervention stage.

The next year Congress awarded Yosemite a half-million dollar annual budget to implement a new program. The park increased staff levels and improved communications and outreach. They also purchased and installed new dumpsters and mandatory bear-resistant storage lockers, and embarked on an aversive conditioning program aimed at teaching bears to avoid people.

Today bear incidents in Yosemite National Park are down an average of 70 percent over 1998. People who deal with human-bear conflicts everywhere would love to know why, and so would the folks at Yosemite. But as an exhaustive research study concluded, no one tactic is clearly responsible. Instead, it's the combination of approaches that gets credit for starting to improve human-bear relations.

HABITUATED HUMANS

The park makes sure every visitor hears about bears. You get literature when you write for visitor information. You get literature at the gates when you enter. You get literature when

SARA TUTTLE

you register for back-country permits. You get literature when you register at any of the hotels; you even have to sign a form stating you've read and understand it. Signs and posters are everywhere. Overall, 98 percent of visitors admitted hearing or seeing some information about bears and bear safety. One tally showed that if you read everything, went to all the programs, hiked all the trails and visited all the facilities, you'd be exposed to 632 bear messages.

But recent research suggests that people have seen—not necessarily absorbed—so much information about bears they've become habituated to the messages. And, after all that, they still think the chances of anything happening to them personally are slim.

Since visitors think problems are unlikely, they often give themselves permission to ignore the rules—especially people who've camped many times without any problems, and think they know it all.

Thinking you know it all and actually knowing it all—never mind doing any of it—are two different matters. In a 1979 study, 92 percent of visitors thought they were storing food correctly; only 3 percent actually were. By 1999 over 80 percent of visitors reported they always used the bear lockers provided at campgrounds. The top two reasons were "will help keep animals wild" and "I'll have food to eat."

Visitors who forget to remove food and other attractants from their cars keep the Yosemite body shop busy. *Photo: Jack Hopkins, National Park Service*

Surveys like this one being conducted by Brenda Lackey help Yosemite understand visitor attitudes towards bears and come up with new ways to improve people-bear relations. *Photo: Heather Fener, Wildlife Conservation Society*

OOPS. I FORGOT TO LOOK UNDER THE SEAT.
Despite the fact that the campers attended a program that night that made them go back to their campsite and thoroughly search their BMW, they missed the bag of peanuts under the passenger seat, and the hard candies and lotion in the glove compartment. The bear didn't miss a bite. The same bear had already snagged a watermelon from a cooler at another campsite.

AN ONGOING BATTLE

Yosemite has worked with Wind River Bear Institute's Carrie Hunt and her famed Karelian bear dogs to try and reeducate the bears at popular backcountry campgrounds like Tuolumne Meadows. The summer of the bear

> ### THROUGH THE VISITORS' EYES
>
> ◆ 92% of the visitors interviewed while picking up their impounded vehicles had seen or heard messages about proper food storage.
>
> ◆ 30% of visitors mistakenly believe that black bears seldom cause damage.
>
> ◆ 48% have an accurate perception of Yosemite bears; 6% believe bears are dangerous and unpredictable.
>
> ◆ 86% of the respondents have never had a problem with black bears in Yosemite. Of the 14% who had problems, over half didn't report them.
>
> ◆ 88% believe black bears symbolize the beauty and wonder of nature found in Yosemite.
>
> ◆ 65% believe that seeing a black bear at Yosemite makes an outstanding trip, and that "black bears at Yosemite should be kept alive no matter what."
>
> ◆ 96% didn't want bears eliminated from Yosemite.
>
> ◆ 20% didn't realize canned goods, bottles and drinks (covered and unopened) were still an attractant.

dogs the park recorded the lowest number of human-bear conflicts in Tuolumne Meadows since they started keeping records.

Park rangers have become skilled practitioners of aversive conditioning as well; the office now issues bulletins explaining the rangers aren't being mean to the bears, so people won't call to complain about "bear abuse."

DING DONG, BEAR IS CALLING

In 2003 Yosemite, working with the National Wildlife Research Center and the Wildlife Conservation Society, started testing a remote alarm system originally developed to minimize problems between ranchers and wolves in Idaho. The system uses radio telemetry to send a message through the park radio network to wildlife management when a bear with a radio collar is in a developed area. The staff

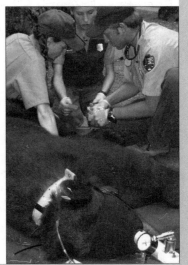

Bears that are having people problems in Yosemite are often trapped and tagged, then monitored to keep tabs on their activities.
Photo: National Park Service

can then quickly respond, aversively conditioning the bear with loud noises and bright lights, and hopefully chase it away with a barrage of harmless-but-annoying bean-bag bullets to the butt. So far it's proved so effective they're now developing a three-stage intervention process. In stage one, the bear is tracked for two weeks to determine its normal habits. In stage two, the bear receives aversive conditioning every time it tries to go after human food. In stage three the bear is tracked for an additional two weeks to make sure it's staying away from people.

People stated repeatedly that they wanted more information about bear biology, and less about storing food properly. But the same survey found that messages about citations and fines and what would happen to you if you didn't follow regulations had more lasting impact than clever messages people enjoyed reading. Yellowstone National Park has found that heftier fines and more frequent citations help people "remember" to store their food properly.

While human-bear incidents are very common in Yosemite, even minor injuries are rare, so most people just don't take "mischief" seriously. They think it's no big deal if a bear goes after their ice chest, or makes off with their leftovers. These same people say they appreciate the bears, and want them protected. They don't think of their coolers and picnic baskets and cars full of food as lethal weapons—but they are. Because the more "mischief" a bear gets into, the better its chances of winding up a sad statistic on Yosemite's annual Bear Report. ❖

YOSEMITE SUGGESTION BOX

These suggestions for reducing human-bear conflicts came from National Park Service and concessionaire employees in Yosemite taking part in a survey and research study:

- Hang pictures of destroyed vehicles in all the bathroom stalls.

- Dart and tranquilize the offending human, and relocate outside the park.*

- Make sure visitors know that "problem" bear will probably have to be killed.

- Step up law enforcement and hand out stiffer fines.

- Since visitors can't seem to follow the rules, limit the number of visitors allowed in the valley, or ban vehicles from the valley.

- Add more bear dog teams, and do more hazing; stop young bears from following in the footsteps of old, habituated bears.

- Public flogging for those who don't follow the rules.

My personal favorite

chapter 16

Fishing and Hunting in Bear Country
Special Precautions for Sportsmen & Women

Going fishing often means heading into great bear habitat. Bears like to feed on vegetation along streams and the shores of lakes and ponds. Bears like to catch and eat fish. Bears like to clean up after sloppy fishermen. Sometimes bears will even let you do the fishing for them. Unless you're fishing from a boat out in the middle of a big lake, fishing in bear country is a good way to encounter bears.

If you're hiking, keep an eye peeled for bear sign and make some noise—especially when you're moving through dense vegetation, or coming around blind curves.

When you get to your destination, see if there are signs you're sharing your fishing spot with bears. Look for tracks and scats, heavily worn trails, birds scavenging along the stream or fish remnants—heads, tails, intestines. If you find a whole fish lying on the bank, leave the area—it probably belongs to a bear that will be back shortly.

A fast-flowing stream makes it tough to hear an approaching bear—or for the bear to hear you. Plus when you're fishing, it's easy to focus only on the water, and not on what's going on around you. You're probably being quiet, and concentrating on watching your line and not your surroundings. Try to take a bear break now and then and look around.

If you have a good day and catch some fish, clean them right away rather than taking them

People fishing alone are often quiet, seldom take their eyes off the water, and frequently have coolers full of food—or fish—at their sides, all reasons to be extra-alert in bear country.
© *Cory Phillips*

back to camp, unless you've got a fish cleaning station. Bear attack expert Steve Herrero suggests piercing the air bladder and tossing the fish guts into deep water in a stream or lake so they won't wash up on shore, unless regulations prohibit it. If that's the case, opt for burning them in a very hot fire, or if you're not in an area with other people, simply leave them in the open to decompose or be eaten by scavengers. Double bag your fish in Ziploc-style freezer bags.

Bear expert Gary Brown strongly recommends you don't keep or cook fish in a backcountry camp. But if you can't resist the idea of a fish fry, then be sure to wrap and pack out all the remains, just like any other garbage.

And after you eat, pack up the clothes you were wearing and store them in a plastic bag, with your food and other attractants. Whatever you do, don't store them in your tent or sleep in them. Wash up with a strong unscented soap before you turn in.

If you're fishing for salmon or other fish that travel up rivers in the summer and fall, you're probably going to be sharing the bank with bears intent on putting on as much fat as they possibly can before they turn in for the winter.

Some black bears frequent popular fishing spots in the hopes of cleaning up discarded fish guts; sometimes bolder bears who've become people-food conditioned will march up to fishermen and demand their catch. Gary Brown recommends that if you're accosted by a bear who wants your dinner, drop the fish and leave the area. This is no time to try to recondition the bear.

If you're going fishing in northwestern Canada, Alaska, or in or around Glacier or Yellowstone National Parks, please check with the local authorities, find out about bear activity in the area, and read up on grizzly bear behavior. Responses that work with black bears often backfire with grizzlies, and vice versa. See Chapter 19 for a quick look at grizzly behavior.

If you're back-country camping overnight, treat the clothes you fish, clean your catch and cook in like smelly food, and store them in a bear-proof canister or bag them and hang them out of bear reach. In front-country campgrounds, bag them and lock them up in your trunk or a bear-resistant container. © Cory Phillips

HUNTING WITH BEARS IN THE NEIGHBORHOOD

Like fishermen, successful hunters put themselves in situations that increase their odds of surprising a bear, usually at a time of year when bears are single-mindedly spending up to twenty hours a day eating and looking for food.

Hunters silently hit the trail before dawn, often disguised like bushes and vegetation, and masked in the scent of prey animals. They often travel off trail, and don't talk or make noise. If they're successful, they end up hiking out with a collection of carcasses.

Big game hunters often leave gut piles; indeed, in places where elk and deer hunting is a popular fall sport, studies show that some of the local bears have learned to follow the gunshot dinner bell to the gut-pile. There's always the chance that a hunter will stumble on a fellow-hunter's kill site, and the bear that's thoughtfully tidying up the forest.

You've got the greatest probability of encountering a black bear if you're out hunting in September or early October, during the season when bears spend more time eating than your average teenager. In many areas by November the bears are hitting their

Early fall when bears are frantically fattening up for the winter is one of the most likely time for hunters—and hikers, campers or other outdoors-minded folks—to encounter bears.

Black bears can get defensive if someone tries to come between them and a carcass they've discovered.
© *John E. Marriott*

dens instead of your kills. In Colorado over half the bears are denned up for the winter by Halloween. So find out how long bears are typically active in the area you're hunting, and take extra precautions. You don't want to come between a bear and its quest for calories.

Tips for Safe Hunting in Bear Country

◆ Pack bear spray, and keep it where you can get your hands on it in a second, not in the bottom of your pack. No matter how great a shot you are, bear spray is easier to get at and use in an emergency, requires little aiming, and disperses over a fairly large area. Black bears seldom attack either offensively or defensively, but if you over-react and wound a bear, you could have a real problem. And don't wait until you actually need your bear spray to practice using it. For more on bear spray, see Chapter 18.

◆ Since you can't make noise, try to stop frequently, look around, and be on the lookout for fresh bear sign.

◆ If you're hunting with dogs, be prepared for your dog to lead you to—or bring back—a grumpy bear rather than that trophy elk or white tail you were hoping for.

◆ If you have to leave your carcass for more than a few minutes, stash it at least 25 to 50 feet (7.6 to 15.2 meters) from your gut pile, cover it with tree limbs or brush and make sure you can see it from a distance. When you come back, make noise, and if a bear has beaten you to the meat, don't try to reclaim it.

◆ Avoid gut piles if you can, and don't leave yours on a trail or road.

◆ If you're in grizzly country, hang carcasses at least 100 yards (91 meters) from camp, at least 10 feet (3 meters) above the ground and 6 feet (1.8 meters) from another tree, and be extra alert when you're approaching a carcass you've left.

BULLETS VS. BEAR SPRAY

Experienced hunters may be tempted to think carrying a firearm is their best protection against an aggressive bear. But extensive studies by the U.S. Fish and Wildlife Service (FWS) show that if you're involved in a bear encounter, shooting the bear usually makes matters worse. Guns can kill bears…but the problem is, they often don't kill bears fast enough.

If a bullet doesn't stop a bear in its tracks, momentum and rage are likely to carry the bear into a full collision with the shooter. The bear may eventually die of its wounds. But by that time, the person may be severely injured, or worse.

It's not about having nerves of steel, or the dead aim of a sharpshooter. FWS says, "Even a skilled marksman with steady nerves may have a slim chance of deterring a bear attack with a gun."

Fish and Wildlife has been studying the results of human-bear encounters since 1992. People defending themselves with a firearm are injured about half the time. During the same study, people defending themselves with bear spray escaped injury most of the time, and if they were injured, their injuries were less severe. These results are very similar to Steve Herrero's research.

Most of the data referenced is from grizzly bear encounters and attacks, but the information applies equally to black bear encounters. So no matter how great a shot you are, experts agree that bear spray beats bullets when it comes to stopping an aggressive bear.

For more about bear spray, see Chapter 18. ❖

Even a sharpshooter with nerves of steel has only a small chance of using a firearm to successfully defend against the rare aggressive black bear.

chapter 17

Bear Encounters and Attacks

Staying Safe in Bear Country

Black bears are normally shy and reclusive; they naturally avoid people and other predators in their territory they sense might be dangerous. For a black bear, looking for food is a full time job; most bears have neither the nature nor the time to go looking for trouble.

Like most people, bears don't like to be surprised. They like their space and don't want to feel crowded. They work hard for their food, and if they think you want to take it away, they might try to stop you. Sometimes, just like people, they react to being scared or startled by striking back first, and thinking about it later.

Although it's rare, black bears have seriously injured and killed people. The more you understand and follow the bear-smart guidelines for camping, hiking, living and playing in bear country, the better your chances of avoiding, or escaping unharmed from, an unpleasant encounter with a bear.

This chapter deals with encounters out in the woods where you're in the bear's territory. Dealing with bears that come into camp is covered in Chapter 15; bears invading your home turf are in Chapter 5.

Bears "hike" many hours a day; it's not uncommon for a black bear to travel a 5- to 15-mile

SARA TUTTLE

(8- to 24-km) daily circuit in pursuit of food. Bears don't like crashing through the brush any more than you do; they often take advantage of trails, particularly in the early morning or early evening, at night and in areas where trails don't get much use by people.

There's some evidence that most bears avoid popular trails during daylight, when they've learned that people are likely to be on them. But bears may still forage near trails, as they often go through areas attractive to both bears and people. If you're bush-whacking and traveling cross-country, a bear doesn't have a clue you might be in its neighborhood until it smells, hears or sees you.

MEETING A BLACK BEAR ON THE TRAIL

If you do meet a black bear on a trail, it will most likely turn tail and run off. If it doesn't, stop, stand still and stay calm.

♦ **Talk to the bear in a normal, calm voice,** in as much of a mon-otone as you can master. You can say anything you want, as

Ears forward and openly and silently approaching or circling can indicate the very rare aggressive or predatory black bear.
© Cory Phillips

there's no evidence bears understand English. "Hey bear, hey bear, we're sorry we bothered you, we're getting out of your way now," is easy to remember. If you're traveling in a group, appoint one person to be your "Bear Talker" before you head out. Several people babbling at once may sound contentious to a bear, no matter what you're saying.

◆ **Don't approach any closer, and don't whip out your camera** and start taking pictures.

◆ **Don't make any sudden, abrupt movements.**

◆ **Don't offer the bear any food.**

◆ **Avoid direct eye contact.** Bears, and many other animals (including domestic dogs) may view this as hostile or aggressive behavior.

◆ **Don't run.** Running triggers a chase response in many animals, including bears. Remember, bears can sprint at speeds of up to 35 mph (56 kph). You can't outrun a bear.

◆ **Don't climb a tree.** Black bears can climb a 100-foot (30-meter) tree in less than 30 seconds. Mother black bears often send their cubs up trees when they sense danger. You don't want to end up in a tree with a couple of bear cubs, and momma bear waiting patiently below for you all to come down. And when a dominant bear chases another bear up a tree in a battle of "whose turf is this, anyway?" the treed bear often gets yanked to the ground and pummeled a few times to teach it a lesson. Bears survive being pummeled by other bears a lot better than people do. Don't climb trees to escape a black bear.

Beck's Bits

In antagonistic encounters between black bears, the submissive bear will often climb a tree. In most cases the dominant bear will follow, attempting to grab the fleeing bear by the hind foot and tug it down. Sound familiar? Human goes up a tree, bear responds as if human is a mangy bear, climbs tree, grabs foot, pulls him down.

If the bear remains in place, it's your turn to back off. If you can, loop around on the uphill side of the trail—you'll make yourself look bigger, and you'll get a better view of the bear. Now back up slowly until the bear is out of sight, or at least a quarter-mile (0.4 km) away. If possible, detour around any very thick, brushy areas, and stick to the most open terrain, where you don't have to keep wondering whether or not the bear is about to surprise you. If you need to keep going in the same direction, make a very wide detour, and try to remain upwind of the bear, so it has your scent and knows where you are.

IF A BLACK BEAR STANDS UP

Despite everything you've seen in the movies, this is not a sign of aggression; even though the bear will probably appear to be 7 feet (2.1 meter) tall, don't panic. Black bears stand up on two feet to use their super-sensitive noses to get a better sniff of things in their environment they're trying to identify.

◆ **Don't run or be aggressive.** Chances are the bear is only trying to figure out what you are, and decide if you're a threat.

◆ **Let the bear see you're a human** and mean no harm, by slowly waving your arms and continuing to talk in a firm monotone. Look at the bear, but avoid direct eye contact.

◆ **Don't turn your back on the bear.** Back away and be prepared to stop and hold your ground if backing away seems to irritate instead of calm the bear. Clacking teeth, popping noises, moaning, woofing or barking sounds are all vocal clues that mean the bear is as stressed out and uncomfortable with the situation as you are. They are not indications of aggressive intent or an imminent attack. Truly dangerous bears are eerily silent.

Beck's Bits

Bear grunts, woofs, moans and other sounds directed at humans mean "I'm not comfortable in this situation." These are not signs of aggression. The truly dangerous bear is silent.

| ## IF A BLACK BEAR CHARGES YOU

Sometimes a black bear will paw the ground, huff, puff, clack and snort, and run directly at you; this is often referred to as a bluff charge.

This is usually a loud message from the bear you've invaded its turf and need to leave, which you'd probably love to do if your feet weren't rooted firmly to the ground, and "don't run" wasn't echoing in your head.

The bear is treating you pretty much like it would treat another bear it considered a possible threat. With black bears, there is a very high probability the bear will screech to a halt a few feet from you, then turn around and run back. If this happens, be prepared; the bear may bluff charge as many as a half-dozen times before backing off, and giving you the chance to do the same.

No matter what happens, don't run. When the bear heads back to the starting line, try slowly backing off while waving your arms and talking in a firm monotone. If that appears to irritate the bear, stop, stand your ground and stay calm.

How Do You Know It's a Bluff Charge?

If a black bear keeps on coming and makes physical contact with you, it's not bluffing. Even in those rare instances when there is contact, a quick, aggressive response on your part will usually drive the bear off. So if you're engaged in a game of chicken with a bear, use your wait-and-see time wisely, and gather your wits, as well as anything you have at hand that can serve as a weapon or could be used to distract the bear.

If you have your bear spray handy, now is a good time to get it out and use it. Remember to flip off the safety and point it at the bear; this would be a bad time to inhale a lung-full of bear spray. Even if the bear just wants you to go away, bears are quick learners; a good dose of bear spray may teach it not to charge another hiker.

Great Smoky's Kim Delozier once went undercover to send a message to a bear that had learned if it charged hikers, they dropped their packs and ran off. He traded his park uniform for hiking gear and hit the trail. When the 260-pound bear spotted Delozier, it launched itself at the biologist in a blur of flying fur, clacking teeth and popping jaws. Much to the bear's surprise, Delozier practiced the advice he preaches and stood his ground. When no pack full of treats went flying through the air, a confused bear hit the brakes and slid to a stop at Delozier's feet.

IF A BLACK BEAR APPROACHES YOU

If a bear approaches on two legs, it's probably trying to get a better look at you. It may turn its head from side to side, all the better to see and smell you. Back away slowly, and try to make sure the bear has a way to retreat. Even though it's approaching you, it probably feels crowded, and wants you out of its space.

If you can back out of sight, keep moving, trying to stay uphill and keep the bear in sight. Then leave the area using your best brisk hiking pace, but don't run.

If backing off irritates the bear further, you are positive you're dealing with a black bear, and it's still approaching, try to chase it off—yell, throw rocks, bang any gear you have with you, blow your handy whistle or pocket air horn, or spray it with bear spray.

IF A BLACK BEAR FOLLOWS YOU

If a black bear follows you down a trail and you're in a national or provincial park, or somewhere else where bears are very used to humans, you are most likely dealing with a highly human food-conditioned bear that's learned people can be bullied into surrendering their packs or food bags.

In that case, your can try to convince the bear you're not an easy mark by calling its bluff. Stop moving, face the bear, yell at it, blow your whistle or air horn, throw rocks or sticks, and generally create the impression you won't be easy to mug, and getting your peanut butter sandwich won't be worth the effort.

If the bear steps up its aggression to the point where you're not comfortable trying to back it down, use anything you have with you to distract it—toss out objects one by one with the idea of getting the bear to stop and investigate them, and buy you time to get your head together, get your hands on anything you have that might serve as a weapon, and get ready to fight back. While it's investigating, you can try backing down the trail, keeping the bear

BEARANOIA

"I was giving a presentation to property managers when one guy says, 'Every bear in Aspen ought to be dead, before something happens to someone.' There are people who believe all bears are like the trained grizzlies they see on TV—big, vicious killing machines. Nothing could be farther from the truth."

KEVIN WRIGHT, COLORADO DISTRICT WILDLIFE MANAGER - ASPEN/SNOWMASS

in sight at all times, but don't turn your back on the bear, and of course, don't run.

WHEN BLACK BEARS ATTACK

The vast majority of black bear "attacks" result in injuries so minor people often don't seek medical attention, although they often make the evening news just the same. That's because even minor injuries are rare enough to be newsworthy, and the very idea of something as big and powerful as a bear hurting a human makes people very uneasy.

Most of the scrapes, cuts and nips inflicted by bears occur around developed campgrounds or other areas where bears have become human-food conditioned. When some bears get too comfortable with people they adopt a "your food is my food, your place is my place" attitude. Sometimes bears become so conditioned to the presence of people they linger by roadsides and picnic grounds in the hopes of getting a handout, and occasionally lose their patience and strike out at someone who tries to take back their bag of Cheetos or cuddle up for a picture. There are cases of people being seriously injured after trying to get overly familiar with bears that seem "tame."

When Black Bears Kill People

Steve Herrero is the world's leading expert on bear attacks. According to his most recent calculations, there are approximately 900,000 black bears in North America. Every year people have millions of interactions with black bears. Yet between 1900 and the summer of 2005 records reveal just fifty-seven people in North America were killed by black bears.

To put that in perspective, fifty people in the U.S. die every year from bee stings. In just nineteen years between 1979 and 1998, 300 Americans died after being attacked by domestic dogs. Man's best friend bites a staggering 4.7 million people a year—nearly a million of whom seek medical attention. Mosquitoes are the deadliest creatures in the world, carrying encephalitis, West Nile, Dengue fever and malaria—diseases that kill two million people a year worldwide. Of course the average person is probably a lot more likely to encounter a bee, dog or mosquito than a bear.

But there are no records of bear researchers or biologists—probably the people who spend the most time with black bears in the wild, often under circumstances that are trying for the bear—being severely injured or killed by a black bear. Yosemite National Park, where there are hundreds, or sometimes thousands, of bear incidents every year has recorded remarkably few injuries, and no fatalities due to black bears.

Statistically speaking, you have a better chance of winning the lottery than being killed by a black bear. But just as people who don't even play dream of winning the big jackpot, stepping off the concrete gives some people nightmares about something even more unlikely—being attacked and eaten by a powerful beast with sharp claws and big teeth.

I discovered you don't even have to spend time in the woods to be afraid of bears. A very intelligent woman I know quite well who lives far from bear country, and is by her own admission "not the woodsy type," confessed that one of her biggest fears is being attacked and eaten by a bear. We humans just don't like the idea that there are still things that go bump in the night that can rip us limb from limb if they want to.

Even though the number of people killed by black bears remains extremely low, it's been creeping up every decade over the past fifty years. According to Herrero, the most likely cause is the fact that ever-increasing numbers of people are camping, hiking, living and working in bear country.

The majority of fatal attacks to date have occurred in remote areas where bears seldom encounter people. At least two people have been killed by bears known to be habituated to human food, although food was not directly involved in the attacks. Herrero believes most

The less you know about bears, the more likely you are to be afraid of them.

of the remaining attacks appear to be cases where the bear had decided the person was prey.

Over half the people killed before 1980 were under the age of eighteen. Since then victims have ranged from loggers and forestry workers toiling alone in very remote stretches of Canada to an elderly woman alone in her cabin in New Mexico.

What makes a black bear decide humans are part of the food chain? Frankly, no one, not even Herrero, knows for certain, although male black bears are the perpetrators in most predaceous attacks. The behavior of an individual bear is dictated not only by bear biology, but by that bear's unique personality and traits, and influenced by everything it's experienced.

Murderers, rapists, child molesters and serial killers are unfortunately all part of the human race, yet few of us look at every stranger we meet as a potential Jack the Ripper or Ted Bundy. Luckily for us, the rare black bear that views humans as prey is a real anomaly; if bears wanted to attack and eat us, hundreds of people would end up on the ursine menu each year.

"It is mainly wild black bears found in rural or remote areas—where they have had relatively little association with people—that occasionally try to kill and eat a human being. The behavior must be exceedingly rare, since I have found so few records of it, given that the population of black bears in North America has probably never been less than half a million bears," explained Herrero in his best-selling book, *Bear Attacks: Their Causes and Avoidance*.

Even though the odds are more than a million to one the average person will encounter the exceptionally rare black bear that means you harm, it's only smart that you know how to recognize the behavior, and what to do in response.

"The black bear's intense motivation to feed on human foods and garbage has probably set up hundreds of thousands of situations that could have led to human injury, yet only a few did."
STEVE HERRERO

HOW TO RECOGNIZE PREDATORY BEHAVIOR

Statistically you may have a better chance of encountering a predatory black bear in a very remote area where it's unlikely bears see people on a frequent basis, but in 2004 a female black bear with her yearling attacked and killed a woman in heavily visited Great Smoky Mountains National Park, so it pays to know what you're doing, no matter where you're going.

If the bear seems to be circling you and is coming closer on each approach, is deliberately following you or openly approaching you on all fours with its ears forward, and is not exhibiting any of the signs of a nervous bear that just wants you to leave—huffing, teeth clacking, blowing, moaning—take the offensive, and do everything you can to drive the bear away. Don't turn your back on the bear, and don't run, unless you're 10 feet (3 meters) away from your cabin or vehicle.

Let the bear know you know it's there, and you're not afraid of it. Act like you believe you can take the bear with one hand tied behind your back. Make noise, make yourself look as big as possible, yell (don't scream or shriek), blow your whistle or air horn, get your hands on anything you're carrying that could be used as a weapon— rocks, pots and pans, trekking poles, knives, heavy flashlights. Convince the bear you're not going down without a fight.

If you're wearing a backpack or daypack, leave it on, unless using it to distract the bear for a few minutes will give you enough time to reach the safety of a sturdy building. In the event the bear attacks you, wearing your pack could provide some protection.

If you're carrying bear spray, and the bear is charging, fire when the bear is 40 to 50 feet (12 to 15 meters) away—that way the bear has to come through a highly irritating orange cloud to get to you. Genuine bear spray delivers a total of at least six one-second bursts, so you can keep spraying if the bear keeps coming. Don't panic and run if the bear initially keeps advancing; it takes a few of what will be some of the longest seconds of your life for bear spray to get into the lungs, especially if the bear is huffing and blowing air out instead of inhaling. See the next chapter for all the details on bear spray.

If the bear responds to your aggression by momentarily stopping or backing off, take the opportunity to do the same, always

"People are rarely chosen as prey. In most areas of British Columbia, large numbers of black bears have coexisted with people without serious injuries or conflicts."

STEVE HERRERO

Of note: When the study containing the above info was done in the late 1990s there were approximately 3.9 million people and an estimated 120,000 – 160,000 black bears in British Columbia.

keeping the bear in view. If you can get downwind so it's harder for the bear to track you, all the better; this is one case where you don't want the bear to know where you are. If this is truly a predatory approach, the bear may disappear for a while, and reappear later. Be very alert until you reach safety.

IF A BLACK BEAR MAKES CONTACT, FIGHT BACK

If you are physically attacked by a black bear that seems to think you're dinner, fight back any way you can. People have successfully defended themselves against a black bear with their bare hands. Use whatever is available; rocks, sticks, camera bags, backpacks, feet, fingernails, nail files, pocket knives (go for the eyes and nose.)

The oft-repeated advice to "PLAY DEAD" is based on deflecting a defensive grizzly bear attack—a sudden encounter at close quarters with a startled bear or a mother grizzly defending her cubs. Studies of black bear behavior have shown this to be a very bad tactic with the atypical black bear that actually attacks a person. Black bears are opportunistic feeders, and often feast on dead animals they find. Playing dead doesn't work with an attacking black bear.

> "During the 1960s and early 1970s I watched people hand-feed black bears along national park roadsides and at dumps. Black bears were sometimes made to stand on their hind legs and "dance" for small edible bits. I've seen people pet, poke and even shake hands with a black bear. The restraint that the powerful black bear normally displayed in these circumstances always amazed me."
>
> STEVE HERRERO

MOTHERS AND CUBS

Black bears will normally send their cubs up a tree if they sense danger; grizzly mothers will often charge. But every once in a great while a mother black bear will attack rather than retreat if she feels her cubs are in danger. If you're positive this is the case—say you've inadvertently stepped in between a mother and cubs, and she's attacking you—treat this as you would a defensive grizzly attack, and either lie on the ground spread eagled to make it harder for the bear to flip you over, or curl up in a ball with your hands laced behind your neck. In a defensive attack, the bear thinks you're a threat; so don't move or show any other signs of life while you count to at least five hundred.

Report all attacks to the nearest ranger, park staff, forest office, the sheriff or the police immediately. ❖

Quick Tips When Meeting A Black Bear

◆ **Don't Play Dead** This advice is predicated on grizzly bear attacks and behavior, not black bears. Except in the rarest of circumstances, playing dead doesn't work with an attacking black bear.

◆ **Don't Climb a Tree** Black bears—even adults—can climb a 100-foot (30-meter) tree in under a minute. If the bear is sufficiently interested in you, you'll have to fend off an aggressive bear in a tree.

◆ **Don't Run** Running triggers a common chase or prey response in bears, as well as most predators. Bears can run up to 35 mph (56 kph) over short distances. You can't outrun a bear.

◆ **Do Fire Your Bear Spray** If you have time to aim and fire your bear spray, this may be the easiest way to turn back or slow down an aggressive bear. The highly irritating spray does a real number on a bear's eyes, lungs and sensitive mucous membranes. For all about bear spray, see the next chapter.

◆ **Do Fight Back** People have successfully defended themselves against a black bear with their bare hands. Use whatever is handy; rocks, sticks, camera bags, backpacks, feet, fingernails, water bottles.

chapter 18

Ready, Aim, Bear Spray

Your Second Best Weapon in Bear Country

I magine a weapon weighing less than a pound that's as simple to fire as a can of spray paint, works at distances of up to 30 feet (9 meters), and is powerful enough to stop a charging bear in its tracks—without doing the bear any permanent damage.

That's what biologists, field officers and bear experts asked for when Bill Pounds set out to develop a non-lethal bear deterrent back in the mid-1980s.

The product he came up with was an ingenious and highly potent pepper-based spray with a unique, expanding-mist delivery system. Well-respected bear biologist Chuck Jonkel headed up the clinical and field testing as part of the University of Montana Border Grizzly Project. Over six years of clinical trials and field testing, bear spray proved to be even more effective than anyone had hoped, turning away a very high percentage of both black and grizzly bears in over 500 tests.

Today the original product Pounds developed is sold under the brand name Counter Assault. A canister is standard gear for many wildlife agencies, including the U.S. Forest Service, along with many seasoned hikers, backpackers, campers and people who work out in the woods.

HOW BEAR SPRAY WORKS

When you pull the trigger, a canister of genuine bear spray emits a loud whooshing sound and sprays out a foggy orange mist of capsaicin and related capsaicinoids—the active irritants in hot peppers.

Sometimes just the noise plus the sight of the strange orange cloud will send a bear off in the opposite direction. If the bear does keep approaching, once it enters the fog and inhales, misery follows. The potent capsaicins and related capsaicinoids inflame the eyes and lungs, making it difficult for the bear to see or breathe well. Think about what happens if you chop up a red-hot pepper and then accidentally inhale and rub your eyes. Now multiply that by one hundred. Rather than press on with aching lungs and streaming eyes, most bears back off or leave the area entirely.

You don't need to be an expert marksman to use bear spray; all you have to do is remember to take the safety off the trigger and spray a burst in the direction of the bear, aiming a little down from the head so the bear will be forced to travel through the widest possible cloud if it continues to approach.

Some people mistakenly think it's best to wait until the last possible moment to fire, but experts say that if the bear is charging, the best time to use bear spray is when it's between 40 to 50 feet (12 to 15 meters) away. The expanding cloud of spray should meet the speeding bear at about 25 or 30 feet (7.6 or 9 meters) from you, so when the bear travels through the mist it will experience the full effects of eyes, nose and lungs full of red hot pepper before it gets close enough to you to do any damage. If the bear is not charging, but instead is approaching slowly—as black bears often do—wait until the bear is about 30 feet (9 meters) away to spray.

If you surprise a bear at such close range there's not enough time for it to breathe in the spray before literally running into you, start spraying and keep spraying anyway. The spray may still affect the bear within the next few seconds, and cause it to back off, or lessen the severity or duration of the attack.

Bears are individuals, and every bear encounter is unique. Bear spray will not stop 100 percent of bears 100 percent of the time, but carrying and knowing how to use it can improve the odds you'll

Your best weapon in bear country is your brain. Bears are smart, but most people are smarter. Make sure you pack your brain full of useful information, and bring it with you.

be able to escape from an aggressive or defensive bear confrontation unharmed.

Carrying bear spray, or any weapon, isn't a license to leave your brains at home. There's no substitute for being bear smart, and doing everything you can to prevent a bear encounter in the first place.

PRACTICE MAKES PERFECT

Carry bear spray in an outside shoulder harness or hanging from your belt, day pack or back pack in a place where you can get your hands on it in seconds. The bear will not patiently stand around waiting for you to dig your bear spray out of the bottom of your pack.

A word of warning: the midst of a bear attack is not a good time to practice using your bear spray. Set up a target and fire off a half-second burst just to get the feel of it. Use something white, and you'll be able to see where the spray ended up, since it leaves an oily orange residue behind. Beck recommends marking off distances of 25 feet, 30 feet and 50 feet (7.6, 9 and 15 meters) so you can get a visual feeling for it while you're brain is actually working. If you fire your test burst and the spray comes out in a stream instead of a mist, you've been had. The product you've bought is probably generic pepper spray which uses water instead of the proper solvents and a poor quality oleoresin capsaicin. Carry your spray in a belt or shoulder holster where you can get your hands on it in seconds, not in your pack or your jacket pocket. I carry mine in a front holster that slips onto the belt of my day pack.

PEPPER SPRAY AND MACE AREN'T BEAR SPRAY

Genuine bear spray is expensive—$45 to $55 USD for a standard canister with enough spray for 6 to 10 seconds. The fact that most people who buy bear spray never need to use it plus the high retail price has tempted some less than reputable companies to illegally mislabel personal defense sprays and misrepresent them as bear spray.

Personal defense sprays and mace type sprays may work well on humans and canines, but tests have shown them to be much less effective on bears. They often use less potent ingredients and water, so instead of hanging in the air in a fine mist, particles quickly drop to the ground. If you ever have to use your bear spray, your life might depend on it doing what it's supposed to do. So take a few minutes to thoroughly read the label, and make sure you're buying an EPA-approved and registered bear spray.

BEAR SPRAY ISN'T BEAR REPELLENT

At $45 to $55 a can, most people won't be tempted to treat bear spray like insect repellent. But just in case you're thinking about blasting your tent or pack, there's some evidence that the powerful pepper scent the spray leaves behind may actually attract bears. There is absolutely no evidence that bears can smell bear spray in the can, or are attracted to the canister itself.

HOW TO RECOGNIZE REAL BEAR SPRAY

By law, only genuine bear spray can use the word bear in its label or instructions. If the product doesn't say "bear defense spray," or "bear deterrent spray," it's a safe bet it wasn't formulated and isn't approved for use on bears.

TRAVELING WITH BEAR SPRAY

You can't take bear spray on a commercial airline in either checked baggage or carry-on. You can ship product to yourself at your destination, or find local retailers by checking your brand's Web site. U.S. citizens are now allowed to cross the Canadian border with bear spray for their own personal use and protection, but not allowed to sell it or leave it behind in Canada. Generally, Canadians are allowed to bring bear spray into the U.S., and take it back with them when they return to Canada.

♦ Label should list an EPA registration number, the manufacturer's number and the state or province where the spray is produced.
♦ Active ingredients are capsaicin and related capsaicinoids.
♦ Active ingredients should be between 1 and 2 percent of the contents. Don't be fooled by a personal defense spray claiming 10 – 30 percent oleoresin capsicum—that's not the active ingredient, and is irrelevant; 1 – 2 percent capsaicin and capsaicinoids is the EPA mandated standard.

◆ Directions should include specific instructions for deterring bear attacks; these instructions are only allowed on genuine EPA-registered bear pepper spray

◆ Personal defense sprays, dog sprays and mace may be cheaper than genuine bear spray, but as is so often the case, you get what you pay for.

CAUTIONS

High winds, extreme cold or heat, heavy rain and dense cover can interfere with the spray. Bear spray can still be your most effective defense under these conditions, but be sure to read the label thoroughly so you understand how to make adjustments when conditions are less than ideal.

Don't store your bear spray in direct sunlight in a closed car, or near a heat source like a fire; extreme heat can expand the contents of the can and cause a loss of propellants. Extreme cold can affect performance; try to keep your spray from freezing.

Bear spray is only EPA approved for use on bears, because all the original testing was done on grizzly and black bears. Some agencies are reporting successful use on cougars and moose. Although it would most likely be highly effective, it's illegal to use bear spray on a person, even in a demonstration.

EPA BEAR PEPPER SPRAY GUIDELINES

Minimum Net Weight:	7.9 ounces / 225 grams
Capsaicin & Other Capsaicinoids	1% – 2%
Minimum Range	25 feet
Time of Continuous Spray	6 seconds minimum

WHERE'S THE SPRAY?

You can find genuine bear spray at sporting and outdoor stores, or order directly from manufacturers, including Counter Assault at *www.counterassault.com*. ❖

Vince Shute Wildlife Sanctuary, Minnesota

Lessons People Can Learn From Bears

On an abnormally cloudless, bugless Minnesota day in late August of 2005 I watched two roly-poly cubs of the year tussle with a much-abused pine cone while their mother alternated between eating sunflower seeds and looking on in what appeared to be amusement.

Suddenly a big male bear appeared, padding deliberately through the sun-splashed forest. With sharp cries of alarm the cubs fled up a tree in the time it took me to blink and turn my head. Their mother held her ground, making a humming sound low in her throat. The male sized up the situation, glanced up the tree where the cubs had sought refuge, and lowered his massive head. With barely a backwards look he melted off into the woods. With a few clucks the mother called her offspring back to earth, and the three of them moved off to paw through the nuts and berries spilling out of a hollow log.

I watched this little drama unfold from less than 25 feet (7.6 meters) away, leaning on the railing of the observation platform at the Vince Shute Wildlife Sanctuary in the remote Northwoods of Minnesota.

It was just one of many bear behavior lessons I learned in the two bear-filled days I spent at the Sanctuary. The bears and I were both in hyperphagia—the bears deep in their annual fall feeding frenzy, me in the final hyperactive work phase of getting this manuscript ready to go to the editor.

SARA TUTTLE

I watched an adult male throw himself into the creek and float with just his head sticking out, looking for all the world like a kid cannon-balling into the pool on a hot summer day. When he came out he shook himself like a dog, and seemed to enjoy the fact that his rump was covered in creek-bottom mud.

At one point there was a tremendous commotion in the bushes. I craned my neck trying to see what it was that had sent four adult bears scurrying up trees, but to my human eyes nothing appeared to be wrong.

"Bears are jumpy," explained Klari Lea, who along with her husband Bill, and Karen Hauserman, is one of the driving forces behind what must be one of the most unusual places in North America. "They don't like to be surprised. I once watched a bear bolt when a chipmunk brushed up against it." A few minutes later a rustling in the trees signaled their descent.

In another clearing a tiny brown fox-faced cub played with his much-larger brother. "He was very sick when his mother came in this spring. We didn't think he'd make it. If the little guy can get up to 30 pounds (14 kg) before winter, he'll have a good chance of surviving," Klari said.

Even the misfits of the bear world seem at peace here; I spy a three-legged bear that looks like a Buddha leaning back against a mound of aromatic cedar chips. I learn he's eight years old, and appeared for the first time as a two-year-old. No one knows how he lost his left front leg; he's always been that way.

"He doesn't seem to have any problems," says Klari. "In June he's quite the ladies' man."

The viewing platform at Vince Shute Wildlife Sanctuary.
© *Bill Lea*

I learn that if I'd arrived then, I might have actually been able to witness the seldom-seen spectacle of bears mating.

Come earlier in the spring and you can watch the mother bears break the family ties with their cubs from the previous year. "I've watched a mother literally throw a persistent yearling out of a tree in order to teach it to quit following her around. It's painful to watch, but the young bears have to learn how to live on their own," explains Klari.

I watch as an octogenarian bear wily enough to survive thirty hunting seasons limps into view, his rangy face scarred from battles long gone by. Beneath his scruffy mahogany coat he seems painfully thin. Klari tells me he's been coming since he was a very young bear, back when there was a real flesh-and-blood Vince Shute.

She suspects it will be his last fall; she only hopes he'll fatten up enough to den up for the winter and die peacefully in his sleep. He'd appeared just a few days before, traveling who knows how many miles with one massive arthritic paw curled up near his chest. Male bears in their prime stalked by, paying scant attention to him. Despite a drought-induced failure of much of the area's hazelnut crop, they didn't challenge him; here there was plenty of food to go around.

Occasionally the Sanctuary's resident dominant adult male swaggers out into the meadow and unceremoniously boots one of

© Tim Halvorson

the lesser males off a feeding station, just to prove he's still king of the woods. Males that seemed to be on more equal footing in the complex bear hierarchy challenged each other, with the one that's more submissive launching into the loudest vocalizations—a throaty humming that sounds like a cross between a revving motor and someone chanting nyah nyah nyah. Sometimes the challenged bear gives way; sometimes not. Occasionally the adult bears indulge in a little horseplay, poking, nuzzling and swatting each other in what looks like good-natured fun.

I blink a few times; it's hard to believe I'm standing on a platform watching upwards of sixty bears of all ages and sizes come and go. The big males favor the big meadow, where they can show off their bulk and see what's happening all around them. The mothers with cubs prefer the surrounding open forest. Adult females with no offspring to tend wander about, occasionally cub-sitting for their harried sisters. The subadults—the teenagers of the bear world—alternate between trying to stay out of everyone's way and testing the waters to see if they've grown up enough to come play with the big boys and girls.

In two short days at the Vince Shute Wildlife Sanctuary I witnessed dozens of different bear behaviors, heard all sorts of vocalizations and watched so many bears for so many hours I lost count.

I first read about the Sanctuary when I started researching this book. My husband and Bear Aware partner, Cory Phillips, obligingly stopped in to check it out on his way to his annual spring walleye fest with brother, Curt, in Canada; for days after he came home he talked not of the fish he'd caught but of the bears he'd seen. He was determined to get me up there one way or the other.

"If everyone in America could spend a day at Vince Shute, we wouldn't have any more bear problems," he told me. His enthusiasm and my own curiosity won out over my reluctance to visit a place I firmly believed shouldn't even exist. In my mind, there was no possible justification for committing the mortal sin of feeding bears.

Then I went to Minnesota, and like so many bear people before me, changed my heart if not my mind. The opportunity to watch bears going about the business of being bears is an almost irresistible lure.

"My head tells me it's wrong, but my heart tells me it's right," said one well-known bear biologist who prefers to remain unnamed, undoubtedly imagining the professional disdain he'd be viewed with for saying something positive about a place that provides food for wild bears.

Vince Shute was a logger who ran a camp on eighty or so acres in northern Minnesota, where bears and wolves still outnumber people. It's 10 miles (16 km) or so from the tiny town of Orr, 60 miles (96 km) as the bear rambles to the Canadian border.

Vince Shute and Klari Lea. © *Bill Lea*

Like a lot of loggers, Vince dealt with the bears that raided his dump by shooting them on sight. Then, in the early 1970s, he decided to try getting along with his furry neighbors instead. Vince opted for keeping the peace by giving the bears what they came looking for: food. Word spread in the ursine population, and the more food Vince put out, the more bears showed up. Soon he was naming the bears and hand feeding them and letting people come and dangle Twinkies and jelly donuts. He didn't charge admission; people just showed up to ogle and take pictures and go away and tell their friends.

By the early 1990s an aging Vince was wondering what was going to happen to his bears when he was gone when a forester with the U.S. Forest Service in North Carolina and his wife were led to Vince Shute by their friend and wildlife biologist Carl Racchini. Bill and Klari Lea were appalled at the fact that Vince was feeding bears, and horrified at the junk he was feeding them. Gradually they convinced Vince it was in the bears' best interests for him to make some changes.

The pair talked to a lot of bear experts, and soon came to realize the Sanctuary had become an important seasonal food source for many bears. Even the bear biologists they consulted were unsure what would happen to the bears if they were suddenly cut off. So instead they switched from junk food to fruits, nuts, seeds and grains that closely mimic a bear's natural diet.

Today a small army of seasonal volunteers who come from as far away as Scotland and Great Britain dispense the food with big grain scoops from bright green buckets. The public no longer mingles with the bears; instead, upwards of 23,000 bear watchers each season ooh and aahh nightly from a viewing platform.

Despite having millions of calories stored in buildings that are far from fortresses, they've never had a bear break in. Visitors park in a remote lot; a shuttle bus delivers them right to the steps of the viewing platform.

Upwards of a hundred individual bears utilize the sanctuary each year, but few take up permanent residence, even though they could clearly sit on their ever-expanding behinds and eat from spring melt to den up. Many bears appear for just a week or two in the spring

© Bill Lea

© Tim Halvorson

before green up and again as fall draws closer and bears enter hyperphagia—the two most critical times for bears in terms of finding food. During years when the natural forage is good, the sanctuary hosts fewer bears, and they arrive later in the season. In years when natural forage is scarce, they come earlier and stay longer—but they continue to eat whatever natural foods are available, and often disappear back into the forest for weeks at a time.

The food at the sanctuary is dispersed throughout a wide circle that has a big open meadow as its center spoke. Feeding areas are hollowed out logs, big slabs of rock and fat upright stumps; food is mixed up into a sort of bear granola and generously dispensed by a tireless staff of volunteers all day long, in order to make sure the bears don't feel any need to get competitive or possessive. Peaceful bear coexistence allows outsiders like the very young, the very old, and the injured to join the

group—providing an unmatched opportunity to observe seldom-seen bear behaviors.

But when the buses roll up to the stairs of the viewing platform and disgorge as many as five hundred tourists on a busy summer evening, the message delivered by the staff is always the same: "We're managing an existing situation as best we can for both people and bears. Please don't leave here thinking it's okay to feed bears." The captive audience is then treated to a lively talk on bear biology and behavior, rounded off with a detailed explanation of why attracting and feeding bears is bad for people and bears.

I had doubts this mixed message would be understood, but none of the visitors I talked to seemed inclined to rush home and put out a bear-feeder, even when I tried to trick them into admitting they thought it would be cool. Most of them seemed awed by the presence of so many bears. Wide-eyed children asked dozens of questions about bear behavior while their parents snapped dozens of photos.

No one would set out to create a place like Vince Shute today. But in this generally remote area of the Northwoods, where there are few people in bear-roaming range and plenty of wild open spaces, there seems to have been remarkably few negative consequences for bears or people.

Vince started feeding bears back in the early 1970s, but since donut-dangling visitors were banned from the meadow in the mid-

'90s, there have been no human injuries. Vince knew almost all the bears by name, and the staff has records and photos that in some cases go back thirty years detailing individual bears' behavior. The high return rate for their bears would indicate that they're not being taken by hunters, or becoming nuisance bears elsewhere.

Apparently the Sanctuary is something of a dirty little secret with some bear biologists— there are photos in their scrapbooks taken by some of the best bear brains in the field who've come to visit not once, but several times, but only a few graduate students have gone on record to say the sanctuary is probably the best place in North America to observe black bear behavior.

After years of letting the public in for free, the Sanctuary has finally started charging a modest admission fee to help pay for the $30,000-plus worth of natural foods they buy every season to supplement the fruits, grains and seeds they receive as donations. They'd like to be able to offer graduate students a competitive stipend, expand their visitor's center and put in an amphitheater. They long for a few modern cabins to host visiting biologists who'd like to observe the bears for several days or weeks at a time, and dream of solar power and running water.

They're always looking for volunteers and donated supplies and funds, and hope someday the professional bear community will recognize them as an unmatched place to observe bear behavior. They welcome photographers, writers, researchers, biologists and other students of bears with open arms. ❖

The author, Linda Masterson at the sanctuary.

VINCE SHUTE WILDLIFE SANCTUARY
Open Memorial Day to Labor Day,
5 p.m. to dusk; closed Mondays.
$5 admission fee for 18 and older; senior discount.
www.americanbear.org
bears@rangenet.com   218-757-0172

chapter 19

The One-Minute Guide to Grizzlies
Understanding the Differences Between Grizzlies & Black Bears

Humans have been having problems coexisting with this powerful bear since Lewis and Clark headed west. An estimated 100,000 grizzly bears once roamed over most of western North America, but today *Ursus arctos* is on the endangered species list in the lower 48 United States, with a total population of somewhere between 800 and 1,000 bears, concentrated in the areas around Glacier and Yellowstone National Parks. Tiny populations also survive in northern Idaho, western Montana and the North Cascades in upper Washington state.

About 30,000 grizzly/brown bears live in Alaska, where the population is healthy and stable enough for the great bears to be classified as a big game species. Another 20,000 – 25,000 grizzlies live in Canada, with over half of the population in British Columbia and the Northwest Territories.

If you're anywhere else in the lower 48 states or eastern Canada, any bears you encounter will be black bears, even if they're very big or very brown. If you live in grizzly country, you're probably already well aware of your big furry neighbors. If you're a newcomer or just visiting, all the same rules about stashing your trash and removing attractants apply equally to grizzly country.

If you're visiting grizzly country, it really pays to know your bears, because the rules of close encounters are different. Grizzly

GRIZZLY BEAR RANGE OUTSIDE OF ALASKA

Small populations of grizzly bears occupy small pockets of land in the lower 48, and are found in greater numbers in parts of Canada and Alaska. *Map Source: www.fs.fed.us/rl/wildlife/igbc/*

bears have shorter fuses than black bears, and are biologically wired to respond to threats and "danger" by fighting back.

HIKING IN GRIZZLY COUNTRY

While many tips are the same, there are some important differences between how black bears and grizzlies relate and react to humans. If you're hiking in grizzly country, make sure you know the latest guidelines and local conditions before you hit the trail.

We treat all bears with the utmost respect. In grizzly country we never ignore trail closures, regularly make noise, and avoid hiking in dense brush where we might surprise a bear.

If you're on a trail that suddenly narrows so much you need to crawl through, you are probably on a bear trail, not a people trail. These grizzly "mazes" are common in grizzly country. Your best bet is to leave the maze to the bears, and hike someplace else.

Grizzly bears seldom attack unprovoked, but grizzlies can be aggravated by behavior that most black bears suffer without retaliating. Most grizzly attacks result from sudden encounters, particularly getting between a mother bear and her cubs, or disturbing a bear defending a food cache. Grizzlies are enormously strong and powerful; even a quick "love tap" meant to tell you to go away can send you to the emergency room.

Most serious grizzly bear injuries result from people being in the wrong place at the wrong time, and surprising a bear at close range, or coming between a bear and a food source or a protective mother grizzly and her cubs.

If you get between a momma grizzly and her cubs, her natural instinct as a good mother is to defend her offspring from what she perceives as danger. This is known as a defensive attack; under those circumstances experts recommend you "play dead," as generally once the mother bear neutralizes the "threat" you pose, she'll go away and leave you alone. Some bears think you need more neutralizing than others, but most eventually back off if you remain absolutely still. Don't move a muscle if you can still hear the grizzly bear in the area; wait at least fifteen minutes before you get up.

Grizzly bears sometimes back off from someone they've mauled, but stay in the area and keep an eye on them. If the person moves

A human mom who killed an intruder she thought was trying to hurt her children would get a medal. A grizzly that hurts a human while defending her cubs usually gets the death sentence. If you're in grizzly country, adopt bear-smart habits, and do your part to avoid conflicts with these great bears.

before the grizzly is satisfied they're no longer a threat, the bear may attack again. Audio evidence from the scene indicates that moving prematurely may have triggered a final and fatal second attack on controversial grizzly-hugger Tim Treadwell, who was killed in Alaska's Katmai National Park in 2003.

Grizzly bears are very defensive of carcasses. If you're in grizzly country and come across a big mound of twigs and leaves with body parts peeking out, leave the area immediately, and remain on high alert. Keep an eye out for a climbable tree; unlike black bears, adult grizzlies seldom climb up into the treetops. This same advice applies to gut piles in hunting season.

Grizzlies really don't like to be crowded. It is not safe to try to creep up on a grizzly to get a better look or a better picture. More than one photographer's final close-up photo has been of a charging grizzly.

CAMPING IN GRIZZLY COUNTRY

Never sleep under the stars in grizzly country; Steve Herrero's research shows that people in sleeping bags on the ground are more likely to be "explored" by a passing bear, and also more likely to be injured or killed.

If your campsite shows obvious signs of recent bear activity, or

A black bear.
National Park Service

A grizzly bear.
© Chuck Bartlebaugh, Center for Wildlife Information

there's trash, garbage and bear scat, leave the area and find another camp site as far away as possible.

Take all the same precautions about storing food, etc. that you'd take in black bear country. If you're camping in an area with high grizzly activity, consider using a portable solar electric fence; there are now models available that weigh less than 5 pounds (2.3 kg).

HOW CAN YOU TELL A GRIZZLY BEAR FROM A BLACK BEAR?

Size and color can be confusing, as plenty of black bears are brown, and a large black bear can easily be the size of a small grizzly. Take a good look at the illustrations below and you'll see there are several points of difference between the two species. ❖

BLACK BEAR

GRIZZLY BEAR

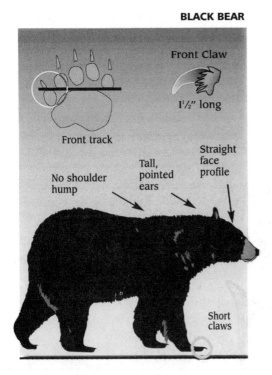

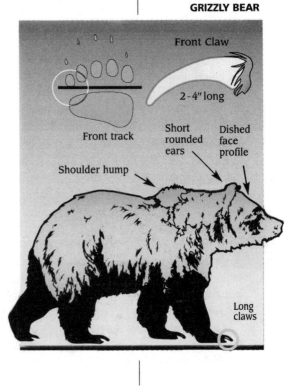

Courtesy of the Center for Wildlife Information

Acknowledgments

I wish I had room to personally thank every one of the hundreds of people who helped me bring this book to life.

Thanks don't begin to cover the debt owed Colorado Division of Wildlife's internationally recognized former bear biologist Tom Beck, who spent untold hours hunched over his computer, dubbed "The Beast," dispensing with wit, wisdom and insight information that only a professional with a couple of decades of experience and a lifetime of passion for his work could impart. Beck reviewed and commented on every chapter, and made *Living with Bears* a much better book. Thanks also to Sandy Rost, for cheerfully letting me take up way too much of her husband's time.

Steve Herrero, the world's leading authority on bear encounters and attacks, talked with me at length, freely shared unpublished or hard to come by information, and reviewed and helped me perfect the chapters on encounters, attacks and human and bear behavior.

Chuck Bartlebaugh at the Center for Wildlife Information urged me to fine-tune the bear spray chapter more times than I care to remember, because he believed this book could make a real difference, and I had to "get it exactly right." He also provided invaluable information, stories, advice and encouragement.

Patti Sowka at the Living with Wildlife Foundation was not only a deep well of practical information but a cheerful and enthusiastic supporter who consistently went above and beyond in her efforts to help me any way she could.

Thanks to many at the Colorado Division of Wildlife, starting Lisa Evans, who created our Bear Aware Program, and volunteer coordinator Danielle Hosler. Thanks also to mammals biologist Jerry Apker, librarian Jackie Boss, and many District Wildlife Managers, especially our Bear Aware partner Aimee Ryel, and Kevin Wright, Jim Jackson, Rick Spowart, and former DWM Sharlene Haeger. Many volunteers provided stories and photos, including Jim Tiffin, Gail Marshall and Jim Boyd.

Sylvia Dolson, the woman behind Canada's Be Bear Smart Society and a driving force in British Columbia's Bear Smart Community Program, offered a wealth of information and was an exacting reviewer.

Ann Bryant, who founded the BEAR League, offered reams of practical information, a candid look at some of the issues communities must deal with if they're going to make room for bears, and unflagging passion and enthusiasm.

Snowmass animal control officers Laurie Smith and Tina White, and DWM Kevin Wright made time during a beary busy summer to do whatever they could to help both book and bears, and offered up the kind of practical advice that comes from long experience.

Sean Matthews of the Wildlife Conservation Society provided thoughtful comments, thorough reviews and lots of help on the

Yosemite chapter. Thanks also to Yosemite's Adrienne Freeman and Jack Hopkins.

In the Smokies, bear biologist Bill Stiver proved an invaluable resource; his experience provided perspective into the evolution of their highly successful bear program. David Brandenburg gave me an inside look at a community on its way to becoming a much safer place for bears and people.

North Cascades' bear biologist Anne Braaten is an eloquent voice for new ways of understanding bears and dealing with human-bear conflicts. Thanks also to biologist Rocky Spencer and his Karelian Bear Dog Mishka. In Florida NFS biologist Carrie Sekarek was a veritable bear network of information, and also connected me to many others throughout the state joined together to help the bears.

Bryan Peterson of Bear Smart Durango is a great example of how one person's commitment and dedication can change a community for the better. Mike Sibio, Mary Beth Connors and the staff at Hemlock Farms show how the right attitude and ongoing education can help a large community successfully coexist with a sizeable bear population for over thirty years.

Wind River Bear Institute's Carrie Hunt was so busy handling real bear "problems" I am amazed she made time for my theoretical ones. Thanks too to her overworked office staff, especially Frank McKinney.

The Vince Shute Wildlife Sanctuary has a special place in my heart. Director Klari Lea is both an amazing woman and a wellspring of information. Tim Halvorson and the Sanctuary staff and volunteers made us welcome and shared everything from suppers to stories.

I would have had a much harder time uncovering people and places to feature in Beary Smart Solutions without Cornell University's Meredith Gore. She is a shining example of an up and coming generation of bear biologists and scientists committed to understanding bear behavior and solving human-bear conflicts.

Thanks to all the photographers, amateur and professional, who freely shared their work. Special thanks to photographer Bill Lea, who provided the great cover shots, and helped perfect the chapter on photography. Big bear hugs for illustrator Sara Tuttle, who created engaging beartoons that bring smiles. And special thanks to authors Wayne Lynch, Kevin Van Tighem, Rex Ewing and David Petersen, biologist Dave Bostick and the Humane Society's Margaret Baird for their help and support.

LaVonne Ewing is far more than a brilliant editor. Her unerring compass for what enhanced the message and what did not made this a much better book. And no matter how tired or discouraged I got, her unflagging enthusiasm kept me glued to my desk chair and hitting the keyboard.

There is no adequate way to thank my husband Cory Phillips, who cheered me on every page of the way, and literally took over virtually all of the tasks of everyday life so I could devote myself to THE BOOK without shorting my clients or volunteer obligations.

To everyone who offered resources, shared contacts or contributed to *Living with Bears* in any way, many, many thanks. I hope after reading the book, you agree the time and energy you spent was well worth it.

Black Bear Populations by State/Territory

State	Bear Population 1991-94*	Bear Population 2005	Trend	Status
Alabama	Fewer than 50	Fewer than 50	Stable	Game
Alaska	100,000	110,000	Stable to Increasing	Game
Arizona	2,500**	2,500**	Stable	Game
Arkansas	2,200	3,000	Increasing	Game
California	20,000	25,000 – 30,000	Increasing	Game
Colorado	8,000 – 12,000	8,000 – 12,000	Stable	Game
Connecticut	15 – 30	"several hundred"	Increasing	Unclassified
Florida	1,000 – 2,000	2,050 - 3,200***	Stable to Increasing	Threatened
Georgia	1,700	2,200	Increasing	Game
Idaho	20,000 – 25,000	20,000	Stable or decreasing	Game
Kentucky	Fewer than 200	Fewer than 200	Slightly increasing	Protected
Louisiana	200 – 400	500 - 600	Slightly increasing	Threatened
Maine	19,500 – 20,500	22,000 – 23,000	Increasing	Game
Maryland	175 – 200	500+	Increasing	Game
Massachusetts	700 – 750	2,000	Increasing	Game
Michigan	7,000 – 10,000	15,000 – 19,000	Stable	Game
Minnesota	15,000	27,000 – 30,000	Increasing	Game
Mississippi	Fewer than 50	25 - 50	Stable	Endangered
Missouri	50 – 130	150 - 300	Increasing	Rare
Montana	15,000 – 20,000	Update not available		Game
Nevada	300	150 - 300	Stable	Game
New Hampshire	3,500	4,500 – 5,000	Increasing	Game
New Jersey	275 – 325	1,777	Increasing	Game
New Mexico	3,000	5,000	Increasing	Game
New York	4,000 – 5,000	5,000 – 6,000	Stable	Game
North Carolina	6,100	11,000	Increasing	Game
Ohio	No Pop.	50 – 100	Increasing	Protected
Oklahoma	120	250	Increasing	Game
Oregon	25,000	25,000 – 30,000	Increasing	Game
Pennsylvania	7,500	16,000	Increasing	Game
Rhode Island	No Pop.	Under 50	Increasing	Protected
South Carolina	200	1,050 – 1,250	Increasing	Game
South Dakota	Unknown	Unknown	Unknown	Threatened
Tennessee	750 – 1,500	1,000 – 1,500	Stable	Game

continued

State	Bear Population 1991-94*	Bear Population 2005	Trend	Status
Texas	50	Unknown	Increasing	Threatened
Utah	800 – 1,000	1,000 –2,500	Stable to Increasing	Game
Vermont	2,300	3,800 – 4,200	Increasing	Game
Virginia	3,000 – 3,500	7,000 – 8,000	Increasing	Game
Washington	27,000 – 30,000	25,000 – 30,000	Stable	Game
West Virginia	3,500	10,000 – 12,000	Increasing	
Wisconsin	6,200	14,000	Increasing	Game
Wyoming	Unknown	2,500 – 4,500		Game

As of spring 2006, Delaware, Illinois, Indiana, Iowa, Kansas, North and South Dakota, Nebraska and Hawaii report no known populations of black bears.

CANADIAN PROVINCE

Alberta	39,600	49,000	Stable	Game
British Columbia	121,600	120,000 – 160,000	Stable	Game
Manitoba	25,000	30,000	Stable to Increasing	Game
New Brunswick	Unknown	12,000 – 13,000	Stable	Game
Newfoundland	6,000 – 10,000	6,000 – 10,000	Stable	Game
Northwest Territories	5,000+	5,000+****	Unknown	Game
Nova Scotia	3,000	8,000	Stable	Game
Ontario	65,000 – 75,000	75,000 – 100,000	Stable to Increasing	
Quebec	60,000	60,000	Stable to Decreasing	Game
Saskatchewan	24,000	24,000	Increasing	Game
Yukon	10,000	10,000	Stable	Game

Bears are not easy to count and don't fill out census forms; biologists caution that all methods of estimating populations are inexact, and numbers are subject to a sizable plus or minus. Current U.S. information based on published reports from agencies as well as current unpublished updates provided by agencies and/or bear or mammal biologists and researchers. Some states are in the midst of DNA or other monitoring studies and were unable to provide updates.

Particularly east of the Rockies, bear ranges and sometimes populations are expanding in many areas and states that ten years ago had no resident bears now report small populations, or regularly report sightings.

Current Canadian information provided by Parks Canada, including the *December 1998 Status Report on the American Black Bear in Canada* by Norman Barichello and data provided by Steve Herrero in 2005.

* U.S. and Canadian numbers from 1995 are based on the research report "Black Bears in North America" by Michael R. Vaughan, National Biological Service, and Michael R. Pelton, University of Tennessee, 1994.

** Arizona estimate is based on actual habitat carrying capacity rather than population estimate.

*** Bear habitat in Florida is currently fragmented, and population trends vary by habitat. Small populations in isolated areas may be at risk.

**** Status report indicates size and trend unknown; 5,000 is a guesstimate cited in McCracken et al., 1995.

Bear Resources

Center for Wildlife Information
www.bebearaware.org
The CWI is a non-profit that's recognized as a national leader in teaching people how to live responsibly and safely with wildlife, especially bears. The Center develops and distributes a wealth of factual, unbiased educational materials to local, state, national and provincial wildlife management agencies, outdoor educators, teachers, environmental groups, hunting, fishing, outfitters and guides organizations and youth organizations focused on encouraging safe and responsible hiking, camping, hunting and living in bear country, and safely viewing and photographing wildlife. Authors of the Be Bear Aware and Wildlife Stewardship campaigns in partnership with state and federal wildlife and land management agencies and associations. Offers "Train the Trainer" workshops and hands-on education. Extensive work with grizzly as well as black bears. Assists the public, as well as organizations, agencies and municipalities. Visit the Web site for details.

National Bear Conservation, Education & Wildlife Stewardship Program
bearinfo@qwest.net
> General H. Norman Schwarzkopf,
>   National Spokesman
> Chuck Bartlebaugh, Executive Director
> PO Box 8289
> Missoula, Montana 59807

Living with Wildlife Foundation
Helping People and Wildlife Coexist
www.lwwf.org
A non-profit focused on providing the latest information on products and techniques that can be used to prevent or deal with human-wildlife conflicts. Developed and manages the Bear Resistant Products Testing Program. Produces a series of comprehensive resource guides that are the yellow pages of products and sources for bear-safe recreating, refuse management, electric fencing and bear behavior modification tools and techniques. Guides available for download from the Web site for a small fee, or on CD. Also lots of free info on the site. Guides also cover wolves and mountain lions. All guides were produced in cooperation with Montana Fish, Wildlife & Parks' Living with Predators Project (Region 2, Missoula, Montana)
> Patti Sowka, Executive Director
> PO Box 1152
> Condon, Montana 59826
> 406-754-0010
> Email: patti@lwwf.org

Available Guides
Recreating in Bear, Wolf and Mountain Lion Country Guide covers products and techniques which can be used while recreating in wild areas. Information about various types of bear-resistant backpacking containers for food and garbage storage, techniques for hanging your gear in the back country, portable electric fencing, outfitters' panniers, and a host of other information is included in this guide. $10 USD

Techniques and Refuse Management Options for Residential Areas, Campgrounds, and Group-Use Facilities covers bear-resistant containers and other products and methods for securing and storing garbage, livestock feed, pet food and other attractants. The guide also contains information on methods for deterring predators from your property, including information about electric fencing, information on ways to scare predators from your property, information on bear-resistant refuse and recycling centers, and information on ways to reduce the volume of garbage that you generate and therefore have to secure. $20 USD

Electric Fencing Guide contains information on electric fencing designs that can be used to help deter predators including bears, mountain lions and wolves. $10 USD

For Wildlife Professionals
Predator Behavior and Modification Tools contains information for wildlife professionals who deal with predator conflicts. The guide contains information on tools and methods for deterring predators, as well as for trapping and aversively conditioning predators when necessary. Wildlife professionals interested in this guide should contact Patti Sowka at 406-754-0010 or patti@lwwf.org $15 USD

International Association for Bear Research and Management
www.bearbiology.com
Covers all species of bears worldwide. Hosts national and international conferences. Publishes *Ursus*, the professional journal for bear and bear management issues. Back issues available on the Web site.

The Get Bear Smart Society
www.bearsmart.com
The beautifully organized Web site for this Canadian non-profit may be the most comprehensive and in-depth source of information about bears and bear management issues available on the Web. Also offers educational and promotional materials you can download.

Get Bear Smart Society
204-3300 Ptarmigan Place
Whistler, B.C. V0N 1B3 Canada
Phone: 604-05-4209
Fax: 604-935-4009
Email: info@bearsmart.com

Bear Smart Community Program – British Columbia, Canada
http://wlapwww.gov.bc.ca/wld/bearsmart/bearsmintro.html
The Bear Smart Community program was designed by the Ministry of Water, Land and Air Protection in partnership with the British Columbia Conservation Foundation and the Union of British Columbia Municipalities. The goal is to address the root causes of bear/human conflicts, and reduce the risks to human safety and private property, as well as the number of bears that have to be destroyed each year. It is a voluntary, preventative conservation program that encourages communities, businesses and individuals to work together. This program is based on a series of criteria that communities must achieve in order to be recognized as being "Bear Smart." Criteria, case histories, brochures, information and more available on the Web site.

The Lake Tahoe BEAR League
www.savebears.org
One of the largest citizen/volunteer bear organizations; comprehensive Web site with bear news from California and Nevada. Comprehensive community bear ordinance available for download.

Wind River Bear Institute
www.beardogs.org
Bear shepherding using Karelian Bear Dogs. Works with individuals, agencies and communities in the U.S., Canada and internationally to peacefully resolve human-bear conflicts. Offers seminars, training and workshops. Headquartered in Montana. See page 141 for more information.
    Carrie Hunt, Director
    Email: windriver@beardogs.org

Karelian Bear Shepherding Institute of Canada
Closely associated with Wind River Bear Institute. Actively working in Alberta.
    Jay Honeyman, Director
    Email: kbsic@telus.net

Bear Smart Durango
www.bearsmartdurango.org
This Colorado-based organization has an excellent and informative Web site, with many resources.

Sierra Interagency Black Bear Group
www.sierrawildbear.gov
Brought to you by wildlife biologists and wilderness managers from the parks and forests of the Sierra Nevada.

Black Bear Conservation Committee
www.bbcc.org
Dedicated to restoring the Louisiana Black Bear.

The Appalachian Bear Center
www.appbears.org
Outside Great Smoky Mountains National Park. Rehabs orphaned or injured black bears and returns to the wild.

Bears in British Columbia
www.bearsinbc.com

Keep Me Wild
California Department of Fish & Game
www.keepmewild.com

The American Bear Association
www.americanbear.org
Website hosted by the Vince Shute Wildlife Sanctuary. Extensive information about bear biology and behavior.

The Vince Shute Wildlife Sanctuary
www.americanbear.org
Safely observe and photograph wild bears from Memorial Day through Labor Day; near Orr, Minnesota. Welcomes visitors. Special accommodations for bear professionals and photographers. Volunteer Opportunities. Accepts donations of appropriate food and supplies. See page 223.

Government Agencies

Search note: When visiting U.S. federal or state agencies or Canadian agencies not solely focused on bears, if you don't find bears on the home page, type "bears" or "black bears" into the site search engine.

U.S. National Parks
www.nps.gov

U.S. Fish & Wildlife Services
www.fws.gov

U.S.D.A. APHIS
Animal Damage Prevention and Control
www.aphis.USDA.gov/ws

State Agencies
www.aphis.usda.gov/ws/statereportindex.html

U.S. Forest Service
www.fs.fed.us
Search: Watchable Wildlife+black bear

U.S. STATE WILDLIFE MANAGEMENT AGENCIES
* indicates easy-to-find bear info

Alabama Department of Conservation and Natural Resources
www.dcnr.state.al.us.

Alaska* Department of Fish and Game
Division of Wildlife Conservation
www.wildlife.alaska.gov

Arizona* Game and Fish
www.azgfd.gov

Arkansas* Game and Fish
www.agfc.state.ar.us

Colorado* Division of Wildlife
www.wildlife.state.co.us

Connecticut* Department of Environmental Protection, Wildlife Division
www.dep.state.ct.us/burnatr/wildlife/

Delaware Division of Fish and Wildlife
www.dnrec.state.de.us/fw

Florida* Fish and Wildlife Conservation Commission
www.floridaconservation.org/bear

Georgia Department of Natural Resources
www.georgiawildlife.com

Idaho Fish and Game
www.fishandgame.idaho.gov

Illinois Department of Natural Resources
www.dnr.state.il.us

Indiana DNR – Division of Fish and Wildlife
www.in.gov/dnr/fishwild

Iowa Department of Natural Resources
www.iowadnr.com

Kansas Department of Wildlife and Parks
www.kdwp.state.ks.us

Kentucky* Fish and Wildlife
www.fw.ky.gov

Louisiana Department of Wildlife and Fisheries
www.wlf.state.la.us

Maine* Department of Inland Fisheries and Wildlife
www.state.me.us/ifw

Maryland* Department of Natural Resources
www.dnr.state.md.us/wildlife

Massachusetts* Division of Fisheries and Wildlife
www.mass.gov/dfwele/dfw

Michigan* Department of Natural Resources
www.michigan.gov/dnr

Minnesota* Department of Natural Resources
www.dnr.state.mn.us

Mississippi Wildlife, Fisheries and Parks
www.mdwfp.com

Missouri* Department of Conservation
www.conservation.state.mo.us

Montana* Fish, Wildlife and Parks
www.fwp.state.mt.us

Nebraska* Game and Parks Commission
www.ngpc.state.ne.us/wildlife/blackbear.asp

Nevada* Department of Wildlife
www.ndow.org

New Hampshire* Fish and Game
www.wildlife.state.nh.us

New Jersey* Division of Fish and Wildlife
www.state.nj.us/dep/fgw

New Mexico Game and Fish
www.wildlife.state.nm.us

New York* Department of Environmental Conservation
www.dec.state.ny.us

North Carolina* Wildlife Resources Commission
www.ncwildlife.org

Ohio* Department of Natural Resources
www.dnr.ohio.gov/wildlife

Oklahoma Department of Wildlife Conservation
www.wildlifedepartment.com

Oregon* Department of Fish & Wildlife
www.dfw.state.or.us

Pennsylvania* Game Commission State Wildlife Management Agency
www.dcnr.state.pa.us/
Good info if you search for *bears*

South Carolina* Department of Natural Resources
www.dnr.sc.gov

Tennessee Wildlife Resources Agency
www.state.tn.us/twra

Texas* Parks & Wildlife
www.tpwd.state.tx.us

Utah* Division of Wildlife Resources
www.wildlife.utah.gov

Virginia* Department of Fish and Game
www.dgif.virginia.gov

Washington* Dept. of Fish and Wildlife
www.wdfw.wa.gov
link to bear home page:
www.wdfw.wa.gov/wllm/game/blkbear/bl kbear.html

West Virginia* Department of Natural Resources
www.wvdnr.gov

Wisconsin Department of Natural Resources
www.dnr.wi.gov/org

Wyoming Game & Fish
www.gf.state.wy.us
note: focused on grizzly bears

CANADIAN AGENCIES

Canadian Wildlife Service
www.cws-scf.ec.gc.ca
grizzly, polar & black bears

Canadian Wildlife Federation
www.cwf-fcf.org

Parks Canada
www.pc.gc.ca

British Columbia Ministry of the Environment
www.gov.bc.ca

Alberta
www.gov.ab.ca

Saskatchewan
www.se.gov.sk.ca/fishwild

Manitoba
www.gov.mb.ca/conservation/wildlife

Ontario
www.mnr.gov.on.ca

Ontario Bear Wise
www.bears.mnr.gov.on.ca

Quebec
www.mrnf.gov.gc.ca

Nova Scotia
www.gov.ns.ca/natr/wildlife

Newfoundland & Labrador
www.env.gov.nl.ca/env/wildlife

Northwest Territories
www.nwtwildlife.rwed.gov.nt.ca

Yukon
www.environmentyukon.gov.yk.ca

Wildlife Education & Information

Colorado State University
www.coopext.colostate.edu/wildlife/bears.html
Cooperative Extension Office has a wide variety of brochures about agriculture, horticulture, livestock and beekeeping.

Cornell University Cooperative Extension Office
www.cce.cornell.edu
Research and informational brochures

The Humane Society of the United States
www.hsus.org

National Audubon Society
www.audubon.org

National Wildlife Federation
www.nwf.org

Managing Bear Damage to Beehives
www.ext.colostate.edu/pubs/natres/06519.html
An excellent publication from Colorado. Also search your state or provincial Web site.

Wildlife Conservation Society
www.wcs.org

Wildlife Management
www.wildlifemanagment.info
Web site created by David Brandenburg, bear biologist and former bear warden for Gatlinburg, TN. A wealth of information about a large number of species, including bears.

Deterrents

BEAR SPRAY
Counter Assault Bear Spray
www.counterassault.com

LIVING WITH WILDLIFE GUIDES
(see pages 238-239 for more details)
www.lwwf.org
◆ *Recreating in Bear, Wolf and Mountain Lion Country Guide* $10 USD
◆ *Techniques and Refuse Management Options for Residential Areas, Campgrounds, and Group-Use Facilities* $20 USD
◆ *Electric Fencing Guide* $10 USD
◆ *Predator Behavior and Modification Tools (for wildlife professionals)* $15 USD

ELECTRIC FENCING

State and Provincial Web sites
Search "electric fence" (diagrams and guidelines)

Living with Wildlife Foundation
Electric Fencing Guide $10 USD
www.lwwf.org

Kencove Farm Fence Inc.
www.kencove.com

Premier Sheep Catalog
www.premiersheep.com

Electric Fence Supplies and Accessories
www.electric-fence.com

Recommended Reading & Viewing

Videos & DVDs from the Safety in Bear Country Society

These videos are endorsed by the International Bear Association, and contain the consensus opinions of the leading experts on living, working and recreating in bear country. Steve Herrero consulted on their production. All three videos are available on VHF or DVD from Distribution Access 1-888-440-4640; *www.distributionaccess.com*

Living in Bear Country

Practical advice on ways people and communities can make simple adjustments that can reduce property damage and increase human safety. Covers living responsibly and safely with black bears and grizzly bears.

Staying Safe in Bear Country

Provides information designed to help reduce human injuries and property damage from black and grizzly bears throughout North America. Lots of information on bear behavior and advice on preventing bear encounters and attacks. Available in English and French.

Working in Bear Country

Designed to be a companion to *Staying Safe in Bear Country*, and provides in-depth information on field safety, including employee responsibilities, camp safety, including location and design, attractant management, bear detection and deterrent systems, firearms, bear response planning. Available in English and French.

Recommended Reading

The Great Bear Almanac, Gary Brown

Safe Travel in Bear Country, Gary Brown

Bear, Daniel J. Cox and Rebecca L. Grambo

The Yellowstone Handbook, Susan and Phil Frank

The Yosemite Handbook, Susan and Phil Frank

Black Bear Country, Michael Furtman

Bear Attacks: Their Causes and Avoidance, Stephen Herrero

Bears: Monarchs of the Northern Wilderness, Wayne Lynch

Mountain Bears, Wayne Lynch

Bear Aware, Bill Schneider

The Bears of Yellowstone, Paul Schullery

Backcountry Bear Basics, Dave Smith

Bears: An Altitude Super Guide, Kevin Van Tighem

Sample Community Ordinances

The Town of Snowmass Village, Colorado — Wildlife Protection Ordinance 1999

CHAPTER 7 ARTICLE VI Wildlife Protection

Sec. 7-151. Definitions.

The definitions and terms used in this Chapter, unless the context otherwise indicates, are herewith defined as follows:

1) *Wildlife* means any medium to large size non-domestic mammal indigenous to the Town of Snowmass Village including but not limited to, black bear, mule deer, elk, raccoon, coyote, beaver, skunk, badger, bobcat, mountain lion, porcupine and fox.

2) *Wildlife Resistant Refuse Container* means a fully enclosed metal container with a metal lid. The lid must have a latching mechanism, which prevents access to the contents by wildlife. Wildlife Resistant Refuse Containers must be approved by the Chief of Police and the Director of Public Works.

3) *Wildlife Resistant Dumpster Enclosure* means a fully enclosed structure consisting of four sides and a roof, with one side accommodating a door. The sides of the structure must extend to the ground and the door can not have more than a two-inch gap along the bottom. The door must have a latching device of sufficient design and strength to prevent access by wildlife. Ventilation openings shall be kept to a minimum and must be covered with a heavy gauge steel mesh or other material of sufficient strength to prevent access. Wildlife Resistant Dumpster Enclosures must be approved by the Chief of Police and the Director of Public Works.

4) *Special Event* means a large, outdoor gathering such as a concert, conference, festival or rodeo.

Sec. 7-152. Wildlife Resistant Refuse Containers or Enclosures Required.

Between the dates of April 15 and November 15, all refuse containers regardless of size, that receive refuse edible by bears or other wildlife shall be either an approved Wildlife Resistant Refuse Container, or a refuse container which is stored within a building, house, garage, or approved Wildlife Resistant Dumpster Enclosure.

Sec. 7-153. Maintenance and Operation of Wildlife Resistant Refuse Containers and Dumpster Enclosures.

a. Wildlife Resistant Refuse Containers and Dumpster Enclosures must be kept closed and secure when refuse is not being deposited.

b. If a container or enclosure is damaged, allowing access by bears or other wildlife, repairs must be made within 24 hours after written notification by the Police Department.

Sec. 7-154. Residential Refuse Disposal.

a. All containers that receive refuse edible by bears or other wildlife must be secured inside the home or garage. Residents unable to keep their refuse container inside the home or garage shall store their refuse in a Wildlife Resistant Refuse Container or Enclosure approved by the Police Department.

b. Residents with curbside pickup shall place their refuse containers at the curb only on the day of pickup. After pickup, the containers must be re-secured inside the home, garage or Wildlife Resistant Dumpster Enclosure by 6 p.m.

Sec. 7-155. Special Event Refuse Disposal.

Outdoor Special Event sites shall be kept free from the accumulation of refuse edible by wildlife. Refuse must be collected from the grounds at the close of each day's activities and shall be deposited in Wildlife Resistant Containers or Enclosures, or be removed to an appropriate disposal site.

Sec. 7-156. Construction Site Refuse Disposal.

All construction sites must have a designated container that receives refuse edible by bears and other wildlife. This container shall be either a Wildlife Resistant Refuse Container, or a container that is emptied at the end of each workday and then securely stored inside a trailer or building.

Sec. 7-157. Feeding of Wildlife.

a. No person shall knowingly leave or store any refuse, food product, pet food, grain or salt in a manner which would constitute a lure, attraction or enticement of wildlife.

b. Birdfeeders are allowed. However, between the dates of April 15th and November 15th, all feeders must be suspended on a cable or other device so that they are inaccessible to bears and the area below the feeders must be kept free from the accumulation of seed debris.

Sec. 7-158. Interference with Animal Control Officer.

No person shall interfere with, molest, hinder or impede the Animal Control Officer in the discharge of his or her duties as herein prescribed, or to violate any of the provisions of this Article. (Ord. 3-1992 §2)

Sec. 7-159. Enforcement.

a. Police or Animal Control Officers shall have the power to issue summonses and complaints for violations of this Article, as well as to issue warning notices to persons in violation of the provisions of this Article.

b. Police or Animal Control Officers shall have the right to enter any premises in the Town at reasonable hours to enforce the provisions of this Article.

Sec. 7-160. Compliance Required and Time Period.

Any dumpster enclosure or refuse container shall be brought into conformity with the wildlife protection provisions of this Article within a period not to exceed sixty days from the effective date of this Ordinance. Upon application to the Chief of Police, and showing a hardship by any owner of a dumpster enclosure or refuse container required to comply with this Article, the Chief of Police may grant an extension, for a reasonable period of time, within which to comply with the provisions of this Article.

Sec. 7-161. Penalty Assessment.

The following penalty assessments are declared to be mandatory and minimum:

Wildlife Resistant Refuse Container (Sec. 7-152):

First offense within 1 year	$50.00
Second offense within 1 year	250.00
Third offense within 1 year	Summons

Maintenance of Wildlife Resistant Refuse Containers and Wildlife Resistant Dumpster Enclosures (Sec. 7-153):

First offense within 1 year	50.00
Second offense within 1 year	250.00
Third offense within 1 year	Summons

Residential Refuse Disposal (Sec. 7-154):

First offense within 1 year	50.00
Second offense within 1 year	250.00
Third offense within 1 year	Summons

Special Event Refuse Disposal (Sec. 7-155):

First offense within 1 year	250.00
Second offense within 1 year	500.00
Third offense within 1 year	Summons

Construction Site Refuse Disposal (Sec. 7-156):

First offense within 1 year	250.00
Second offense within 1 year	500.00
Third offense within 1 year	Summons

Feeding of Wildlife (Sec. 7-157):

First offense within 1 year	$50.00
Second offense within 1 year	250.00
Third offense within 1 year	Summons

Secs. 7-162—7-175. Reserved.

Hemlock Farms, Pennsylvania — Wildlife Ordinance

CHAPTER 102 –
FEEDING WILDLIFE PROHIBITED/
SECURE TRASH MANDATED
(Adopted 4-28-01, Amended 12-15-01, 4-24-04)

A. It shall be prohibited to place or offer any food or enticement on any property located within Hemlock Farms which results in attracting or feeding deer, bear or geese.

B. Assessments:
First Offense $25.00
Second Offense $50.00
Third and Subsequent Offenses $100.00

C. This will be effective July 1, 2001.

115-4   Disposal Methods

a. Solid Waste deposited at Curbside locations shall be secured in a rigid, tightly sealed, covered container; not plastic bags or cardboard boxes.

b. Quantities of Solid Waste placed Curbside for disposal shall not exceed three (3) 32 gallon containers per pick-up.

115-7   Solid Waste Storage
Storage of Solid Waste, on residential property, that is not confined within a building structure, is prohibited except Solid Waste stored as described in 115-4.

115-8   No Dumping
Disposal of Solid Waste (Dumping) on HFCA property including common areas adjacent to HFCA roads is prohibited, except at Curbside locations at times of scheduled Curbside pick-ups and in the Refuse/Recycling Center when Center is open.

115-9   Disposal at HFCA Facilities
Disposal of Solid Waste, generated at residence, is prohibited at HFCA facilities, except at the Refuse/Recycling Center when Center is open.

115-10   Enforcement
In the event of nonconformance with, or violation of one or more of Code Sections of this Chapter a fine of $50 will be assessed per section per incident to the property owner's account. Consistent with Bylaw provision 2.4 (C), the member (property owner) shall be responsible for any damages or violations attributable to his or her immediate family, his or her guests, tenants and invitees.

Bibliography

Books

Beecham, John J., and Jeff Rohlman. *A Shadow in the Forest.* Moscow, Idaho: Idaho Department of Fish and Game and the University of Idaho Press, 1994.

Brown, Gary. *The Great Bear Almanac.* New York: Lyons & Burford, 1993.

_____. *Safe Travel in Bear Country.* New York: Lyons & Burford, 1996.

Cox, Daniel J., and Rebecca L. Grambo. *Bear.* New York: Sierra Club Books, 2000.

Frank, Susan, and Phil Frank. *The Yosemite Handbook.* Rohnert Park, Calif.: Pomegranate, 1998.

_____. *The Yellowstone Handbook.* Rohnert Park, Calif.: Pomegranate, 1999.

Furtman, Michael. *Black Bear Country.* Minnetonka, Minn.: Northwoods Press, 1998.

Herrrero, Stephen. *Bear Attacks: Their Causes and Avoidance.* Guilford, Conn.: The Lyons Press, 1985, 2002.

Lynch, Wayne. *Bears: Monarchs of the Northern Wilderness.* Seattle, Wash.: The Mountaineers, 1993.

_____. *Mountain Bears.* Calgary, Alberta, Canada: Fifth House, 1999.

Mills, Enos. *The Grizzly.* New York: Ballantine Books, 1919.

Petersen, David. *A Hunter's Heart.* New York: Henry Holt and Company, 1996.

Schneider, Bill. *Bear Aware.* Guilford, Conn.: Globe Pequot Press, 2001.

Schullery, Paul. *The Bears of Yellowstone.* Worland, Wyo.: High Plains Publishing Company, Inc., 1992.

Smith, Dave. *Backcountry Bear Basics.* Seattle, Wash.: The Mountaineers, 1997.

Van Tighem, Kevin. *Bears.* Canmore, Alberta, Canada: Altitude Publishing Canada, 1999.

Articles, Bulletins, Papers, Reports

Andelt, W. F.. *Livestock Guard Dogs, Llamas and Donkeys.* Colorado State University Cooperative Extension Program, 2004.

Barichello, Norman. *Status Report on the American Black Bear in Canada.* Prepared for the Committee on the Status of Endangered Wildlife in Canada. National Parks Documentation Center, 1998.

Beck, Thomas D.I. *Black Bears of West-Central Colorado.* Technical Publication 39. Colorado Division of Wildlife, 1991.

Beckmann, Jon P., Carl W. Lackey, and Joel Berger. *Evaluation of Deterrent Techniques and Dogs to Alter Behavior of "Nuisance" Black Bears.* Wildlife Society Bulletin, 2004.

Black Bear Task Team. *Black Bear Management Plan.* Whistler, British Columbia, Canada, 1998.

Clark, Jay E., Frank T. van Manen, and Michael R. Pelton. *Correlates of Success for On-site Releases of Nuisance Black Bears in Great Smoky Mountains National Park.* Wildlife Society Bulletin, 2002.

Delozier, Kim. *Black Bear Management Guideline.* Great Smoky Mountains National Park, 2002.

Dolson, Sylvia. *A Guidebook: Non-lethal Black Bear Management,* 2000.

Eastern Black Bear Workshop Proceedings. 2001, 1997, 1994, 1984.

Gill, R. Bruce and Thomas D.I. Beck. *Black Bear Management Plan.* Colorado Division of Wildlife, 1990.

Gore, Meredith. *Comparison of Intervention Programs Designed to Reduce Human-Bear Conflict: A Review of Literature.* Ithaca, N.Y.: Cornell University, 2004.

Great Smoky Mountains National Park. *Backcountry Food Storage Cable System,* 1999.

Havlick, David. *Roadkill.* Case Study. Vol. 5, no. 1, 2004.

Hebblewhite, Mark, Melanie Percy and Robert Serrouya. *Black Bear Survival and Demography in the Bow Valley of Banff National Park, Alberta,* 2002.

Herrero, Stephen, and Andrew Higgins. "Field Use of Capsicum Spray as a Bear Deterrent." *Ursus.* 10:533-537, 1998.

_____. "Human Injuries Inflicted by Bears in British Columbia: 1960-97." *Ursus.* 11:209-218, 1999.

Huijser, Marcel P. *Animal Vehicle Crash Mitigation Using Advanced Technology.* Oregon DOT, Federal Highway Administration et al., 2005.

Hygnstrom, Scott, and Scott Craven. *Bear Damage and Abatement in Wisconsin.* University of Wisconsin, Cooperative Extension Office, 1996.

Inman, Robert M., and Michael R. Pelton. "Energetic Production by Soft and Hard Mast Foods of American Black Bears in the Smoky Mountains." *Ursus.* 13:57-68, 2002.

Lackey, Carl. *Nevada's Black Bear. Ecology & Conservation of a Charismatic Omnivore.* Biological Bulletin No. 15, 2004.

Matthews, Sean, Brenda Lackey, Schulyer Greenleaf, H. Malia Leithead, John J. Beecham, Sam H. Ham, and Howard B. Quigley. *Human-Bear Interaction Assessment in Yosemite National Park.* Wildlife Conservation Society. University of Idaho. National Park Service. The Yosemite Fund. Yosemite Association, 2003.

Meadows, L.E., W.F. Andelt and T.D.I. Beck. *Managing Bear Damage to Beehives.* Colorado State University. Bulletin 6.519, 1998.

Mississippi State University Extension Service. *Ecology and Management of the Louisiana Black Bear,* 1996.

Nelson, Ralph A., and Thomas D.I. Beck, *Hibernation Adpatation in the Black Bear: Implications for Management.* Proceedings, Seventh Eastern Workshop on Black Bear Research and Management, 1984.

New Jersey Department of Environmental Protection, New Jersey Division of Fish and Wildlife, *Black Bear in New Jersey.* Status Report, 2004.

New Mexico Department of Game and Fish. *A Study of Black Bear Ecology in New Mexico with Models for Population Dynamics and Habitat Suitability.* New Mexico Department of Game and Fish, Hornocker Wildlife Institute, New Mexico Cooperative Fish and Wildlife Research Institute, 2001.

Peine, John D. *Nuisance Bears in Communities: Strategies to Reduce Conflict. Human Dimensions of Wildlife.* Taylor & Francis, 2001.

Peyton, Ben, Peter Bull, Tim Reis, and Larry Visser. *Public Views on Bear and Bear Management in the Lower Peninsula of Michigan.* Wildlife Division, Michigan Department of Natural Resources, 2001.

Proceedings from the Parks Canada Atlantic Region Black Bear Workshop. *Black Bear Ecology and Management Issues for Atlantic Canadian National Parks.* Report 103, 1999.

Robinson, Sandra A., James A. Parkhurst, and James E. Cordoza. *Co-existing with Black Bears in Massachusetts.* University of Massachusetts, USDA, 1993, 2003.

Rogers, Lynn. *Watchable Wildlife: The Black Bear.* USDA Forest Service, 1992.

_____. *Home, Sweet-Smelling Home.* Natural History, Wildlife Research Institute, RV 2005.

Scheick, Brian K., and Mark D. Jones. *Locating Wildlife Underpasses Prior to Expansion of Highway 64 in North Carolina.* Undated.

Sekarak, Carolyn, Thomas Eason, and Christine Small. *Using Partnership to Address Human-Black Bear Conflicts in Central Florida.* Proceedings, Annual Conference of the Southeast Association of Fish and Wildlife Agencies. 56:136-147, 2002.

Settlage, Katie. *Measurement and Data Collection in the Field.* Field Trip Earth, 2002.

Sowka, Patti. *Living with Predators Resource Guide.* RV 2005.

Ternent, Mark A. *Management Plan for Black Bear in Pennsylvania.* Bureau of Wildlife Management. Pennsylvania Game Commission, 2005.

Texas Parks and Wildlife. *East Texas Black Bear Conservation and Management Plan.* 2005.

Tinker, Daniel B., Henry J. Harlow, and Thomas D.I. Beck. "Protein Use and Muscle-Fiber Changes in Free-Ranging, Hibernating Black Bears." *Nature*, vol. 409, 2001.

Ursus, Volumes 15 (2) 2004, 14 (1&2) 2003, 13 (2002), 12 (2001), 11 (1999). An Official Publication of the International Association for Bear Research and Management.

U.S. Fish & Wildlife Services. *Bear Spray vs. Bullets.* Fact Sheet 8.

Vashon, Jennifer, "IFW Management Ensures Healthy Bear Populations." *IFW News, Maine Sunday Telegram,* 2003.

Vaughan, Michael R., and Michael R. Pelton. "Black Bears in North America." Pages 100-108 in E.T. LaRoe III, ed. *Our Living Resources.* Washington, D.C.: USDI, NBS, 1995.

Quartarone, Fred. "Bear Facts." *Colorado Outdoors,* 1993.

Western Black Bear Workshop Proceedings. 2000, 1997, 1993, 1991.

Other Sources

The nature of this book involved the review of hundreds of Web sites, bear informational brochures and newspaper and magazine articles far too numerous to list. I also interviewed and/or corresponded with hundreds of people involved in bear management, education and conservation throughout North America. adaptable bears,22

Index

Professional Photographers

Thanks to all the professional photographers and talented amateurs who provided the photos
that help bring this book to life. Many went far above and beyond the call of duty to help me locate
images that made a point. Many of the pros have Web sites; I encourage you to visit them
and enjoy more of their exceptional work.

Paul Conrad *www.photo.net/photos/pabloconrad.com*
Mike Fox *(970-493-0372) no Web site*
Tim Halvorson *www.timhalvorsonphotography.com*
Nelson Kenter *www.kenterphotography.com*
Bill Lea *www.BillLea.com*
John E. Marriott *www.wildernessprints.com*
Alan Olander *aolander@arvig.net*
Derek Reich/Zöoprax Productions *www.zooprax.com*
Jenny E. Ross *www.jennyross.com*

Meet Linda Masterson

Linda Masterson has been helping people learn to peacefully coexist with bears since she joined the Colorado Division of Wildlife's Bear Aware Team in 2001. Her award-winning work has appeared in the *New York Times Sunday Magazine*, *Animal Kingdom*, *Ranger Rick*, and many others. After a couple of decades as a creative director at Chicago advertising agencies, she moved to Colorado, and quickly learned that some of her most interesting new neighbors were big and furry. She's an experienced outdoorswoman, and has hiked in more than a hundred national parks and forests in the U.S. and Canada. Linda is a partner in Phillips Group, a marketing and communications firm, and lives in bear country west of Fort Collins with her husband and Bear Aware partner Cory Phillips. She can be reached by email at *LiveWithBears@aol.com*.

And Tom Beck

Bear biologist Tom Beck is an internationally recognized, highly respected expert; *U.S.A. Today* refers to him as "One of America's leading authorities on black bears." In his twenty-five years with the Colorado Division of Wildlife, Beck authored many scientific publications and statewide management plans, and conducted widely cited field research studies that advanced our understanding of bears. He's an avid outdoorsman, river runner, hiker, camper, fisherman and hunter, and has recently taken up organic farming. In addition to his expertise, he's known throughout the bear world as a straight-shooter who doesn't mind stomping on a few toes in pursuit of the truth. He served as both scientific and real-world advisor on *Living with Bears*. Tom lives with his wife and fellow outdoor-enthusiast Sandy Rost on their organic orchard near Dolores, Colorado.

A solar and wind-powered independent publisher

PixyJack Press LLC

To order autographed copies or multiple copies for your organization:
PO Box 149 • Masonville, CO 80541
info@pixyjackpress.com
www.PixyJackPress.com